The Evolutionary Epic

The Evolutionary Epic

SCIENCE'S STORY AND HUMANITY'S RESPONSE

Edited by

Cheryl Genet,
Russell Genet, Brian Swimme,
Linda Palmer, and Linda Gibler

Collins Foundation Press

The Evolutionary Epic: Science's Story and Humanity's Response

Published by the Collins Foundation Press
4995 Santa Margarita Lake Road
Santa Margarita, CA 93453
www.CollinsFoundationPress.org

Managing and Production Editor - Cheryl Genet
Organizing Editor - Russell Genet
Technical Editors - Linda Gibler, Brian Swimme, and Linda Palmer
Copy Editors - Linda Palmer, Vera Wallen, and Bette Carnrite

Cover and book design by Cheryl Genet
Cover graphics by John Davidson

Includes biographical references

ISBN 0-9788441-2-2

Printed by Sheridan Books in the United States of America

The Humanity Participants' Conference Series website is:
www.EpicandFutures.org

CONTENTS

8

Contributors

The short biographies that were submitted by contributors can be found on the Evolutionary Epic conference website. (www.EvolutionaryEpic.org)

Nancy Ellen Abrams – Attorney at Law, lecturer, University of California, Santa Cruz; co-author (with Joel R. Primack) of *The View from the Center of the Universe*. (p. 107)

Stephen Allen, Ph.D., LEED AP – Associate Professor of Chemistry, Environmental Science Program, College of Natural Sciences, Hawai`i Pacific University. (p. 279)

Craig Benjamin, Ph.D. – Associate Professor of History, Grand Valley State University. (p. 147)

Jane Bramadat, M.A. – (Religious Studies), MEd (Counselling); Ordained Unitarian Universalist Parish Minister, First Unitarian Church of Victoria, BC, Canada. (p.193)

Cynthia S. Brown, Ph.D. – Professor Emerita of Education and History, Dominican University of California; author of *Big History: From the Big Bang to the Present*. (p. 153)

Josefina Burgos, M.A., Ph.D. candidate – (Philosophy and Religion) at the California Institute of Integral Studies, San Francisco. (p. 321)

Carlos A. Camargo, M.D. – Emeritus Clinical Professor of Medicine, Stanford University School of Medicine. (p. 61)

Katie Carrin, C.M.T. – Instructor, Acupressure Institute, Berkeley and The Healing Arts Institute, Sacramento; self-published author. (p. 243.)

Fernando Castrillon, Psy.D. – Clinical Psychologist, Instituto Familiar de la Raza (IFR)-San Francisco; Adjunct Assistant Professor, Interdisciplinary Studies Department, Community Mental Health Masters Program at the California Institute of Integral Studies (CIIS). (p. 221)

David Christian, Ph.D. – Professor of History, Macquarie University, Sydney, Australia (Until Dec 2008, Professor of History at San Diego State University). (pp.11 & 91)

Dwight Collins, Ph.D. – President, Collins Family Foundation; founding faculty member and lecturer, Sustainable Operations Management, Presidio School of Management, San Francisco. (p. 15)

Christopher Corbally, S.J. – Vice Director, Vatican Observatory; Adjunct Associate Astronomer, University of Arizona. (p. 79)

Richard L. Coren, Ph.D. – Emeritus Professor of Electrical Engineering, Drexel University. (p. 201)

Jon Davidann, Ph.D. – Professor of History, Director, International Exchange and Study Abroad Program, Hawaii Pacific University. (p. 279)

Drew Dellinger, M.A. – Founder of Poets for Global Justice; author of *love letter to the milky way: a book of poems*. (pp. 87 & 297)

Rob Duisberg, Ph.D., D.M.A. – Lecturer, E-Commerce & Information Systems, Albers School of Business and Economics, Seattle University. (p. 71)

Todd Duncan, Ph.D. – Director of the Science Integration Institute; Adjunct faculty, Portland State University Center for Science Education and Pacific University Physics Department. (p.329)

Phyllis Frus, Ph.D. – Associate Professor of English, Hawai'i Pacific University. (p. 279)

Cheryl Genet, Ph.D. – Adjunct Professor of Philosophy, Cuesta College; Managing Editor of the Collins Foundation Press; Director of the Orion Institute. (pp.17, 21, 37, 89, 133, 183, 251, 301)

Russell Genet, Ph.D. – Research Scholar in Residence, California Poly-technic State University; Adjunct Professor of Astronomy, Cuesta College; Director, Orion Observatory. (p. 23)

Linda Gibler, OP, Ph.D. – Dominican Sister of Houston; Doctor of Ministry Program Director and Associate Academic Dean, Oblate School of Theology; Adjunct Professor, Loyola Institute of Ministry. (p. 291)

Marc Jason Gilbert, Ph.D. – National Endowment for the Humanities' Endowed Chair in World History and the Humanities, Hawaii Pacific University. (p. 279)

Ursula Goodenough, Ph.D. – Professor of Biology, Washington University, St. Louis; author of *The Sacred Depths of Nature*. (p.175)

Paul A. Harris, Ph.D. – Professor of English, Loyola Marymount University; President, International Society for the Study of Time. (p. 101)

Louis G. Herman, Ph.D. - Philosopher; Professor of Political Science, University of Hawaii West Oahu. (p. 253)

Peter M. J. Hess, Ph.D. – Faith Project Director, National Center for Science Education; Professor in Graduate Liberal Studies, Saint Mary's College, Moraga, California; Fellow, International Society for Science and Religion. (p. 335)

Barbara Marx Hubbard – Co-founder of The Foundation for Conscious Evolution and Conscious Evolution Chair at Wisdom University. (p.125)

Jeff Jenkins – California Institute for Integral Studies. (p. 303)

Pauline Le Bel – Playwright, novelist, singer; Executive Director of *Voices in the Sound*. (p. 119)

Elaine Leilani Madison, Ph.D. – Associate Professor of English, Hawaii Pacific University. (p. 279)

John A. Mears, Ph.D. – University of Chicago; Associate Professor of History, Southern Methodist University; Past President, World History Association. (p.135)

Gregory Mengel, M.A. – California Institute of Integral Studies. (p.213)

Gary Moring, M.A., Ph.D. candidate – California Institute of Integral Studies; 1984-2004 Professor of Philosophy and Comparative Religion, University of Phoenix; author. (p. 237)

Winslow Myers, M.F.A. – Artist and retired teacher. (p. 311)

Jack A. Palmer, Ph.D. – Director of Graduate Studies, Professor of Psychology, College of Education and Human Development, University of Louisiana at Monroe. (p. 265)

Linda K. Palmer, M.S. – Researcher, writer; editor: Edition Naam Publishing, Collins Foundation Press, Jiva Institute, India. (p. 265)

Joel R. Primack, Ph.D. – Distinguished Professor of Physics, University of California, Santa Cruz; co-author (with Nancy Ellen Abrams) of *The View from the Center of the Universe*. (p. 107)

Sheri Ritchlin, Ph.D. – Free-lance writer, editor and lecturer. (p. 185)

Loyal Rue, Ph.D. – Professor of Philosophy and Professor of Religion, Luther College. (p.175)

Kathy Schick, Ph.D. – Professor, Anthropology Department and Cognitive Science Program, Indiana University; Co-Director, CRAFT Research Center, Indiana University; Co-Director, Stone Age Institute; co-editor, Stone Age Institute Publication Series. (pp. 39, 43)

Brian Swimme, Ph.D. – Professor in the Philosophy, Cosmology, and Consciousness Program at the California Institute of Integral Studies. (p.273)

Nicholas Toth, Ph.D. – Professor, Anthropology Department and Cognitive Science Program, Indiana University; Co-Director, CRAFT Research Center, Indiana University; Co-Director, Stone Age Institute; co-editor, Stone Age Institute Publication Series. (pp. 39, 43)

Trileigh Tucker, Ph.D. – Associate Professor of Environmental Studies, Seattle University. (p. 159)

Art Whatley, Ph.D. – Professor and Program Chair, MA/Global Leadership and Sustainable Development, College of Professional Studies, Hawaii Pacific University (p. 279)

John Wilkinson, Ph.D. – Liberal Studies Instructor, Art Institute of California, San Francisco. (p. 229)

Alan T. Wood, Ph.D. – Professor of History, University of Washington, Bothell. (p. 169)

Contributor's information is listed as submitted.

Foreword
Celebrating the Birth of a New Creation Story

The conference from which most of the papers in this volume are drawn met at the Makaha Resort in Hawaii on January 3 – 8, 2008. It was organized by Cheryl and Russ Genet. The conference was about a story, and it was the power, the beauty, and the importance of that story that drew the participants together. The story has many different names; Evolutionary Epic is just one. It has also been called a Modern Creation Myth, The Universe Story, Big History. Whatever the name, the core idea is the same: there is emerging today a coherent story, based on modern, scientific information that tells the history of our universe, from its very beginnings to today. That story can help each one of us understand our place in a larger universe. The evolutionary epic links modern accounts of the origins of the universe, the Earth, life, and human societies into a single story about origins, so it can play in modern society a role similar to that of traditional creation stories in all earlier societies.

Creation stories are immensely important. They provide large maps of reality, and by tracing the origins and evolution of our world, they explain how things came to be as they are. Maps tell us where we are and, in some sense, who and what we are. The largest maps, those attempted in creation stories, are as fundamental to our sense of history as maps of the world are to our sense of geography. Like a world map, the evolutionary epic provides a frame within which we can better understand the smaller maps with which we navigate our way through life. The evolutionary epic is important because it is the largest possible map of time.

A conference like this would not have been necessary if the evolutionary epic had been widely known. The strange thing (strange, at least, to those at this conference) is that the evolutionary epic is not taught in every school in every country in the world! Instead, schoolchildren throughout the world are presented either with bits of the story (the history of my country, for example, or a bit of geography or geology or astronomy) with little attempt to describe the larger story that threads these smaller stories together. Or they are taught creation myths that worked well for hundreds, sometimes thousands of years, but don't work so well today because we have so much more information, and much of that information contradicts what is said in traditional creation stories. The Earth was not created 6,000 years ago, or just a few generations ago. Nor was it created countless billions of years ago. We now know when it was created: about 4.5 billion Earth years ago. The evolutionary epic builds on a vast amount of new knowledge generated in recent centuries (much of it in recent decades) through careful and rigorous scientific research conducted throughout the world in many different disciplines, from nuclear physics to cosmology, to biology, to human history.

The fact that so much of the definitive information needed to construct the evolutionary epic has been gathered very recently suggests one reason why the evolutionary epic is not widely taught today (yet!). A modern scientific account of the origins of the universe became available only in the twentieth century, and only in the last decade or two could it be based on a solid foundation of empirical observation, much of it from new, space-based satellites. The modern study of genetics became possible only after the discovery of the crucial role of DNA in heredity by Crick and Watson in 1953; now, genetic knowledge is helping transform our understanding of the origins and early history of our own species, *Homo sapiens*. A modern understanding of the evolution of our Earth became possible only after the clinching of the theory of "plate tectonics" in the 1960s.

Above all, we can now date the whole of the past. Before the appearance in the 1950s of new methods of dating, most of them based on measuring the regular breakdown of radioactive materials, it was impossible to assign reliable dates to any parts of the story before the appearance of the first written documents a few thousand years ago. In the last few decades, our timelines have expanded from just a few thousand years to almost 14 billion years, reaching back past the civilizations of Sumer, to the evolution of our human ancestors several million years ago, to the appearance of the first multi-celled organisms almost 1,000 million years ago, to the formation of our Earth itself, some 4,500 million years ago and finally to the origins of our universe, about 13,700 million years ago.

These recent changes explain the sense of excitement shared by all of us who have been involved in the attempt to construct the evolutionary epic and to make it more widely accessible to others. How can it best be told? How can we link the science with the spirit? How can the story be acted out, re-told and taught so that its power is palpable? What meaning does the story contain for humans today? How can we link the science that underpins so much in our society with our personal experience of life as felt and experienced?

For me, one of the revelations of the conference was that there are so many questions to be asked about the evolutionary epic, and even more answers. Like all creation stories, the evolutionary epic contains within itself great diversity and can be received and appreciated and taught in many different ways, a bit like a complex crystal being slowly turned and turned and turned in front of many people, each of whom will see in it slightly different things. That diversity is reflected in the diversity of approaches, styles, questions, and struggles in the essays collected here. Don't be surprised if you find dissenting positions here, or essays that seem to contradict other essays, or essays that raise unexpected questions or approach the evolutionary epic from unexpected angles. The evolutionary epic, we found, is capacious enough to absorb such differences with ease.

You will find essays on the construction of the evolutionary epic, on philosophical and spiritual ways into it, on scientific approaches to its various components, on what it might mean in different contexts and to different people, on the challenge of bringing out the story's beauty and the challenge of teaching the epic, on ways of rendering it in poetry, in images and in theatre, and on its implications for the future of our species and our biosphere. This is not a monolithic story even though, like all great creation stories, it has a narrative core that can be recognized in all versions.

Another revelation was the repeated reminder both of the smallness and insignificance of our species, and of our centrality to the evolutionary epic. We are, after all, the only creatures of which we know that can begin to grasp the story of the universe and infuse it with meaning and feeling. In his paper, Winslow Myers offers a powerful image of this relationship in a wonderful Vermeer painting that depicts a figure (perhaps the pioneering biologist Anthony van Leeuwenhoek) leaning forward and touching a celestial globe. For me, Vermeer's painting inverts Michelangelo's image of God touching the finger of Adam. However cool-headed we may remain as we try to piece together the scientific evidence for the evolutionary epic, it is hard to resist a sense of awe as we realize that we, in our tiny corner of the universe, represent the universe becoming aware of itself.

I hope these essays can convey something of the majesty, beauty, and power of the evolutionary epic, and also something of its diversity and capaciousness. Finally, I want to offer my personal thanks to Russell and Cheryl Genet for bringing together this diverse assembly of people to celebrate the birth of a new creation story.

David Christian
Professor of History
Author of *Maps of Time*

Publisher's Note
The Evolutionary Epic and a Sustainable Future

The mission of the Collins Family Foundation (www.collinsff.org) and its publishing segment, the Collins Foundation Press, is to provide leadership in humanity's efforts to live sustainably. As CEO of the press, my interest in publishing this book arises from my belief that developing, teaching, and celebrating the evolutionary epic can contribute to the task of moving our human family and our fellow living species toward a condition of sustainability on our planet.

A recent Worldwatch Institute study indicates that in about 1985, humanity's "ecological footprint," a measure of the rate at which we are consuming the Earth's resources, began to exceed the rate at which the Earth is able to renew them. This disparity continues to grow. A majority of our natural scientists worldwide agree that we have begun to witness the first major collapse of species diversity since an asteroid collided with the Earth 65 million years ago.

A June 2008 special issue of *National Geographic* states that "the scientific consensus on the basic facts of climate change is virtually unanimous. Hard data such as temperature records, CO_2 concentrations, and sea level rise, can't be denied." These facts indicate that all living species have entered a new era of uncertainty and intensified challenge for survival that is unprecedented in human history. Humans have difficulty perceiving most of these changes because the time frame of our lives is so short relative to the time frames over which environments and civilizations collapse.

It may be that our genetic-cultural co-evolution as hunter-gatherers has not wired us to perceive the impact of outcomes that are beyond the scope of our relatively brief lives. We tend to take action to preserve our loved ones and ourselves only when a threat is imminent. A number of past civilizations have collapsed because certain conventional behaviors of their culture depleted the ecosystems on which their survival depended. Knowledge of the consequences of these behaviors came too late, if perceived at all, for compensating initiatives.

The difference between our time and times past is that humans have developed a rich culture of scientific inquiry, much of it in just the last few centuries. Science has generated technology that has enabled humankind, in the geological blink of an eye, to establish dominion over the Earth. Relatively recent discoveries confirm that we are but one of many interdependent parts of a complex web of life on our planet and that we can no longer consider our natural resources to be in infinite supply. It is clear that certain human behaviors seriously jeopardize the base of natural resources on which we depend for survival. Unlike earlier cultures, we *know* that we are destroying the means of our survival.

While science has provided us with the means to know our limitations intellectually, many of us appear paralyzed from taking action because the danger is not imminent enough in terms we are equipped to perceive from day to day. It would seem that our wiring, evolved in simpler times, devoid of the complexities of civilization, has not equipped us well to face the challenges of global climate change and ecological collapse across broader expanses of time.

Nevertheless, our history of genes and culture evolving together has also provided us with the ability to take action when events are set within the meaningful context of a story or narrative that defines who we are in reference to the world around us. Throughout history, humanity has found solace, wisdom, inspiration, and calls to action in the form of rich stories. The world's great mythologies and religious traditions have enabled humans to join together in great numbers to take action on behalf of values and causes having little connection with imminent physical danger. Yet, however helpful they may be, these great stories have never before been asked to provide guidance in coping with the global challenges we now face. Nor have the stories had the benefit of the facts that science has recently revealed. This does not diminish the stories' value, but it gives us the opportunity to write a new story, one that might help us to evade our own global civilization's proverbial "end-time."

In contrast to stories of the past, the evolutionary epic is based entirely on science. Yet it still provides a narrative in which we can each find our own rich meaning, and with it the resolve to identify and respond to future dangers, even when they may lack immediacy that we are able to feel at a primal level. Developing this new resolve will require us to learn how to perceive our relationship to our environment differently. As Brian Swimme points out in his insightful essay, *Cosmology and Environmentalism*, learning the evolutionary story helps us to see ourselves as a part within a whole—as depending for our existence on the ability of so many other life forms to thrive while also keeping our nonliving resources in balance within our planet's ecosystem.

It was an honor for me to participate in the January 2008 conference on The Evolutionary Epic and to sponsor the publication of this book, *The Evolutionary Epic: Science's Story and Humanity's Response*. I applaud its authors and editors for coming together and for their scholarship in producing this comprehensive update on the status of this remarkable story of all stories.

Dwight Collins, Ph.D.
President, Collins Family Foundation

Preface
Journey to the Evolutionary Epic

I grew up with the companionship of my brother Richard and his best friend Russell Genet. Richard and Russell started me, at the advanced age of six, on my quest to understand the scientific and spiritual dimensions of the universe. They were more than five years my senior, yet they included me in their philosophical musings, stamping me with an insatiable desire to *know*. My mentors left for the Air Force when I was twelve, and I did not see Russell again for nearly forty years.

When we reconnected, he invited me to attend one of the first Epic of Evolution conferences—which he and Brian Swimme had organized—at a time when the "story" was just beginning to be told. Building on the work of Connie Barlow, Thomas Berry, Eric Chaisson, Ursula Goodenough, Loyal Rue, Brian Swimme, Mary Evelyn Tucker, E.O. Wilson, and other early "epicers" like Russell, the conference began to shape the epic's future. And I began the journey with Russell that led to our romance and marriage. Then, inspired by his book, *Humanity: The Chimpanzees Who Would Be Ants*, together we launched the Humanity Participants' Conference series and the edited volumes that are now emerging from them.

So *The Evolutionary Epic: Science's Story and Humanity's Response* has roots deep in the history of the concept of "science as story" but also reflects how this "true tale" has been taken up by a new generation of epicers. I am deeply humbled by the opportunity to make a small contribution, as the Evolutionary Epic conference co-chair along with Russell and as the managing editor of this volume along with my co-editors, to the ongoing process of developing, exploring, and celebrating the science story of our origins.

This book has several unique characteristics. It is a collection of many different authors of diverse perspectives and is written in several different styles—from research, to narrative, to poetry. Therefore, some minor variations in referencing, formatting, and presentation have been preserved to retain the author's disciplinary character and creative freedom. The arrangement of chapters is designed to capture, to the degree possible, the sense of the fruitful and synergistic interaction that took place between the authors as they shared their unique perspectives at the conference.

I have organized the chapters into thematic sections (parts) which can both stand alone and yet be part of the larger presentation. While a cover-to-cover approach is often the most productive way to read a book, it is not required in this case—the sections can be enjoyed in any order or selected individually for specific research or study purposes. I have provided an introduction for each section to give a sense of its content and to draw out the connection between the chapters. To enhance the section's continuity throughout the book, I begin each introduction with an epigram taken from David Christian's comprehensive foreword. There are also several quotes in each of these introductions taken directly from their corresponding chapters and therefore not further referenced.

In addition, I have provided an extensive index, based on the author's choice of important words or concepts in their chapters, but expanded considerably to give significant depth to the entries. Since the range of topics covered in this volume is vast, I encourage the reader to peruse the index to spot topics of interest or to pique curiosity. The index is a veritable banquet of intellectual delights.

I extend my gratitude to my co-editors for their dedication to the production of this volume and their always prompt responses to all that was asked of them. Brian Swimme, a veteran epicer who was our conference's keynote speaker, brought many new voices to the dialogue and provided a timely and important chapter on the epic and environmentalism, as well as valuable technical advice. David Christian provided editorial support and drew the many diverse perspectives of this book together into a comprehensive foreword. Russell Genet co-chaired the *Evolutionary Epic* conference with me and was largely responsible for gathering together the distinguished group of presenters who ultimately became the authors of these many chapters. He also provided invaluable guidance in production and editorial processes. Linda Gibler proved to be a highly competent technical editor, able to spot difficulties in the most amazing range of topics. This was a critical input, as all the editors agreed from the outset that while the authors might have a wide variety of views on the epic, we felt it was important to make sure the science on which their views were based was as accurate and current as our capacity to do so would allow.

Finally, I wish to acknowledge the unfailing support and editorial expertise of Linda Palmer, who served as the first line of defense in our battle against copy, technical, and formatting errors. In addition, she was invaluable in helping me work through the multitude of production tasks, processes, and timelines. I am deeply in her debt.

About the authors in this volume I can only say that I am in awe of the breadth of their knowledge, their literary and presentation skills, and their cooperation with every phase of the production process. I could not have asked for more. Many thanks as well to Vera Wallen who quickly and efficiently copy edited every chapter and piece and served as an additional line of defense against errors, a few of which will inevitably slip through in any case, and for which I take sole responsibility. My appreciation goes to my son, John Davidson, whose graphic talents brought to fruition my vision for the cover of this book. A special thank you to Drew Dillinger for permitting the inclusion in this volume of his wonderful poems, which delighted conference participants. They have been placed in "interludes" for contemplative savoring. And thank you to Kathy Brown at Sheridan Press for her cheerful competence and great patience.

Finally, I acknowledge with heartfelt gratitude, the financial and behind-the-scenes support, for both the conference and this book, of Dwight Collins and the Collins Family Foundation. I am honored to be a part of the ongoing mission of his family's foundation and the Collins Foundation Press to promote and support various efforts directed toward building a sustainable and flourishing Earth.

In the evolutionary epic, the scientific naturalist experiences wonder and awe, the traditional theologian experiences the power of nature, the philosopher finds wisdom in the infinitesimal, and the soul of the artist soars on the wings of grandeur. In time, it can be hoped, this compelling and globally assembled scientific story of how we came to be will provide for the community of humanity what no peoples have ever been without—a cosmological story that illuminates the past, inspires both ethic and imagination, and guides its believers on their path to the future.

Cheryl Genet
Managing Editor

We now know, in quite some detail, how the Darwinian story of life's ever increasing complexity played out on Earth, the third planet orbiting an ordinary G2-type star, one of hundreds of billions of stars in an only slightly larger than average spiral galaxy, which in turn is only one of hundreds of billions of galaxies in the visible universe, ...a fleck of gold on a grain of sand in a remote corner of a vast cosmic beach.

Russell Genet

Science's Story of How We Came to Be

Cheryl Genet

> Creation stories are immensely important. They provide large maps
> of reality and by tracing the origins and evolution of our world, they
> explain how things came to be as they are.
>
> David Christian

This book presents many perspectives on the teaching, telling, sharing, and celebrating of what has become known as the evolutionary epic. Brian Swimme reminds us in the first paragraphs of his chapter in this volume—"Cosmology and Environmentalism"—that there are many ways to tell the epic story of evolution:

> How one tells the new epic of the universe will be determined at least in
> part by the aims of the storyteller. [The stories] will all require their own
> telling, their own epistemology, and their own rhetorical skills—their
> own artistic or intellectual genre.

One of those intellectual genres is to simply lay out the science story of how humanity came to be, tracing our path from stardust to planetary stardom through physical and biological evolution, and focusing especially on our cultural evolution. This genre informs and intrigues all who wish to know just what it is that science says about becoming human in a vast cosmos. The following "story," a synopsis of astronomer and cosmic evolutionist Russ Genet's book *Humanity: The Chimpanzees Who Would Be Ants*, tells the story in such a way, based on our latest scientific knowledge. But he also treats the reader to a look at four possible futures for humanity, the remarkable creature that is, in many ways, the universe come to know itself.

So, before launching into the multi-faceted ways that the authors in this book address the possibilities presented by our emerging twenty-first century cosmology for a global community, settle back as though you were gathered around a campfire under a starry-night sky for a old-fashioned story-telling, a tradition as old as humanity itself.

The evolutionary epic is probably the best myth we will ever have.

Edward O. Wilson

Despite all the stars and galaxies that form a backdrop,
cosmic evolution is a story that places life and humanity on
center stage—and that's not an anthropocentric statement
as much as an honest statement about
human curiosity and inventiveness.

Eric Chaisson

C. Genet

Go to the ant thou sluggard;
Consider her ways, and be wise.

Proverbs 6:6

The roots of politics are older than humanity.

Frans de Waal

The evolution of the human species is
one of the greatest dramas in the unfolding of life on Earth—
a tale of passion, challenge, and high adventure,
with everyone's favorite character, themselves, in the lead

William F. Allman

I would contend that if something
fits in with common sense it almost certainly isn't science.
If scientific ideas were natural,
they would not have required the difficult and
protracted techniques of science for their discovery.

Lewis Wolpert

Humanity
The Chimpanzees Who Would Be Ants
Russell M. Genet

What Came Before Humanity? Setting the Stage
Once upon a time there was a Big Bang. Quarks, the fundamental building blocks of matter, instantly condensed from the intense energy. In the blistering heat of the young cosmos, quarks attempted to join together to form higher-level entities, but were quickly knocked apart almost as soon as they were formed by super-energetic photons. The porridge was simply too hot. However, as the universe expanded and cooled, the porridge became just right, and quarks combined to form the next highest level of matter, atomic particles. On further expansion and cooling, atomic particles combined to form the nuclei of the simplest atoms, hydrogen and helium.

One would have thought that even more complex nuclei than hydrogen and helium, such as those for carbon, oxygen, and iron, would have also formed as the universe continued its expansion and cooling but, as Goldilocks would have noted, the porridge had now become too cold. And all this occurred within three minutes of the Big Bang! It is not clear why the universe was in such a hell-fire rush, but at the three-minute point it looked like it was a bust, a simple sea of photons, electrons, and hydrogen and helium nuclei fated to expand and cool forever. Yawn, how boring!

As the universe continued to expand, its early, frenetic, heat-driven particle motions were gradually stilled. At about the 300,000 year point, the plasma fog cleared as negative free electrons were captured by positive nuclei. Photons, no longer ricocheting off free electrons, now traveled in a straight line, on and on for billions of years. The expansion of space itself stretched the wavelengths of the initial, highly energetic ultraviolet photons into radio invisibility, and total darkness fell upon the face of the deep. What a bust! Double yawn, how infinitely boring! What was wrong with the universe, anyway? Some sort of design flaw?

> *Had I been present at the Creation, I would have given some useful hints for the better ordering of the universe.*
> Alfonse the Wise

But wait, there was movement! Diffuse hydrogen and helium atoms, not to mention mysterious dark matter, were, ever so slowly, gathering into increasingly concentrated clumps, thanks to the gentle yet remorseless and far-reaching force of gravity. Gravity was slowly acting on the ever-so-slight cosmic irregularities—only one part in 100,000—that were the result of tiny quantum fluctuations in the initial Big Bang. These quantum-induced irregularities, originally subatomic in size, had now, thanks to the incredible expansion of the universe, been inflated into fluctuations the size of entire clusters of galaxies! Ever so slowly, gravitational attraction gathered local concentrations of matter into stars and, nearly a half billion years after the Big Bang, the first young stars blazed forth to light up the dark universe. Let there be light, and there was light! The once-stalled cosmic story continued.

Deep in the dense hearts of these young stars, the high temperatures and pressures of the early universe were reestablished, and, with the leftover porridge reheated, the creation of atomic elements beyond hydrogen and helium continued onwards after the almost half billion year hiatus. No three-minute limit this time: there were millions of years for nuclear reactions to build up the heavier elements. But were these elements hopelessly trapped in the hearts of stars? Fortunately, with their fuel exhausted, the more massive stars collapsed and then exploded as supernovae at the end of their short lives, generously spreading their heavier elements into space. These heavier elements formed the raw and now enriched material for the next generation of stars and—drum roll, please—planets with iron cores and rocky mantels!

Some of these planets were "Goldilocks planets," neither too hot nor too cold, positioned at just the right distance from their parent stars such that liquid water—as opposed to either steam or ice—existed on their surfaces. Under these benign conditions, and with planetary ocean water as a solvent, stardust, the raw elements from exploded supernovae, combined to form ever more complex molecules. Because these molecules were very delicate and fell apart as fast as they were formed, however, a limit to complexity was soon reached.

Once again, in its climb towards ever greater complexity, the universe had come to an impasse to which there seemed no solution. Soon, however, some clever molecules hit on a cyclical chemical process that allowed them to continuously reproduce more of themselves. Growth industries were founded. It wasn't long before various types of self-replicating molecules were vying with one another for the increasingly scarce raw material, stardust, in the planetary oceans. Life had been born. Life competed with life, and as less successful lines lost out, the Darwinian saga was launched, we presume, on many favored planetary surfaces throughout the vast and still expanding universe.

What evolution does is to give the arrow of time a barb,
which stops it from running backward,
and once it has this barb, the chance play of errors
will take it forward of itself.
Jacob Bronowski

We now know, in quite some detail, how the Darwinian story of life's ever increasing complexity played out on Earth, the third planet orbiting an ordinary G2-type star, one of hundreds of billions of stars in an only slightly larger than average spiral galaxy, which in turn is only one of hundreds of billions of galaxies in the visible universe, ...a fleck of gold on a grain of sand in a remote corner of a vast cosmic beach.

On planet Earth, which formed almost five billion years ago, life began soon after the ocean-vaporizing impacts of large asteroids finally came to a halt. As the chemical systems of early life became more complex, life soon discovered that reproducing the plans for building and running its tiny but complex chemical factories was more effective than cloning the entire factories themselves. Encoding vast quantities of factory construction and operation details within compact DNA blueprints allowed single-celled life on Earth to take a quantum upward leap in complexity, eventually filling every possible life-supporting niche on the planet.

However, physical restrictions on practical cellular size eventually limited the growth of complexity on Earth. Another roadblock. This time, evolution really struggled. It took over a billion years for a work-around—multicellular life—to be discovered. Quarks had combined to form atomic particles which, in turn, combined to form atoms, then molecules, and, finally, single cells—a hierarchical pyramid of increasing complexity with each higher level based on the broader base of the components from the level below. Now single cells combined to form the next higher level, multicellular life.

One key to successful multicellular life was the nearly total suppression of competition between formerly fiercely independent single cells. The other key was providing a common shared (identical) DNA blueprint across all cells while still allowing various cells in the collective to specialize in different functions. One-for-all and all-for-one. Another dead end avoided!

The lines of multicellular life of greatest interest to our story of humanity were the animals that developed specialized sensor organs and motor capabilities. To effectively pursue a meal or avoid being eaten, these animals developed brains to coordinate sensors and movement—tiny brains in the case of insect ganglia, but relatively enormous brains in mammals.

When multicellular animal life eventually hit up against practical limitations of what a single individual or small family could accomplish, insects were the first to discover yet another work-around. Individual animals evolved to become mere cogs in the highly organized entities scientists call superorganisms. Although composed of individual insects, superorganisms act as single entities, and, typically, individual members cannot survive for long outside of the superorganism. As with the transition to multicellularity, individuality is suppressed for the good of the group. The most complex of the genetically organized superorganisms on Earth were the social insects such as bees, termites, and ants.

Ants, the descendents of solitary wasps, have evolved colonies (superorganisms) which practice highly organized agriculture by raising fungi "mushrooms" in vast underground gardens. These leafcutter ants practice large-scale, production-line farming. They have been farming in the New World for over 25 million years. A physically large caste scissors out leaf sections and transports them to the nest. Ever smaller castes, in turn, dice the leaves, mulch them into pellets, and tend the ants' fungi garden. Henry Ford would have approved. The bountiful harvests sustain entire colonies of millions on a diet of pure mushrooms. The all-for-one, one-for-all principle perfected.

Other types of ant superorganisms have ingeniously domesticated animal, as opposed to plant life. Aphid-herding ants "milk" their wards for honeydew, the aphid's sugar-loaded waste. In return for this sustenance, these ant dairy farmers not only protect their livestock from predators, but shift them from one plant pasture to another and, at night, to the sheltering barn of the ants' own nest. Whether raising mushrooms or herding aphids, ant superorganisms make a living on what to them are indigestible plants at the base of the food chain, thus becoming numerous instead of rare. Totally selfless, these ants are the perfect little communists.

Concentrated into colonies of millions, ant superorganisms endlessly engage one another in ruthless, all-out warfare. The many parallels between ant colonies and human cities are both instructive and frightening. In the overall scheme of life on Earth, ant colonies—especially the leafcutters and aphid-herders—can be considered as modern humanity's closest organizational analogue, although they became agriculturalists and reached superorganism status some 25 million years before we did.

If ants had nuclear weapons,
they would probably end the world in a week.
Bert Holldobler and Edward Wilson

Although agricultural ant colony superorganisms represent the pinnacle of genetically orchestrated complexity and display many characteristics of human civilizations, their genetic relationship to us is distant. In fact, we have to go back 600 million years to the Cambrian explosion—back to the initial branching point for the different types of animals—to find a common ancestor between ourselves and the ants.

In ants, increasingly complex behavior evolved solely via genetic information passed from one generation to the next. On the other hand, the behavior of chimpanzees, our closest genetic relative, evolved both genetically and culturally—cultural information being passed extra-genetically, via learning, from one generation's sizeable brains to the next. An excellent example of such cultural transmission is the chimpanzees of the Tai forest in western Africa. They eat nuts with shells so hard they can only be cracked open with a stone hammer and log anvil after years of a mother's patient lessons. Nearby forests have the same stones, nuts, and patient mothers, yet their nuts go unharvested for lack of an appropriate cultural tradition. These other chimpanzee tribes, however, have their own distinct and enduring traditions, such as probes to extract termites, picks to remove bone marrow, and leaves to sponge up water, keep off rain, or wipe away unseemly messes.

How Did We Come to Be? Cultural Evolution Takes Command

From the Big Bang, over 13 billion years ago, our story took us to the beginning of animal life in the Cambrian era just 600 million years ago. It then took two parallel paths. One path led to our closest organizational analogues, the mushroom-growing and aphid-herding agricultural ant superorganisms with their highly organized, million-strong colonies—true biological superstars. The other path led to our closest genetic relative, the tool-making, independent minded yet socially skilled chimpanzees that lived in small tribes. Rare, they were at best a minor biological footnote. So how, in only a few million years, did a few thousand bipedal "chimpanzees" in East Africa manage to become ant-like superorganisms of billions of humans, harnessing most of the planet's resources to meet their own ends as the planet's all time biological superstars? How did they manage to out-ant the ants?

The common ancestor of contemporary chimpanzees and humans was an extinct ape that earned an easy living as a frugivore in the African jungle. Then, just six million years ago, a few of these chimpanzee-like apes became geographically isolated in eastern Africa. The newly formed Rift Mountains not only cut them off from the rest of chimpdom, but also heartlessly cast a rain shadow over their eastern jungle, transforming it into scattered woodlands. Compelled to traverse ever-longer distances on the ground between their life-sustaining and increasingly scarce fruit trees, our evolving ancestors became bipedal. Sprinting soon became an evolutionarily-favored sport, as the laggards were eaten by the lions. In other ways, however, our ancestors remained *bona-fide* chimpanzees, even retaining their ability to climb trees, spending their nights in the safety of the branches.

When, only 2.5 million years ago, the Earth was plunged into an ice age, the East African climate turned even drier, and the bipedal chimpanzees lost their trees altogether. Fruitless, our ancestors enlisted their stock chimpanzee cultural traditions of tool manufacture and cooperative hunting to forge a new livelihood on the open savanna. Broken rocks served as hide-slashing "teeth." A hundred rock throwing hominids made even lions think twice about their dinner menu! Freed from the necessity for immediatly cling to their formerly tree-climbing mothers, newborns now benefited from increasingly prolonged periods of rapid postnatal brain growth as still helpless babes in their mother's arms.

Larger brains allowed our hominid ancestors to keep track of a greater number of favors due and paybacks owed. Larger, more lion-proof social groups emerged which, in the natural course of evolution, favored even larger brains. While chimp cultural information remained constant at a rather low level, hominid cultural traditions snowballed. A new and highly effective cultural channel, in parallel with the ancient genetic channel, had been created for the storage of information and its transfer to the next generation

Round and round went the merry-go-round of brain enlargement and cultural transmission until, about 100,000 years ago, out popped our own species, *Homo sapiens*. Soon a wave of weapon-making, highly cooperative, top-predator humans swept the planet. Our glory days as the planet's top predator were short-lived, however, as we soon hunted many species of large mammals to extinction. As the human population rose and big game disappeared, we were forced into the hard life of agriculture.

The good news was that farming, as contrasted to hunting and gathering, allowed the same parcel of land to support many more humans. The bad news, as the ants could have told us, was that raising domesticated plants and animals required extensive organization, hard work in the sun all day long, and the suppression of individuality. However, once an un-chimpanzee, ant-like exertion was applied to farming, a modest surplus was created.

Agricultural-based civilizations were soon controlled by kings and priests who collected the modest surpluses to amply support themselves and their newly established cities. As was the case with the leafcutter and aphid-herding ants, agriculture allowed humans to tap the bottom of the food chain, so we, like them, became numerous instead of rare. The beginnings of biological success for the two-legged chimps! Only five thousand years ago, writing was invented by the priest-accountants who kept track of taxes. The first IRS Form 1040s were written on clay tablets. Schools were inaugurated to teach the accountants how to write, and professional armies were established. Soon, like so many fiercely defended anthills, the plains of Mesopotamia and other river valleys sported the walled cities and temple-capped mounds of the planet's first cultural superorganisms. Ants had their colonies. We had our city-states. Our civilizations thrived on the perpetual disruption of nature we called farming, as did our camp-following weeds, rats, and measles. Taken together, farming and disease were an unstoppable combination, and, in a second, overwhelming wave, the most militant civilizations spread about the planet, supplanting the thinly spread hunter-gatherers who had preceded them.

> *Human history is a story of cultural takeover.*
> Kevin Kelly

Finally, only a few hundred years ago, the machines arose. Thousands of times more powerful than humans, horses, or beasts of burden, machines quickly evolved beyond meager wind and water power to tap vast bonanzas of buried energy—coal and oil. Machines found fertile ground in the capitalist West where their power and efficiency were swiftly harnessed to accumulate vast personal fortunes. As each new generation of machines became more fit, they rapidly proliferated and, with their Western human sidekicks, swept the planet yet again, subjugating the non-industrialized societies before them.

> *The tractor, unlike the horse, does not eat when not in use.*
> *A machine can work tirelessly and uncomplainingly,*
> *and can be scrapped rather than put on a pension.*
> Bruce Mazlish

Thanks to the machines, not to mention the raw materials from the rest of the planet, wealth in the West—for the first time ever—won the race against an ever-increasing population. Heretofore, civilizations had primarily benefited the elite because the surpluses had been so meager. Now, in the Golden Age of Machine Plenty, almost everyone was well off—at least in the industrialized nations. Machines did the strenuous work formerly consigned to hapless serfs, while domestic chores previously assigned to slaves were accomplished at the touch of a button. The West, not to mention Japan and other industrialized countries, luxuriated in a sea of machine-produced goods.

But as rapidly proliferating chain saws and bulldozers consumed the last forests, and as a vast army of machines filled the air, water, and land with their effluents, it finally dawned on us, the chimpanzees who would be ants, that we might have been had. Machines, initially few, had gained our confidence as faithful servants, and we had gladly helped them evolve and proliferate. But were the tables now being turned on us? Were machines now enslaving us and consuming the planet to boot?

Things are in the saddle,
and ride mankind.
There are two laws discrete,
not reconciled, –
law for man, and law for thing;
the last builds town and fleet,
but it runs wild,
and doth the man unking.
Ralph Waldo Emerson

What Is Our Fate? Four Alternative Finales

It is amazing that, in only a few hundred years, our science, books, and computers have allowed us, the first predominantly cultural life on Earth, to accrue more information than did the four billion years of genetic life that preceded us. Has life's genetic era been superseded? Are we in charge of evolution now, heading toward a grand and glorious future? Or, as we log the last trees, pump the last oil, and drain our water aquifers dry, does mindless human competition reign supreme? Will our vast stores of accumulated cultural information merely hasten our own demise, triggering a return to the genetic era?

What will be the end to our story? What will happen to the upstart chimpanzees who both out-aped the apes and out-anted the ants? Although we cannot predict the future, we can contemplate alternative endings to humanity's story. Stories need endings, and the four endings provided below are better than one because, oh lucky reader, you get to pick your favorite ending!

Chimpanzee Paradise High-tech Garden of Eden

In the first alternative future, we come to understand that we are, at heart, just laid-back chimpanzees. We, the chimpanzees who would be ants, finally recognize we weren't cut out to be highly competitive, hard-working, ant-like superorganisms. Billions of us huddled in perpetual contact with tiers of bureaucracy just doesn't seem to be our thing. At heart we remain proud individualists, not identical, subservient cogs in some gigantic, smoothly running machine.

As Earth's self-appointed Gaia, we rescue the planet from our own former profligacy. In firm control of ourselves now, our numbers rapidly drop from billions to millions. Machine life, demoted to subservient, green-conscious helpers, is brought to heel before it usurps us. We discover that it is not too late to find our way back home to the chimpanzee virtues of individual freedom and close-knit family and tribal ways.

> *Are not the mountains, waves, and sky a part*
> *of me and my soul, as I of them?*
> George Gordon, Lord Byron

Science's parting gift is not only a continuing power over nature that allows us to lead healthy lives with trivial effort, but also a frank, unvarnished vision of ourselves and our only home, Earth, that is so compelling that we forevermore exercise our god-like powers with Gaian wisdom and the utmost restraint. The best of both civilization and nature, of culture and genes, is ours. We regain our chimpanzee souls.

Science, key discoveries completed, discreetly fades into the background. Freed from the incessant blind-siding of headline-grabbing, indisputable scientific discoveries, our imaginations soar beyond mere factual knowledge as we enter a golden age of cultural diversity. Once again we become fun-loving chimpanzees. In our species' adulthood, the fable of the chimpanzees who would be ants (but changed their minds before it was too late) reestablishes us as responsible citizens of Earth's living community. With our dreams of planetary antdom empire forever stilled, we live happily ever after.

Boom and Bust *May the Punishment Fit the Crime*

Chimpanzee paradise? What a pipe dream! At the dawn of civilization, we sold our chimpanzee souls to Devil Efficiency for a shot at planetary stardom. It worked. Our cultural blitzkrieg promptly overwhelmed mere genetic life, but now we are grossly overextended. As fossil fuel junkies, we're totally dependent on fertilizers and pesticides, not to mention tractors, trucks, and trains. We literally eat oil. Already the chimpanzees who would be ants are consuming 40% of the planet's organic productivity, even as our machines slurp up the last easy oil. With our population doubling every forty years and machines proliferating like rabbits, it doesn't take a rocket scientist to figure we will soon crash head on into the brick wall of planetary finiteness.

> *Competition is racing along in high gear,*
> *but the train is running off the track.*
> Hubert Reeves

While there are still those do-gooders who think we can save ourselves by recycling a few beer cans, in actuality they're just spitting upwind into the rising hurricane. We are not about to regain our souls, and soon we will all drown in the final tidal wave of unbridled global competition as our mindless over-consumption destroys the planet.

As the first species to fathom its evolutionary destiny, it is ironic that we are trapped in a slow-motion nightmare, powerless to avoid our likely biological fate—following the dinosaurs to extinction. Like all other temporarily unrestrained life before us, we will go bust even faster than we boomed, machines and humans biting the dust together. As the last chain saws and bulldozers fall silent, what remains of genetic life will, breathing a sigh of relief, move on without us. May the punishment fit the crime.

Planetary Superorganism All Together on the Global Farm

All this worry about crashing, about self-restraint, is just so much flamboyant, headline-grabbing gloom and doom. Since the birth of civilization, prophets have routinely forecasted our imminent demise. Naturally we are experiencing a few minor adjustments as we transition from the genetic to the cultural era. A few billion years ago photosynthetic life, like us, renovated the planet when it first tapped its own immense new energy source, sunlight. Photosynthetic life quickly forced all other life forms to adapt to the greatest pollution event of all time—the wholesale emission of highly toxic and inflammable oxygen into the Earth's atmosphere. The oceans literally rusted as oxygen combined with free iron, and oxygen-enabled fires often raged on land, yet the planet prospered. Today's minor human-induced pollution pales in comparison. Other life will soon adjust to us and our New World Order.

We can avoid the crash. Instead of using our scientific knowledge to totally usurp all other life and swamp ourselves with needless consumer frills, we could act decisively on our understanding of our current evolutionary predicament. We could stop using the planet as a crash-test dummy and provide the restraint that other life so kindly furnished the ants but inconsiderately failed to supply us. We could—for the first time ever—become self-restraining life. Biologically perverse and unprecedented, such self-restraint would open up a virtual infinity of possible futures.

We might, for instance, apply the minimal necessary self-restraint; just enough to survive, cheek-by-jowl, without a bust. But by restraining ourselves more aggressively, and thereby unnaturally limiting our numbers to a mere twenty billion or so, we could, even more than the ants, become biological superstars with a record-breaking, single-species share of the planetary pie. The chimpanzees who out-anted the ants. Such bust avoidance would, of course, require that most every planetary resource be channeled as directly as possible to us. But why not? We are the winners!

Star Trek Our Descendents Inherit the Cosmos

Do we really want to restrict ourselves to planet Earth? What of our dreams of traveling to other stars? What can we do before our home is no longer habitable, before our Sun turns into a red giant and literally melts the Earth? We can reach for the stars!

> *The only people who really felt the tug,*
> *the gravitational attraction of outer space,*
> *were the dreamers, the trekkies,*
> *and various Californians.*
> Joel Achenback

Already we have traveled to the Moon and have sent our robotic machine partners to nearby planets. Recently our telescopes have detected planets by the score orbiting distant stars. We are reaching out to other life in the universe. If there are planets circling stars with detectable signs of life, we will observe them. If there are signals from extraterrestrial sentient beings to be heard, we will hear them. And if it is even remotely possible to travel to the stars, we will travel to them. We, the chimpanzees who would be ants, will boldly go where no chimp has gone before.

> *If seed in the black earth can turn into such beautiful roses,*
> *what might not the heart of man become in its long journey*
> *toward the stars.*
> G. K. Chesterton

Epilog Futures Most Likely and Desirable

For many years I have presented my take on the evolutionary epic as a short course or a one-hour talk at high schools and universities around the planet. To wrap things up I always asked my students two questions. First, which of the four futures did they consider most likely? They invariable elected *Boom and Bust* by an overwhelming majority.

Second, which future, even if unlikely, would be most desirable? They always split their vote almost evenly between *Chimpanzee Paradise* and *Star Trek*. I had initially expected that *Chimpanzee Paradise* would be their nearly unanimous choice because rejoining nature as responsible and modest planetary citizens seemed to be the logical counter to their fears of a bust. I didn't think that *Star Trek*, a much more aggressive "Masters of the Universe" alternative would receive many nods. But I was wrong. So I asked the students who unexpectedly voted for *Star Trek*, why, if they thought the most likely future was *Boom and Bust*, hadn't they voted for *Chimpanzee Paradise*? They suggested that *Chimpanzee Paradise* would be too boring, even somewhat mindless.

Turnabout being fair play, they always asked me for my opinion. I told them that, as a species, I believed we faced two challenges. Our first is to avoid becoming victims of our own success, while our second is to venture forth from our birth planet to habitable homes circling distant stars well before our local star turns into a red giant and the Earth melts. I call these two challenges the Greenie Challenge and the Trekkie Challenge. These challenges are interrelated. It will take us a very long time to reach the stars, so we must, meanwhile, take good care of our only home, planet Earth.

I feel that while green preservation and self-control *a lá* Chimpanzee Paradise is vital, it isn't enough. We also need the motivation and inspiration of our Star Trek vision of a grand and glorious future. We are a venturesome species, and we dream of immortality, of inheriting the cosmos. We can have the best of both. Our green thumbs and starry eyes naturally go together. Hand in hand, arm in arm, the Greenies and Trekkies will lead us to our destiny. The universe is young, we are young, and our cosmic evolutionary future stretches before us—an immense banquet we will savor for eons.

Author's Note

I dissipated my teenage years searching through philosophy, history, and science for human meaning in a vast universe with my buddy Rich and his little sister Cheryl. Then a morbid fascination with self-acting machines diverted me into years as an electrical-engineering rocket scientist and then, as an astronomer, many more years developing automated telescopes that I used at a mountaintop observatory to observe eclipsing and pulsating stars.

In retirement of sorts, I reverted back to my teenage search for human meaning in the cosmos, and spent almost two decades researching and writing a book that presents my synthesis of science's evolutionary epic. My "feature-length" recounting of our cosmic evolutionary story is available as *Humanity: The Chimpanzees Would Be Ants* from www.CollinsFoundationPress.org.

In my other "back to the future" move, I tracked down my secret teenage sweetheart, Cheryl, and courted and married her. Contemplating the cosmos together again, we are happily living out our story at Rainbow's End, our cozy little home on California's picturesque Central Coast.

For my part I know nothing with any certainty,
but the sight of the stars makes me dream.
Vincent van Gogh

The Epic Emerges Through Research and Wonder

Cheryl Genet

The evolutionary epic builds on a vast amount of new knowledge generated in recent centuries (much of it in recent decades) through careful and rigorous scientific research conducted throughout the world in many different disciplines from nuclear physics, to cosmology, to biology, to human history.

David Christian

The Big Bang birth of the universe was followed in time by the "Little Bang" of the first biped making a simple tool—the birth of technological and environmental control in what would become the human species. Eventually our technology would help us understand the pieces of our own past and draw them together into our scientific creation story. This section considers how we have learned our own story through painstaking research driven by a capacity to wonder and question. It traces our ancestral spread out of Africa, illuminating the critical contribution of technologies such as tool use and the harnessing of fire to the ability of Homo species to move into areas of the planet with much colder climates. "The Little Bang" discusses our earliest use of tools while "Fire and Civilization" specifically describes the role fire use has played in the building of civilization and its eventual ties to global warming.

As our technology has allowed humans to explore our world from the depths of our past to the vastness of outer space, it has also permitted the quantification of both relationships and meaning to aid in the understanding of their importance and implications. "Toward an Information Morality: Imperatives Derived from the Statistical Mechanics of Meaning" is one such effort in quantification. "Having such a means of evaluation [of meaningful relations] suggests implications of applying such a measure to our actions in this world—that is, it can provide a basis for normative, objective values, a form of 'moral realism,' informing, for example, choices between preservation and exploration."

Astronomy, physics, and cosmology have provided us with a greatly expanded understanding of the evolution of the physical universe from the Big Bang to the formation of planets capable of bearing life. How many a young dreamer has been inspired to a career in one of these sciences by the simple persuasion of a star-filled night sky? How many have been driven by the wonder of what they explore to interpret the universe in terms of meaning? One such theological interpretation is found in "An Astronomer's Faith," yet it is also pointed out that exploration may lead to alternate interpretations:

> One may not be able to join...in...an explicitly theological interpretation of, say, the stages in stellar evolution that their spectra outline, but surely an appreciation of the immense energies and essential wonder of these physical processes must be everyone's reaction.

> This was a world in which most of them would, sooner or later, be killed and eaten by the large cats that prowled the semi-open woodlands and open grasslands.
> Kathy Schick and NickToth

Imagining a Day in the Lives of Our Evolutionary Ancestors

Kathy Schick and Nicholas Toth

The bipeds move along the margin between the dense riverine forest and the less dense woodland searching for the seasonably available fruit and berries, two of the staples of their diet. There are over three dozen members in this social group: adults, adolescents, and infants being carried by their mothers, who bore children by the time they were fifteen years old and were usually dead by thirty.

The serpentine ribbon of foliage along the stream course, with close access to climbable trees, provided relative safety from a host of predators. This was a world in which most of them would, sooner or later, be killed and eaten by the large cats that prowled the semi-open woodlands and open grasslands. This grim reality was rarely far from their thoughts as they foraged.

These cats would sometimes leave behind parts of animal carcasses of browsing or grazing herbivores that they had killed. Their jaws and teeth were evolved to be consummate flesh-cutters, but not the bone-crushing organs of the contemporary species of hyenas. Normally only the larger, denser bones of the skeleton and scraps of meat were left behind. This could provide the bipeds with a source of marrow and brains, as they would crack open the long bones and skulls with stone hammers and anvils if they could beat the hyenas to the kill.

Today, however, was something different. A pride of saber-tooth cats has killed a hapless, young buffalo in the woodlands. But this time they had been driven off by a number of irate members of the buffalo herd, whose thundering hooves shook the ground as they charged and pursued the large, retreating cats for some distance. The young buffalo had weighed about a half ton. Only the viscera of the animal had been consumed by the cats. An almost complete carcass of such a large mammal was an unusual bonanza for these bipeds, more accustomed to hunting smaller game such as gazelles, spring hares, or lizards, and collecting slow-moving tortoises and bird eggs.

The bipeds see their opportunity. They go to an exposed gravel bar in the shallows on the inner curve of the stream. With dexterous, deft hands they choose some of the larger, dark lava cobbles and quickly run out to the kill. Using a spherical cobble as a hammer, one of the bipeds strikes a violent, glancing blow to the edge of a flatter, disc shaped cobble, removing a large cortical flake. A dozen more blows are struck from that same cobble edge, producing a shower of sharp-edged flakes and fragments on the ground. Three of the largest, sharpest, and most comfortable flakes are chosen as knives. Soon most of the other adults and adolescents are banging on similar rocks, creating a cacophony of percussion that had become a unique sound and sight in this primeval world, and could be heard up to a half mile away.

Cutting quickly through hide and muscle, the bipeds are able to disar-ticulate much of the carcass into smaller, transportable parts and take them back to the safety and shade of the riverine forest. Two individuals share in dragging each meaty hind limb by gripping the shank above the hoof, and oth-ers carry portions of forelimb, rib cage, backbone, and pelvis. Two adolescents playfully drag the severed, wide-eyed buffalo head, each grabbing one of the large black horns.

Under the trees they consume the portions of buffalo at a slower pace, either ripping meat off with their bare teeth or using stone flakes to cut through hide and cut meat off the bone. The long bones are cracked with large cobble hammers, using the massive exposed root systems of the trees as anvils, exposing the red marrow inside...

Editor's Note:

This wonderful vignette is the introduction to Schick and Toth's fasci-nating chapter that follows: "The 'Little Bang': The Origins and Adaptive Significance of Human Stone Toolmaking." Billions of years after the Big Bang, our bipedal ancestors struck one stone against another and the Little Bang ushered in the evolutionary tool-making path to all modern technology and civilization itself.

When the latest glaciation ended approximately 10,000 years ago, human populations were poised in a novel position in the course of their evolutionary development: they were fully modern in physical form, apparently possessed modern cognitive abilities, had developed and maintained social organizations supporting adaptation to a wide range of environments, and had managed to spread to virtually every continent on the Earth (except Antarctica).

KathySchick and Nick Toth

The "Little Bang"

Figure 1. The "Little Bang": Hitting one stone against another to produce sharp-edged stone flakes. This is a relatively simple, though not intuitively obvious, way to produce a cutting tool. The earliest known archaeological sites show that stone toolmakers 2.6 million years ago were remarkably skillful in such flaking activities.

The "Little Bang"
The Origins and Adaptive Significance
of Human Stone Toolmaking

Kathy Schick and Nicholas Toth

Introduction

Beginning around two-and-a-half million years ago, our proto-human ancestors embarked upon a novel evolutionary journey that has never been traveled by any other species in the history of life on Earth. This journey involved a new adaptive pattern, one that emphasized the making of flaked stone tools produced by hitting one stone with another (the "Little Bang") and that was transmitted by cultural learning (Figure 1, opposite page). Technology and culture have truly transformed our species from a small-brained, ape-like creature restricted to a small portion of Africa to the large-brained modern humans now inhabiting every continent and almost every habitat on our planet.

This transformation is a vital component of our evolutionary epic, one with critical phases that have unfolded over the past several million years, with each phase serving as the foundation for the next in our biological and cultural evolution. In the course of this journey, our biological evolution (changes in our genome with dramatic consequences on our bodies, brains, and cognition) and our cultural evolution (including our technologies, our cultural capacity, and our social groups) have become deeply intertwined and inextricable. Starting two-and-a-half million years ago, our species' evolutionary journey emerged as a new kind of adaptation in organic evolution on Earth, one depending on the co-evolution of our technology and our biology, which we have called "*techno-organic*" evolution (Figures 2 through 6 on next two pages; Schick and Toth 1993). Through regular, inventive use of external tools, hominids were able to expand their repertoire of food resources and their overall niche deftly and rapidly, using tools as 'synthetic organs' so to speak, to access foods usually available to more specialized animals.

Here we will explore critical junctures and elements in this evolutionary journey. We will include evidence concerning technology and culture (from the archaeological record), hominid biological evolution (from the fossil record and, within the past few hundred thousand years, DNA studies), and ancient environments (from the geological record, animal fossils, and indicators of climate and habitat). Interestingly, the pace of human evolution has not been constant over time—rather, it has quickened markedly over the past several million years, producing rapid changes in some aspects of our biology (such as our brain), along with especially dramatic, accelerating changes in our technology and culture.

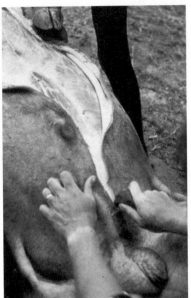

Figure 2. (left) Using a simple stone flake to cut through the hide of a wildebeest. (The animal had died of natural causes.)

Figure 3. (right) Using a stone hammer and anvil to access nutritious marrow within a limb bone.

Figure 4. Using the simplest stone technology to butcher the world's largest terrestrial animal, an elephant. (The animal had died of natural causes.)

Figure 5. Using a stone hammer and anvil to process hard-shelled nuts.

Figure 6. Using a sharp-edged cobble (a "chopper") in wood working, as for preparing a digging stick or a spear.

Human 'Hallmarks' Emerged in a Sequence, Not as a Package

For some time it had been assumed that the evolution of bipedal walking, the invention of stone technology, and the dramatic increase in hominid brain size evolved in tandem as a package, so to speak. One line of argument was that bipedal locomotion perhaps evolved to free the hands for manipulative tool use, and then such tool use quickly selected for a surge in brain size to support intelligent tool behaviors, so that these developments appeared almost simultaneously on the scene. Interestingly, paleoanthropological research in the past few decades has successfully decoupled these evolutionary developments as far as the time of their emergence, with upright, bipedal walking appearing very early in the evolution of the human lineage (over 4 million years ago), stone tools emerging much later (by 2.5 million years ago), and then a significant increase in brain size beginning even later (starting by about 2 million years ago) (Figure 7).

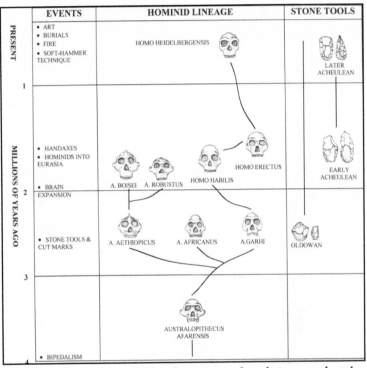

Figure 7. Major hominid fossils, stone tool traditions, and evolutionary events between four million years ago and 250,000 years ago. The "Events" column also includes more recent developments up to about 10,000 years ago, including the emergence of burial practices in the past 100,000 years and of artwork starting 30,000 to 40,000 years ago.

Thus, these three "hallmarks" of humans that help distinguish us among our animal relatives—our strange mode of walking, our dependence on tools to survive and adapt, and our unusually large brains—have evolved at different times in our evolutionary past. This is not to say that they are totally unrelated, or that the evolution of one did not impact in some way the later evolutionary developments (e.g. hands freed from locomotion could usefully be put to other tasks, and intelligent tool use quite likely enhanced significantly selection for a larger brain). Nevertheless, mechanisms of natural selection appear to have acted on these adaptations at somewhat separate times in our evolutionary past, so that some of our ancestors were walking bipedally but showing no reliance on tools for two million years or more, and, subsequently, relatively small-brained bipedal ancestors were making stone tools for thousands of generations, over the course of several hundred thousand years, before the human brain apparently began its explosive evolutionary expansion.

Divergence of hominids from the African apes
Molecular evidence strongly suggests that the last common ancestor of humans and the African apes (gorillas, chimpanzees, and bonobos) was between 5 to 7 million years ago. Recent fossil finds from Chad and Kenya at around six million years ago suggests that these forms were already derived towards the human condition and may represent very early hominids.

Bipedal Walking Emerges Early, Predating Stone Tools
We now know that bipedal walking emerged among hominids millions of years before we see the first stone tools. There is good evidence in the forms of functional morphology of hominid postcranial bones of *Australopithecus afarensis* (for an overview see Ward 2002) and footprints in volcanic ash at Laetoli, Tanzania, that human ancestors were upright-walking between 4.2 and 3.0 million years ago. In addition, a proximal femur from Baringo, Kenya may indicate that this form of locomotion may even go back to 6 million years ago.

What is important to note here is that bipedal walking appears to emerge millions of years before the earliest recognizable stone artifacts in the prehistoric record. Thus, ancient hominids were walking bipedally for at least 1.5 million years before we see stone tools emerge in the archaeological record at 2.6 million years ago. It is also important to realize that a variety of forms—a number of species—of early hominids were bipedal walkers, some of them contemporary with the ancestors of *Homo sapiens*. Only one lineage of these bipedal apes, however, has survived to the present day, represented by *Homo sapiens sapiens*, or modern humans.

Stone Tools Predate Encephalization
The earliest stone tools are now well documented at 2.5 to 2.6 million years ago at the site of Gona in Ethiopia. These consist of flaked pieces of stone, rocks that have been hit, one against another, to strike off chips or flakes from a cobble or chunk of stone. The earliest flaked stone artifacts in Africa are

commonly called "Oldowan" technology, named after the famous site of Olduvai Gorge (Figure 8). It was a very simple, yet significant, beginning for human
technology, signaling a shift toward repeated reliance on external tools beyond
our biological equipment in order to accomplish some tasks and ultimately,
adapt. A large number of such stone 'artifacts' (materials produced by deliberate, artificial means rather than by natural forces), numbering normally in the
hundreds, are generally found at the earliest sites. Several sites have now been
found at Gona bracketed within this time period.

Figure 8. A range of Oldowan artifact forms. Top row: Hammerstone and typical types of cores commonly found at early sites. Bottom row: A range of typical flakes struck from such cores.

Only two hominid forms are known from Ethiopia during the time period
of the earliest stone tools, *Austalopithecus garhi* (within the same general region
of Ethiopia) and *Australopithecus aethiopicus* (further south in Ethiopia) (for a recent overview of early sites and contemporary fossils, see Schick and Toth 2006).
If one of these were responsible for the stone tools (discussed further below), it is
significant that neither shows appreciable brain size increase or encephalization
far beyond that of other australopithecines. The first definite sign of significant
encephalization in hominids is only seen several hundred thousand years after
these earliest stone tools, in early forms of *Homo*. As discussed further below, it
may well be that the use of early stone tools paved the way to encephalization, but
only after many generations of selection for this behavior over several hundred
thousands of years. This may well be a classic case of a behavioral adaptation
preceding the biological adaptation that would help support it.

Who Were the Earliest Stone Toolmakers?

At our current state of knowledge, the complete 'line-up' for potential tool-makers in the early period, i.e. fossil hominid species contemporary with early archaeological sites during the first million years of stone tools, would include a number of species (see Figure 7 and Klein 1999). Several of these are major candidates. However, not all of these major candidate species are contemporary with the very earliest sites, and others later go extinct while stone toolmaking continues, so it is easier to narrow down the known possibilities for the earliest toolmakers. In East Africa, where the earliest stone tools sites are found by 2.5-2.6 million years ago, two hominid forms are roughly contemporaneous with the early stone tools from Gona: *Australopithecus garhi* from the Middle Awash of Ethiopia and *Australopithecus* (*Paranthropus*) *aethiopicus*, known from the Omo Valley in Ethiopia and West Turkana in Kenya.

Thus far, however, the so-called "robust australopithecines," including *A. aethiopicus*, are found within the East African region, but they are not known as far north in the African rift as the early archaeological sites at Gona, and so it becomes harder to argue their case as the prime candidate for makers of the earliest stone tools. Also, the robust australopithecines in East Africa and in South Africa continue to survive and evolve for more than a million years after the beginning of stone technology, but throughout this time manifest biological adaptations in their jaws and teeth (e.g., large molars, large chewing muscles) that indicate adaptation to chewing tough foods. Selection for such strong features in the robust australopithecines would argue for an adaptation still based largely on biological mechanisms rather than technological innovation and mediation. Coupled with this evidence for profound biological adaptation they were pursuing, a lack of a profound increase in brain size in these robust australopithecine lineages over a span of more than a million years, while other hominids were manifesting significant brain expansion, would suggest they were not engaging in an intelligence-mediated, technological adaptation, and are not the primary makers of early stone tools. They are contemporary, however, with early stone tools, and, even if not the principal tool-maker, may well have observed the making and use of tools on occasion, and it cannot be ruled out that they could have incorporated some manipulation of such tools in their lives and adaptation.

So who are the other major candidates for earliest stone toolmakers? Some palaeoanthropologists have argued on paleontological grounds that *A. garhi* is a likely candidate for the ancestor of our genus, *Homo*. As *A. garhi* is found in 2.5 million-year-old Bouri deposits in the Middle Awash region of Ethiopia, it could be responsible for cut-marked bones at Bouri and for the stone tools in nearby deposits of similar age at Gona. In South Africa, the hominid form known from 2.5 million years ago is *Australopithecus africanus*, known from the cave sites of Sterkfontein, Makapansgat, and Taung. However, no stone tools have ever been found in *A. africanus*-aged cave deposits in this part of Africa, making it hard to support this species' candidacy as maker of the earliest stone tools. Thus, despite the fact that *A. garhi* still has a relatively small, more ape-size brain, as it is arguably ancestral to later *Homo* species, which show significant brain expansion within a few hundred thousand years, and is contemporary in the same region with early stone technologies, *A. garhi* is presently a very good candidate for the earliest stone toolmaking species.

It has sometimes been argued that perhaps some other lineage, representing an early form of *Homo*, may have been evolving in Africa during this time but has not yet been discovered, and that such an early, yet-undiscovered early *Homo* species may have been responsible for the earliest stone tools. This could yet be proven with future exploration and discovery, but at present it would appear that *A. garhi* may well represent such an early lineage that led to *Homo*, though without the brain expansion that was soon to be seen within this evolutionary group.

The Origins and Significance of Hominid Toolmaking

Origins of Stone Toolmaking

Chimpanzee behavior has given us some possible models for early hominid flaked stone technologies. Chimpanzees use rocks for nut cracking (hammers and/or anvils), and for throwing in defense or display; both of these behaviors could accidentally produce sharp-edged spalls from fracture. It would appear likely that the earliest fractured rocks may well have been generated as by-products of operations such as these. Other early hominid behaviors that could have produced accidentally fractured rock include breaking open animal bones (acquired through scavenging or hunting, or both) with stone hammers and anvils to access marrow and brains, and the aimed throwing of rocks.

Once such fractured rocks were produced, perhaps initially inadvertently and intermittently, early hominids would have been able to explore the usefulness of their sharp edges, particularly for cutting activities. It would appear likely that such behavioral advances—hammering or other activities producing sharp-edge flakes as byproduct, then trial-and-error experimentation with the functional cutting edges at hand—may have finally led to the intentional, goal-directed flaking of stone, so to produce stone 'knives.'

Although chimpanzees show a range of tool using and tool-making in the wild, including such hammering activities, they have not yet been observed flaking stone. It has been possible, though, to conduct experiments teaching captive modern apes to make and use stone tools (Figure 9). These studies indicate a basal level of technological ability in our closest living ape relatives that may well have 'pre-adapted' our ancestors for stone tool manufacture (Toth et al. 1993; Schick et al. 1999; Toth et al. 2006). A three-way comparison, however, of stone tools made by modern humans, by the earliest tool-makers in Africa, and by modern apes indicate that the early tool-makers 2.6 million years ago already had a surprising level of skill, closer to that exhibited by modern humans than that developed thus far in experimental tool-making among modern apes (Toth, Schick, and Semaw 2006).

Figure 9. Kanzi, a captive bonobo (*Pan paniscus*), making stone tools. Kanzi began to make such stone tools in 1990 in an experiment teaching him through modeling to make such tools and use them in cutting activities. He and his younger sister, Panbanisha, are both quite proficient stone toolmakers, although their skill level is still somewhat less than that of the early hominid toolmakers 2.6 million years ago.

Adaptive Significance of Early Stone Tools

Experimental archaeological studies (Jones 1994; Schick and Toth 1993; Toth 1985) have demonstrated that early stone artifacts could have been used for a range of activities, including stone tool manufacture, animal butchery (hide-slitting, disarticulation, meat cutting, and marrow-processing), hide-scraping, nut-cracking, and wood-working to make simple digging sticks or spears (see Figures 2 through 6). Prehistoric evidence for tool-related activities include cut-marks and stone hammer/anvil fracture patterns on fossil animal bones as well as micro-wear polished on stone tool edges consistent with meat-cutting, wood-scraping, and the cutting of soft plant matter. The development of cutting implements in the early hominid tool repertoire is almost certainly one of the most important adaptive elements in our techno-organic evolution.

More complex tool-use would have ultimately allowed early hominids to significantly expand their diet breadth and make these tool-using populations better adapted to rapidly changing environments. Archaeological sites become much more numerous and complex through time as a co-evolution of biology, intelligence, social behavior, culture, and technology occurred (Washburn, 1960; Lumsden and Wilson, 1981; Schick and Toth, 1993).

Hominid Cognition and Early Technology

Within a half-million to a million years after the first known stone tools, new forms of hominids begin to be seen in the fossil record, ones with larger cranial capacities usually exceeding 600 cc. These new forms are usually assigned to the genus *Homo* (*H. rudolfensis*, *H. habilis*, and *H. ergaster/erectus*).

Numerous models for encephalization in human evolution have been proposed to try to explain this dramatic pattern through time. Aiello and Wheeler's "expensive tissue" hypothesis (1995) suggests that a higher-quality diet (higher in protein and fat and lower in cellulose and toxins) through more omnivorous foraging and tool-use could have decreased gut size and energetic costs for digestion, allowing for larger brains. Dunbar's "social intelligence" model (1995, 1998) correlated higher neocortex ratios in primate brains with larger group sizes, arguing that increased social complexity from larger group sizes drove such encephalization. Barrickman *et al.* (2008) found a correlation between larger brain size and an increase in reproductive lifespan, as well as a decrease in adult mortality due to more complex foraging patterns and social behaviors and better avoidance of predators.

A quantum change in stone technologies can be seen in the emergence in Africa of new tool forms called Acheulean technology by approximately 1.6 to 1.7 million years ago. Acheulean technology involves the production of tools such as 'handaxes' and 'cleavers,' indicating the deliberate shaping of large flakes or cobbles into large, sharp cutting tools (Figure 10). Such tool forms are remarkably long lasting in the prehistoric record, produced over a span of more than a million years and spread over great distances, from the southern tip of Africa to as far north as England and as far east as India. In the latter phases of Acheulean technology, between about 500,000 and 250,000 years ago, many of these tools show superb technological finesse and often-refined symmetry, suggestive perhaps of some aesthetic sense in their production.

The Spread of Hominids out of Africa

By approximately 1.8 million years ago, hominid populations had spread out of Africa and into Eurasia. The site of Dmanisi in the Republic of Georgia, in the foothills of the Caucasus Mountains, has yielded five hominid crania, an abundance of fossil animal fauna, and Oldowan stone tools from deposits between 1.8 and 1.7 million years old. Interestingly, these hominids appear to be intermediate between *Homo habilis* and *Homo erectus* (some paleoanthropologists call them *Homo georgicus*), with cranial capacities between 600-700 cc. Also of great interest, one adult individual is missing all of its upper and lower dentition, yet managed to survive for some time (Lordkipanidze *et al.* 2005).

In East Asia, some of the *Homo erectus* fossils in Java may be well over one million years old (Swisher *et al.*, 1994), as well as a number of archaeological localities in the Nihewan Basin of northern China (Zhu *et al.*, 2004). Stone tools from East Asia from this period are characterized by simple Oldowan-like technologies. Other early Eurasian archaeological sites with fragmentary hominid fossils dating to between 1.4 and 1.0 million years ago include Ubeidiya, Israel, Atapuerca (Elephantine locality), Spain, and Orce, Spain.

Figure 10. A range of Acheulean tool forms (in the top row: two handaxes, a cleaver and a pick), which emphasize the shaping of a large flake or cobble into a tool with a long, sharp cutting edge. Bottom row: A hammerstone ("spheroid"), a flake scraper, and trimming flakes produced in making such large cutting tools.

Migration, Expansion, and Transformation

Getting Established

By approximately 500,000 to 200,000 years ago, hominid populations had established at least transitory populations in much of Africa and the southern to middle latitudes of Eurasia. Many sites in this time period contain extremely well-made artifacts, including highly symmetrical handaxes which not only show expert control of the tool-making process but also possible evidence of the emergence of an aesthetic sense. Some sites also show special tool-making procedures (such as 'soft-hammer' flaking that produces more refined tools, and sophisticated 'prepared core' techniques designed to produce consistent types of flakes).

Significant technological innovations that emerged during this period include new tool forms such as wooden spears, as well as good evidence of controlled use of fire. These would have added greatly to hominid ability to adapt to changing environments of the time, enabling hominids to successfully hunt large animals and to secure heat, light, and protection, as well as to cook food. Hominids during much of this time include *Homo heidelbergensis* in Europe and *Homo rhodesiensis* and, late in this period, *Homo helmei* in Africa. Towards the end of this period, Neandertal-like forms also appear.

Becoming Human

In the period between about 200,000 and 40,000 years ago, prevailing hominid forms include early anatomically modern humans (*Homo sapiens*) and Neandertals (*Homo neandertalensis*) (Trinkaus and Shipman 1993). Early modern human remains are relatively uncommon, with remains reported in East Africa, South Africa, and Israel. Studies of mitochondrial DNA of modern populations appear to indicate that all modern humans descended from a population in East Africa about 200,000 years ago (Cann *et al.* 1987). Studies of both mitochondrial DNA and Y-chromosome DNA indicate that the ancestors of modern human populations in Eurasia spread out of Africa approximately 60,000 to 70,000 years ago, with subsequent group migrations afterwards.

Interestingly, there is little distinct archaeological difference between sites associated with Neandertals and early modern humans (Middle Palaeolithic, Middle Stone Age). They seem to share similar technologies (prepared cores, flake tools, and stone points), although some sites associated with early modern humans have also yielded sporadic evidence of possible jewelry (e.g., perforated shells), bone points, simple engraved objects, or systematic exploitation of shellfish; such traits, however, do not become common until the last 40,000 years. Of note, the earliest evidence of almost certain intentional burials is documented from a number of Neandertal sites.

A Creative Explosion

Starting after 50,000 years ago there develops a more widespread presence of modern humans, although Neandertal forms continue to overlap with *Homo sapiens* in parts of Western Europe for almost 20,000 years. During this period, the last phase the Ice Age between about 50,000 and 10,000 years ago, the prehistoric record reveals what has often been regarded as a "creative explosion" (Pfeiffer 1982). This refers not only to new technological devices but also to the sudden appearance of a variety of forms of impressive artwork as well as widespread evidence of personal adornment and ornaments.

The earliest definitive art emerges full-blown and well executed in the archaeological record over 30,000 years ago. This early art is also remarkable in terms of the mastery the prehistoric artists had achieved in diverse media, each of which must have had precursors, although earlier and theoretically cruder developmental stages of these artistic traditions have not been found. These include figurines of various Ice Age animals (including horses, mammoths, bear, and felids) as well as apparent therianthropic (part human, part animal) figurines sculpted out of mammoth ivory dating to more than 30,000 years ago, as found at Vogelherd and neighboring sites in the Upper Danube region of southwest Germany (Conard 2003). Also dating to approximately 32,000 years ago, finely detailed cave paintings, drawings, and engravings of various animal species (including lion, bison, reindeer, extinct cattle, rhinoceros, mammoth, and cave bear) have been found within the cave of Chauvet in southeast France (Chauvet *et al.* 1996). During this period, musical instruments also appear in the form of apparent 'flutes' of perforated animal limb and finger bones, and there is widespread occurrence of decorative items made from beads of shells and teeth. It has sometimes been suggested that fully modern language emerged during this time period. Although there is no definitive evidence that earlier human populations lacked modern language, it is clearly arguable that these Ice Age artists possessed fully modern means of communicating and maintaining cultural traditions with use of a fully developed language.

Significantly, during this period at the end of the last Ice Age, human societies also show enhanced technological prowess and diversity, with a range of new devices and technologies appearing, including spear throwers, bone needles (implying more finely-made clothing and materials), the bow and arrow, harpoons, and stone lamps. While these late Ice Age peoples still made their 'living' by hunting and gathering, they appear not only to have achieved modern physical form but appear also, by at least this time, to have developed modern ways of thinking, behaving, and creating.

Amazingly, the creative traditions of these Ice Age artists, encompassing cave art, portable art such as figurines, decoration of utilitarian items such as spearthrowers, lasted for over 20,000 years in Western Europe. These disappear, however, at the end of the last glaciation. It would appear that environmental changes, including profound reduction in open grasslands and large herds of grazing animals, spurred profound changes in human subsistence patterns and, ultimately, in the cultural systems of values and rituals that had supported these Ice Age societies for tens of thousand of years.

The End of the Beginning

When the latest glaciation ended approximately 10,000 years ago, human populations were poised in a novel position in the course of their evolutionary development: they were fully modern in physical form, apparently possessed modern cognitive abilities, had developed and maintained social organizations supporting adaptation to a wide range of environments, and had managed to spread to virtually every continent on the Earth (except Antarctica). In no previous interglacial had humans been so well developed in all of these realms—physical, cognitive, societal, and geographic—and prepared to adapt to the rapidly changing ecosystems as the ice sheets retreated.

Very soon within the ensuing postglacial (or better, interglacial) period—often called the Holocene—these wide-ranging human populations engaged in a great cultural experiment. Widely dispersed and even on different continents, within several thousand years, diverse human populations embarked on a new pathway to survive: controlling the reproduction of select groups of plants and animals, i.e., domestication and food production. Most of such domestication was for food sources, although some also eventually provided labor (e.g., animals for work or transport) or hunting and protection (e.g., dogs). The earlier societies that embarked on this route did so with the local populations of plants and animals in their particular regions—e.g., wheat, barley, goats and sheep in the Near East; rice, millet, and pigs in China; corn, beans, and maize in Mexico—though over time domesticates eventually spread far beyond their original regions.

In each of these developing regions of food production, we eventually see broadly similar "ripple effects" of this transformation in subsistence: development of larger populations, significant and long-term settlements, more complex social structure, role specialization and craftsmen, organized religion, centralization of power, often large-scale or even 'monumental' architecture, sometimes armies and periods of expansion and conquest, and, in some instances, even taxes. Thus, within regions where food production produced large-scale, ever-more complex societies, these trappings of civilization emerged over time.

But our hunter-gatherer past is not long behind us, and it has shaped our bodies, brains, and our psyches over the long haul of evolutionary time. Humans have lived in large-scale, complex societies only within the past 400 generations or so, at the very most. In contrast, our Stone Age ancestors, living off the land in smaller and more closely-knit groups and depending on stone tools in their adaptation, extend back over 100,000 generations to those early tool-makers in Africa. We are still very new and very inexperienced in this novel way of life we have developed. We are cramming ourselves into gigantic settlements, sprawling over most of the Earth, developing ever more complex technologies, entering into global economies, exploiting a number of critical food and energy resources to near-exhaustion, endangering many other species through direct competition or indirect effects of our expansion and food needs, and putting incredible strain on our political and social systems. Energy—fuel for our technologies and food for our massive, ever-growing population—has understandably and necessarily become a central and prominent concern worldwide that will certainly become ever more pressing over time.

There obviously is no way of going back to our Stone Age way of life (at least deliberately…), with modern population densities requiring ever more efficient means of food production, and with our value systems oriented in countless ways around this new way of life we have created. Looking back on our technological trajectory, it is nothing short of incredible how we have transformed ourselves in a mere 2.5 million years—from that rather insignificant-looking biped knocking two rocks together in East Africa to the present world population of 6.7 billion *Homo sapiens* in an increasingly complex, technological world. Hopefully we will give ourselves sufficient time to learn to cope with the brave new world we have created. We *are* smart—but *are we smart enough?*

References

Aiello, L. C. and Wheeler, P. 1995. The expensive-tissue hypothesis. *Current Anthropology* 36 (2), 199-221.

Barrickman, N. L., Bastian, M. L., Isler, K., and van Schaik, C.P. 2008. Life history costs and benefits of encephalization: A comparative test using data from long-term studies of primates in the wild. *Journal of Human Evolution* 54, 568-590.

Cann, R. L., Stoneking, M., and Wilson, A. C. 1987. Mitochondrial DNA and human evolution. *Nature* 325, 31-36.

Chauvet, J.-M., Deschamps, E. B., and Hillaire, C. 1996. *Dawn of Art: The Chauvet Cave, the Oldest Known Paintings in the World*. New York: Abrams.

Conard, N. J. 2003. Palaeolithic ivory sculptures from southwestern Germany and the origins of figurative art. Nature 426 (6968): 830-832.

Dunbar, R. I. M. 1995. Neocortex size and group size in primates: A test of the hypothesis. *Journal of Human Evolution* 28, 287-296.

Dunbar R. I. M. 1998. The social brain hypothesis. *Evolutionary Anthropology* 6, 178–190.

Jones, P. R. 1994. Results of experimental work in relation to the stone industries of Olduvai Gorge. In *Olduvai Gorge—Excavations in Beds III, IV and the Masek Beds (1968-1971), Vol. 5*, ed. M.D. Leakey. Cambridge, UK: Cambridge University Press.

Klein, R. G. 1999. *The Human Career: Human Biological and Cultural Origins*, 2nd edition. Chicago, IL: University of Chicago Press.

Lordkipanidze, D., et. al. 2005. Anthropology: the earliest toothless hominin skull. Nature 434 (7034): 717-8.

Lumsden, C. J. and Wilson, E. O. 1981. *Genes, Mind, and Culture: The Coevolutionary Process*. Cambridge, MA: Harvard University Press.

Pfeiffer, J. E. 1982. *The Creative Explosion*. New York, NY: Harper and Row.

Schick, K. and Toth, N. 1993. *Making Silent Stones Speak: Human Evolution and the Dawn of Technology*. New York, NY: Simon & Schuster.

Schick, K. and Toth, N. 2006. An overview of the Oldowan Industrial Complex: the sites and the nature of their evidence. In *The Oldowan: Case Studies into the Earliest Stone Age*, eds. N. Toth and K. Schick, 3-42. Gosport, IN: Stone Age Institute Press.

Schick, K. D., et. al. 1999. Continuing investigations into the stone tool-making and tool-using capabilities of a bonobo (*Pan paniscus*). *Journal of Archaeological Science 26*, 821-832.

Toth, N. 1985. The Oldowan reassessed: A close look at early stone artifacts. *Journal of Human Evolution 16*, 763-787.

Toth, N., et. al. 1993. Pan the tool-maker: Investigations into the stone tool-making and tool-using capabilities of a bonobo (*Pan paniscus*). *Journal of Archaeological Science 20*, 81-91.

Toth, N., Schick, K., and Semaw, S. 2006. A comparative study of the stone tool-making skills of *Pan*, *Australopithecus*, and *Homo sapiens*. In *The Oldowan: Case Studies into the Earliest Stone Age*, eds. N. Toth and K. Schick, 155-222. Gosport, IN: Stone Age Institute Press.

Trinkaus, E. and Shipman, P. 1993. *The Neandertals: Changing the Image of Mankind*. New York, NY: Knopf.

Ward, C. V. 2002. Interpreting the posture and locomotion of *Australopithecus afarensis*: where do we stand? *Yearbook of Physical Anthropology 119* (45), 185-215.

Washburn, Sherwood L. 1960. Tools and human evolution. Scientific American 203 (3): 3-15.

Without fire, no Homo species would have been able to leave Africa and move into areas of the planet with much colder climates. Certainly during the prolonged periods of glaciation in the late Pleistocene, it would have been very difficult for humans to survive in areas partly covered by glaciers without the artificial warming of their habitats resulting from domesticated fire.

Carlos Camargo

Fire and Civilization

Carlos A. Camargo

As insisted over many years by the Dutch scholar Johan Goudsblom, the domestication of fire has not received the importance it deserves in understanding its role in the process of human evolution, the development of language,
the socialization and cultural processes leading to civilization, and the development of multiple technologies that have brought *Homo sapiens* to the present state of the species (Goudsblom 1992), and, one could add, to the present
quagmire. This brief paper will try to put things into a better perspective.

Fire, as we now know it, did not exist on planet Earth for at least 4100
million years. It requires three elements: fuel, oxygen, and the heat of ignition
(Rossotti 1993, 1-32). There was plenty of heat as the Earth formed 4,567
million years ago (mya), but there was no oxygen in the atmosphere and no organic material to be oxidized with production of more heat and flames. It was
only after the appearance of life on the planet that, very slowly, circumstances
changed that made possible the development of fire. The Earth's atmosphere
3,500 mya did not contain oxygen but had plenty of methane, ammonia, water
vapor, carbon dioxide, and other gasses. When cyanobacteria (formerly called
green-blue algae) evolved 3,000 mya, they used water, carbon dioxide, and
sunlight to produce calcium carbonate and oxygen. This oxygen dissolved in
the ocean water and was combined for millions upon millions of years with
the gigantic amounts of iron and other minerals present in the planet. The
calcium carbonate produced by the cyanobacteria accumulated as stromato-
lites. Eventually oxygen, a product of photosynthesis, began to escape into the
atmosphere, very gradually increasing its concentration.

About 542 mya the long Precambrian period (80% of the Earth's history)
ended. The unparalleled life explosion of the Cambrian and subsequent periods began (Ordovician, Silurian, and Devonian). Precursors of all the major
phyla made their appearance. Why? An increasing concentration of oxygen in
the atmosphere appears to have been a major factor. Many millions of years
later, during the Devonian period, seed-bearing plants spread over the land
and forests developed. The first evidence of forest fires in the form of charcoal
deposits appeared in the Devonian period (416 to 359 million years ago).
Spontaneous, natural fires have been a feature of this planet ever since, the
most common and frequent cause being lightning.

When and how did the first hominid domesticate fire? This is controversial! Many sites and dates have been proposed, as old as over one million years ago for places in Kenya and China. A recent paper from Israel shows strong evidence for anthropogenic (human made) fire near 790,000 years ago (Gore-Inbar 2004, 725). Terra Amata, near Nice, is a place where repeated habitation by *H. erectus* is associated with charcoal deposits. These have been dated to about 200 to 400 thousand years ago (Johanson 2006, 97). The Swartkrans cave in South Africa also has good evidence for anthropogenic fires with dates ranging from 200 thousand to one million years ago (Johanson 2006, 97).

Most scholars attribute the domestication of fire to *Homo erectus*. This has very important consequences. Was fire used for cooking initially? For heat? For illumination? As protection against predators? Against mosquitoes and other pests? As help in hunting? Whatever the reason, fire was found to be exceedingly useful by *Homo erectus* in the Pleistocene.

Cooking

One of the clearest elements to determine whether a fire was natural or anthropogenic is the presence or absence in the charcoal of remains of animal bones that were clearly cooked and show evidence of having been scratched by stone tools as the fire-makers scraped the meat off the bones. This makes it clear that cooking must have been one of the most important uses of early anthropogenic fire.

+ Wood was the preferred, perhaps the only source of fire.
+ From scavengers, hominids became hunters. Fire hunting has been used by practically all aboriginal groups on the planet. Groups of hunters with torches could also cause stampedes of large animal herds, leading the animals over cliffs or into bogs, where they could be butchered.
+ As a result of improved hunting, protein intake increased.
+ Furthermore, cooking made tubers, stems, roots, tendons and other animal and vegetable foods softer and much more easily digestible. Whereas chimpanzees have to chew for many hours every day to fulfill their energy requirements, humans chew for less than one hour daily. Cooked food also lasted longer before becoming spoiled. Eventually, humans learned that smoking of some foods would cause them to be preserved for much longer periods of time.
+ Fire removed toxins and killed agents of disease present in food. Examples include cyanide compounds found in raw cassava, tannins found in acorns, and the multiple parasites and bacteria that would be found in raw and often semi-rotten meat available to scavengers.

It is likely that the nutritional benefits achieved by cooking food played a significant role in some of the evolutionary changes seen in the Pleistocene after the use of fire became prevalent. The cranial capacity of genus *Homo* and therefore its brain size dramatically changed in the last 700,000 years from late *Homo erectus* (Figure 1) to *Homo sapiens*: it increased in size (900 to 1400 cc) and changed its shape and proportions (Johanson 2006, 80-83). The facial structures were also altered, with the teeth becoming smaller and the jaws less powerful, as the forehead expanded and became more vertical.

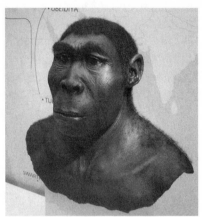

Figure 1

Fire and Socialization

From the most remote antiquity until the early 1800s it was easier to maintain a fire than to create it *de novo*. The fire had to be tended, nursed, and protected from rain, mist, and wind. Wood had to be added at regular intervals to keep it alive. The wood pieces had to have a certain size, so as to not smother the fire, etc. This led to specialization: some people became specialists in doing just that, and if we are to believe the multiple myths emerging in very different societies much later, these keepers of the fire were likely to be women, the Roman Vestal Virgins, keepers of the sacred fire of Rome, being the best known example (Buttita 2002, 75).

As human groups met day after day at the fire to enjoy the warmth and light, to cook and eat, for thousands upon thousands of years, it is not hard to imagine that this led to socialization and contributed to development of language. This may be hard to prove, but it is logical to think that the hundreds of thousands of years of engagement in this pattern of daily gathering at the hearth certainly would have helped to transform the hisses and grunts of the remote ancestors into phonemes, words, and sentences. And as Prof. Goudblom has suggested, the process of civilization began there (Goudblom 1992, 1-12).

Other Uses of Fire in the Paleolithic

Since the overwhelming majority of animals avoid and are repelled by fire and smoke, a fire would provide protection against predators and make a cave safe from attack.

Without fire, no Homo species would have been able to leave Africa and move into areas of the planet with much colder climates. Certainly during the prolonged periods of glaciation in the late Pleistocene, it would have been very difficult for humans to survive in areas partly covered by glaciers without the artificial warming of their habitats resulting from domesticated fire.

And of course, illumination was another superb benefit of anthropogenic fire. No better examples of this exist than the magnificent paintings deep in the interior of caves such as Lascaux, Altamira and in the most recently found (December of 1994) Chauvet cave, with its magnificent horses, lions, aurochs, etc. The latter cave's charcoal from torches used for illumination gives dates of 30,000-32,000 BP (Figure 2).

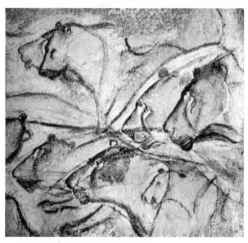

Figure 2

Megafaunal Extinction

+   As *Homo sapiens* improved their hunting techniques, cooked their food, and migrated to different continents and regions, a massive extinction of large animal species took place between 40,000 years ago and the present (Alroy 2001,1893).

+   In Europe, the mammoths disappeared, along with the woolly rhinoceros, cave bears, lions, aurochs, and many others.

+   In the Americas, the horses, quadrupeds that evolved in North America, disappeared soon after the Clovis people appeared on the scene 12,000 years BP. Horses did not return to the American continent until they were brought by Spaniards after 1492. American mammoths were also exterminated. In fact, the highly refined Clovis points were first found in a dried lake near Clovis, New Mexico, among the ribs of slain mammoths (Johanson 2006, 47). Giant sloths, toxodons, smilodons, and other large animals also vanished about 10,000 BP.

* This disappearance pattern, chronologically associated with the arrival of humans has continued until the present time in many islands: moas and 40 other species of birds disappeared in New Zealand after the arrival of the Maoris. Dodos disappeared in Mauritius, elephant birds in Madagascar, etc.

* Controversy exists as to whether climatic changes or other natural phenomena were partly responsible for the disappearance of many of the species mentioned.

The Agricultural Revolution

About 11,000 years ago in several areas of the planet *Homo sapiens* began to settle in agricultural societies. As barley, wheat, and rye were domesticated in the Old World, and potatoes and maize on the American continent, fire played a crucial role by clearing land for planting and transforming forests into fields. This process would be repeated century after century later, as *H. sapiens* expanded their habitat to virgin areas of the planet, such as Australia, New Zealand, and the Americas, and continues to this day in the forest areas of Indonesia, Brazil, and other tropical countries.

Figure 3

Ceramics and Metals

No one knows exactly when this happened. But at some time, a remote ancestor found out that some of the wet clay that happened to be in the hearth had become a hard, very solid, though brittle, material. And pottery was born! The earliest examples are from Japan: the Jomon pottery (Figure 3), named after the decoration used on it by applying ropes to the clay before heating (Jomon means rope in Japanese). The earliest specimens date back to about 13,000 BP.

And then, about 6,000 years ago, someone noticed a reddish, bright, hard lump at the bottom or side of a campfire underneath the dying embers, perhaps after a windy night that increased the temperature of the fire. And this person marveled at the sight of copper and had the insight to recall what kind of rock or ore had been there below the fire. And metallurgy began! A thousand years later, somehow, somewhere, a similar process happened for tin, and the two metals were mixed in different proportions and bronze came to be (Figure 4). Iron smelting first took place in Asia Minor about 1,300 BC and rapidly spread to Europe and the East around 1,000 BC. Humankind also transmuted sand into glass, limestone into mortar, and mud into bricks, as in the Greek myth of Prometheus, the Titan who stole fire from Heaven to give to humanity, his creatures, and thus provided them with the means for all of the arts and technology! (Figure 5)

Figure 4   *Figure 5*

Modern Times

The need to protect and nurse the common fire decreased when *H. sapiens* discovered a variety of methods to create fire *de novo*. When this first happened is uncertain, but for thousands of years people have used friction of wood against wood or the percussion method, hitting a hard rock like flint against a pyrite (an iron containing mineral) so that sparks are produced. After steel became available, flint and steel kits were used until the mid-nineteenth century, as well as magnifying lenses to focus the Sun's rays upon very dry and porous tinder (Figure 6). Needless to say, these methods were not effective in windy and wet conditions. So, we should be eternally thankful to John Walker, an English chemist and apothecary, who in 1827 invented the friction match!

23 (p. 111).

Figure 6

The Industrial Revolution

The control and domestication of fire continues even now—from Watts' steam engine to Rudolf Diesel's engine, from the controlled burning of coal, petroleum, and natural gas to produce electricity, to the jet engines that power our airplanes, and even to the thermonuclear weapons that need detonators of controlled, domesticated fire. Anthropogenic fire in the form of controlled burning of fossil fuels in the last 200 years and the dramatic increase in the world population since 1800 (there were 978 million people on the planet in 1800, whereas there are 6,678 million people in May of 2008, according to the US Census Bureau, Population Division) further emphasizes the dramatic importance of that first step on the road to civilization. The increased production of carbon dioxide, with accumulation of this gas in the atmosphere and the resulting green-house effect and global warming, represent the negative side of the control and domestication of fire by humankind.

And so, in the words of Stephen J. Pyne: "Out of the campfire and hearth arose the kiln, the furnace, the forge, the crucible, the oven and the metal-encased combustion chamber. From cooking food it was a short step to cooking other matter—stone, wood, clay, ore, metal, the air, even seawater, whatever fire could transmute into forms more usable to people. In effect, humanity began to cook the Earth" (Pyne 2001, 129).

References

Alroy, J. 2001. A multispecies overkill simulation of the end-Pleistocene mega-faunal mass extinction. *Science 292*, 1893-1896.

Buttita, I. E. 2002. *Il Fuoco: Simbolismo e Pratiche Rituale.* Palermo: Sellerio Editore.

Goudsblom, J. 1992. The civilizing process and the domestication of fire. *Journal of World History,* 3(1), 1-12.

Goren-Inbar, N., Alperson, N., Kislev, M. E., Simchoni, O., Melamed, Y., Ben-Nun, A., and Werker, E. 2004. Evidence of hominin control of fire at Gesher Benot Ya'aqov, Israel. *Science 304,* 725-728.

Johanson, D. C. and Edgar, B. 2006. *From Lucy to Language.* New York, NY: Simon and Schuster.

Pyne, S. J. 2001. *Fire: A Brief History.* Seattle, WA and London, UK: University of Washington Press.

Rossotti, H. 1993. *Fire.* Oxford, UK; New York, NY; Tokyo, Japan: Oxford University Press.

Having a measure of a quantity establishes the basis for the ability to evaluate, literally to associate a value with that property. So the importance of a measure of this kind is that it gives us a quantitative way to value the encoding of relationships associated with the development of meaningful understanding.

Robert Duisberg

Toward an Information Morality
Imperatives Derived from a Statistical Mechanics of Meaning

Robert Adámy Duisberg

Introduction

The Evolutionary Epic describes the great arc from the initial singularity onward to the ultimate end of the universe. The Big Bang in its extreme improbability is effectively the zero point of entropy from which the universe unwinds, entropy ever increasing. However, within the closed system of our planet and its diaphanous aura, the steady influx of our sun's energy is able to locally drive the entropy down, consistent with thermodynamics' second law, leading to the improbable, myriad order of life on earth. This ordering of life is manifest not only physically, but also in the cognitive capacities of sentient beings—in their creation of mental representations of their experience. These cognitive patterns too constitute diminutions in the ineluctable flux of entropy.

We strive to make sense of the world, to find patterns and discern form in our perceptions of experience. Our understanding of how we manage to do this, to construct meaningful relations out of incoming streams of sensations, has deepened in recent years through research in neurology and artificial neural networks of the kind that now informs cognitive psychology. This chapter proposes a measure of such "meaningful relations" as represented in cognitive systems. Having such a means of evaluation suggests implications of applying such a measure to our actions in this world—that is, it can provide a basis for normative, objective values, a form of "moral realism," informing, for example, choices between preservation and exploitation.

The Mathematical Theory of Information

To understand how we make sense out of information, we may begin with our best understanding of information itself. Information Theory, as formalized by Claude Shannon (1948), has valuable applications in communications. For example, its theorems are useful in the design of optimal digital encoding and compression algorithms for data transmission. In this theory, information is defined in terms of the statistics of symbols in messages in a way that turns out to be mathematically isomorphic to the definition of entropy that comes out of statistical thermodynamics. Specifically, information is defined to be equal to the negative entropy—the "surprise value"—of symbols in messages.

To understand what this means, consider a source of messages M, sending out messages consisting of symbols chosen from a given alphabet of n symbols x_i, where $i=1,...,n$, each with a probability $p(x_i)$ of occurring anywhere in a message. For example, in English, $p(x = \text{`e'}) > p(x = \text{`q'})$. When we read any new symbol in a message, the "surprisal" of the new symbol is taken to be just the inverse of its probability, $1/p(x_i)$. The more unlikely a symbol is to occur, the more surprised we are when it does. The information entropy of the message source as a whole is then taken to be the expectation value for this sense of surprise averaged over all symbols in a large sample of messages, thus:

$$H(M) = \sum_{i=1}^{n} p(x_i) \log(1/p(x_i)) = -\sum_{i=1}^{n} p(x_i) \log p(x_i).$$

This expresses a value of the average surprise imparted by each symbol in the stream as a whole. It is usually measured in "bits" when the logarithms are chosen to be of base 2, and the conventional symbol H is borrowed from thermodynamics where it signifies entropy.

So for example, if the data stream comprises an endless repetition of one character, 'b' say, there is no surprise at all when the next character in the stream arrives. The arrival of 'b' is a complete certainty; the probability of reading 'b' is one. Since $\log(1) = 0$, and since $p(x_i) = 0$ for all other symbols but 'b', the value of the sum above is zero—this corresponds to the *maximum* level of entropy (general sameness), from which it decreases (going negative) for more unpredictable signals. Surprisal and information then increase according to the minus sign above.

For an example at the other extreme, if in another message source the occurrence of each character in the ASCII alphabet is equiprobable, (i.e. if each character were found $(1/128)^{\text{th}}$ of the time), then each successive character will convey a full seven bits of information (an ASCII character is an 8-bit byte with 1 bit reserved as a parity bit). As we can see, the value of the sum is:

$$H = -\sum_{i=1}^{128} \frac{1}{128} \log_2 \left(\frac{1}{128} \right) = \log_2 128 = 7.$$

But consideration of these two extrema of information content point up a sharp disjunction between the information in a message and how meaningful it is, since clearly the upper bound of maximal information corresponds to a condition of gibberish—what might be expected from the proverbial monkeys at typewriters. In fact, Shannon estimated the information rate of English text to be between 0.6 and 1.3 bits per character, far below our 7-bit maximum. This low information rate for meaningful messages reflects the redundancy that necessarily arises from the internal coherence and linguistic structure that are related to meaning. This limitation of information theory, that the measure of information says nothing about its import or significance, suggests that it may be useful to devise a measure, analogous to the statistical measure of information, that can begin to assess and evaluate elements involved in creating meaning in communications. Let us consider some systems that display abilities relating to this question.

Artificial Neural Networks

Research in a relatively new branch of Artificial Intelligence has patterned an entire family of mathematical models after what is known about biological neural networks (DeWilde 1997; Rumelhart, McClelland, and PDP Research Group 1986). These offer an alternative methodology to that of "classical AI," with its emphasis on *a priori* rule-bases or "expert systems," providing particularly efficacious applications aimed at pattern recognition in variable, noisy, or incomplete data sets. Systems based on artificial neural networks find application in such areas as machine recognition of handwritten characters and feature detection in photographs or voice recordings.

Common to all members of this family of models is the notion from graph theory of an array of N nodes, often suggestively referred to as "neurons," formed into a network by a set of connections or directed arcs, also called "axons" or "synapses" in keeping with the metaphor. The arcs are labeled with values called "weights" that represent the strength of synaptic connections, which can be either excitatory or inhibitory. The weights compose a matrix $\mathbf{W}$ of values w_{ij} between each pair of nodes i and j, where $0 < i, j <= N$. Each node i has an associated "activation level," a_i, representing its state of excitation. Each node's excitation is in turn considered to be dependent upon its incoming "stimulus," computed in a straightforward way as the aggregate of the activations of all the other nodes connected to it, weighted by the strength of each such connection, w_{ij} from the j-th node to the i-th. This weighted sum is typically passed through some thresholding function to give the activation level of the node in question.

$$a_i(t) = F\left(\sum_{j \neq i}^{N} w_{ji} a_j(t-1)\right)$$

The time dependence, (t), of the activation levels indicates the manner in which activations tend to propagate through the network, in that a current activation is derived from previous activations of the input nodes. In artificial networks, the propagation dynamics are often synchronously "clocked" through the network in discrete time increments, while in truly distributed implementations, as well as natural systems, the dynamics are likely to be asynchronous. The thresholding function $F(x)$ is sometimes taken to be a step function, as if the nodes were simple switches, but more often it is chosen to be a sigmoid function (so named for its S-like shape, smoothing out the corners of the step function) of the form $F(x) = 1/(1 + e^{-x})$, the differentiability of which is advantageous for algorithms by which these networks "learn." A variety of learning algorithms exist, typically involving the propagation of some feedback from experience or training back through the network to enhance the connection weights that have contributed to correct or advantageous decisions, and to diminish the weights on connections that contribute to errors in recognition.

Whatever the process of learning in either artificial or natural cognitive networks, its results are the modification of connection strengths between neurons so that the resulting networks are characterized by clusterings of nodes that are mutually excitatory. It is this quality in trained artificial neural networks that affords them behaviors we value, such as being able to correctly identify partial or variable inputs; if only part of a mutually excitatory cluster is stimulated, the whole will nonetheless tend to become active. Marvin Minsky (1986), in the model he describes as a "society of mind", roughly associates such mutually excitatory clustering with representations of concepts or fundamental percepts. We may recognize in this our own ability to respond to synecdoche, the poetic device in which reference to a part evokes the whole.

Similar phenomena can be observed as learning occurs in artificial networks. For example, in a system that has learned to recognize handwritten characters, a common subset may exists among the internal nodes that become activated during the recognition of the letters 'A' and 'H.' This common cluster may be associated with the perception of the middle cross-bar in both characters. Thus it is as if, through its exposure to the training data set, the learning algorithm has enabled discernment of the salient components in the data stream upon which to base its decisions, essentially expressing logic of the form "if the character has a cross-bar with vertical side-bars, it is probably an 'H,' but a cross-bar with side-bars that slant in toward the top is more likely an 'A.'"

Note in the above example that the "cross-bar percept" was not pre-programmed into the system. Rather, the salient structure in the information stream impressed itself into the network through learning recognition and finds itself represented in the network as a self-exciting cluster of nodes. Notice also that the clustering of nodes in a network can be considered as a statistical property of the associated graph (Albert and Barabasi 2002). If we imagine an initial state as a fully connected graph in which all connection weights are equal, an effective *tabula rasa* with maximal entropy, and compare this to a well tutored network, we expect to see that salient concepts in the tutorial information stream have become represented as changes in the distribution of weights, effectively implementing the self-excitation of the cluster. This ordering of the weights will be manifest as a reduction in a form of entropy.

Thus the passage of information through a responsive cognitive network can be seen to physically lower the entropy of the network itself, as concepts become represented in mutually excitatory sub-networks. This is analogous to the reduction in entropy of a thermodynamic system as energy is passed through it, indeed just as our stream of solar energy has made possible the ordering of life on Earth.

The Concept of Salience in a Cognitive Network

We saw that information theory gives us a useful measure of information content, but tells us nothing about the meaning in the messages. A measure of the entropy reduction over a matrix of weights can reflect the structuring of the cognitive network so represented, when it has learned to recognize what is meaningful in the information environment it experiences. This reduction in entropy is due to the clustering of weights associated with the learning of salient concepts from experience and provides a means of quantifying that quality. We may define a quantity, call it "salience," which is a direct measure of this organizing of a network as it learns to represent the salient elements in its information environment via mutually excitatory weighting clusters.

Having a measure of a quantity establishes the basis for the ability to evaluate, literally to associate a value with that property. So the importance of a measure of this kind is that it gives us a quantitative way to value the encoding of relationships associated with the development of meaningful understanding. Thus ascribing a value to order and our understanding of it, in a consideration of values or ethics, may stand as a counterweight, for example, to mere economic evaluation.

Formally, a definition of "salience" grows out of an extension to Shannon's approach, by looking at the probability distributions not of the frequencies of symbols in a message, but of the values of the synaptic strengths in a cognitive network that has learned to understand (i.e. correctly categorize) elements of an information stream. Also our entropy measure must be over a two dimensional matrix rather than over Shannon's one-dimensional channel. For simplicity, let the allowed values for the w_{ij} be restricted to a domain of K discrete values $\{w_1, \dots, w_K\}$ (otherwise the outer sum below could be replaced by an integral). Then we have,

$$S(\mathbf{W}) = -\sum_{k=1}^{K} \sum_{i \neq j}^{N} p(w_{ij} = w_k) \log p(w_{ij} = w_k)$$

where $p(w_{ij} = w_k)$ is the probability that a given matrix element in $\mathbf{W}$ has a particular value w_k, in the domain of allowable values for synaptic weights. S is the common symbol for thermodynamic entropy, and is suggested here by association with the notion of "salience."

According to this measure then, the aforementioned *tabula rasa* case will have value of $S = 0$, again because the certainty of that value of $w_{ij} = 1$, for all i unequal to j, by definition.

Consider by contrast, an end case in which the network has condensed into a set of loosely connected, internally tight sub-clusters, in what Barabasi calls a "small worlds model." With a suitable change of basis, the matrix can therefore be arranged so that it has an appearance resembling that sketched below (in which we make the simplification that the domain of weights is $\{0,1\}$).

$$
\mathbf{W} = \begin{pmatrix}
0 & 1 & 1 & \cdots & 0 & \cdots \\
1 & 0 & 1 & \cdots & & \cdots \\
1 & 1 & 0 & 1 & 1 & \cdots \\
& \cdots & 1 & 0 & 1 & \cdots \\
0 & \cdots & 1 & 1 & 0 & \cdots \\
\vdots & \vdots & \vdots & \vdots & \vdots & \ddots
\end{pmatrix}.
$$

In this fragment, there is shown a cluster size of three nodes per cluster. The matrix has a total of $(N^2 - N)$ relevant weights (excluding the diagonal elements, since nodes are not considered to connect to themselves). We can see in this case, by counting six ones in each cluster around three diagonal zeros, that the number of nodes with value 1 is $(6 N / 3) = 2N$. Therefore,

$$
p(w_{ij} = 1) = \frac{2N}{N^2 - N} = \frac{2}{N - 1}, \quad p(w_{ij} = 0) = 1 - \frac{2}{N - 1},
$$

and, for large N,

$$
\log p(w_{ij} = 1) = 1 - \log(N - 1), \quad \log p(w_{ij} = 0) = \log(1 - \frac{2}{N - 1}) \to 0.
$$

Then in this simplified case, again for large N,

$$
S(\mathbf{W}) = -(N^2 - N) \left(\frac{2}{N - 1} \right) (1 - \log(N - 1))
$$

$$
= 2N (\log(N - 1) - 1) \approx 2N \log N.
$$

This displays a marked increase in the value of salience as the matrix has condensed, through learning, into a set of self-exciting clusters.

Conclusion

It follows from a statistical definition of meaning that the reductions in physical entropy associated with sentience and the cognitive awareness of meaningful relations are fundamental, universal, and measurable values. If we lose these ordered states assembled in their myriad diversity, whether through extinctions or environmental destruction or book burning or museum looting, it is a universal loss. We can assert a fundamental and measurable value associated with that loss, and this measurement affords such losses a moral weight in ethical questions of value and conservation.

References

Albert, R. and Barabási, A-L. 2002. The statistical mechanics of complex networks. *Reviews of Modern Physics*, 74, 47-97.

De Wilde, P. 1997. *Neural Network Models*, 2nd ed. New York, NY: Springer Verlag.

Lewis, T., Amini, F., and Lannon, R. 2000. *A General Theory of Love*. New York, NY: Random House.

Minsky, M. 1986. *The Society of Mind*. New York, NY: Simon & Schuster.

Rumelhart, D.E., McClelland, J.L., and PDP Research Group. 1986. *Parallel Distributed Processing: Explorations in the Microstructure of Cognition*. Cambridge, MA: MIT Press.

Shannon, C.E. 1948. A mathematical theory of communication. *Bell System Technical Journal*, 27 (July & October), 379-423, 623-656.

I found that I was undecided whether to treat first the *beauty* of the evolutionary cosmos or its *energy*. Then I realized that the beauty of the universe is a result of the energy within it, and the flow of this energy enhances its beauty. So beauty and energy are intertwined, as can be their treatment.

Christopher Corbally

An Astronomer's Faith Within an Evolutionary Cosmos

Christopher Corbally

Introduction

I am addressing a question that was, in essence, put to me some years ago by a fellow member of a Spiritual Support Team for people living with AIDS. As we were driving to a meeting he asked, "What difference does astronomy make to your faith?" My answer, mindful of an evolutionary cosmos, is from the perspective of an astronomer and a Christian, but I invite you to use the "filter" of your own particular expertise to reflect on your own belief, whether this is in a personal God or some other description of the source beyond your-self that is fundamental to the universe's existence.

Two points can be made about one's "filter" or perspective of expertise. First, just as a polarizing filter can beautifully enhance the effect of clouds for a color picture, whether digital or photographic, so our expertise-filters can enhance our faith, bringing out aspects that would otherwise be less obvious. Secondly, one's own filter is not to be seen as privileged. The astronomer's filter is not better than, say, that of an anthropologist or a poet. Hopefully the various filter-views will become complementary when shared, as I am attempting now with my own.

Beauty and Energy

I found that I was undecided whether to treat first the *beauty* of the evolutionary cosmos or its *energy*. Then I realized that the beauty of the universe is a result of the energy within it, and the flow of this energy enhances its beauty. So beauty and energy are intertwined, as can be their treatment.

The Beauty of Evolutionary Form

Hubble Space Telescope has given us so many beautiful pictures of the universe, and I am sure you will be able to see in your mind's eye some favorite.[1] Perhaps this picture is of a galaxy or maybe a nebula within our own Milky

---

1   If not, go to the HST web site now, <http://hubblesite.org/gallery>, and enjoy looking at some.

Way. In contemplating this picture, the words of Gerald Manley Hopkins can come to mind: "Give beauty back, beauty, beauty, beauty, back to God, beauty's self and beauty's giver" (Hopkins 1967).

Yet a further understanding that comes from astrophysics can enhance, at least for me, this immediate appreciation of beauty, and so of God. The glowing pink parts of a nebula are the result of the interaction of intense radiation from the embedded young stars with the hydrogen gas left over from the birth of those stars. And the blue colored wisps are the result of the scattering of this same intense radiation off the similarly leftover dust particles, in the same manner as makes our Earth's skies blue. The beauty we see is the signature of radiation interacting with the electrons that compose atomic hydrogen and with the particles that make up dust clouds. The radiation alternately energizes electrons and then is released by them, all at most precise frequencies or colors. We are witnessing radiation at play, as it were, with matter.

Not just the colors, but also the shapes and swirls of the nebula are also the result of astrophysical processes. In this case the processes are those of thermodynamics, and so of how hot and cool matter interacts. As Alejandro García-Rivera describes, "Nature tends to flow into the cool and it does so beautifully" (2007, 129). Earlier he opined, "Focusing on form rather than cause gives us a more effective framework to understand the significance and truthfulness of evolutionary theory and a powerful guide in articulating a theology of evolution" (2007, 126). Perhaps this is just a matter of focus, since the cause, at least the immediate or efficient cause from the laws of thermodynamics, is a powerful complement to the perceived form and to its implications. The filter of astrophysics is enhancing what the eye first sees.

(Divine) Energies and the (Divine) Milieu of Evolution

Even more so than in the kind of direct pictures that we have been considering, the beauty of stars is enhanced for me by examining their spectra or rainbows. The history of stellar spectroscopy started with Josef von Fraunhofer in 1814, observing Sirius with a one-inch telescope and spectrograph. Then it continued nearly 50 years later with Father Angelo Secchi, S.J., and fellow pioneers Giovanni Battista Donati, William Huggins, Lewis Rutherford, and George Airy. It culminated in work at the end of the nineteenth century at the Harvard College Observatory, which established our current ordering of stars with respect to their surface temperatures. The movement is one of coming to understand the fascinating personalities of stars via their spectra. In turn, it was discovered in the first part of the twentieth century how those personalities could only be understood in relation to how stars evolve through their lifetimes. Such a picture is dynamic, with one energy source of atomic fusion replacing another as a star progresses from a newborn, to a middle-aged, and then to a giant star nearing its final stages. It is varied, with extremes in surface temperatures and stellar radii and consequently of outputs of radiation, and with different pathways in evolution and huge variations in timescale that depend on initial differences in masses.

An early voice raised in appreciation of the diversity displayed in the universe was that of St. Thomas Aquinas, who wrote that God "produced many and diverse creatures, so that what was wanting to one in representation of the divine goodness might be supplied by another... hence the whole universe together participates in the divine goodness more perfectly, and represents it better than any single creature whatever" (1920, Ia, q. 47, a. 1).

Contemporarily, Philip Hefner (2007) reflects how "the processes and theories of evolution are examples of the energies of God, and scientific study and interpretation of evolution is exactly the appropriate work of the human mind." He goes on to consider how the energies of God are both various and paradoxical, that evolution is the divine milieu in which we have our being, and that the rule of apophasis (attempting to describe the divine, since it is ineffable, in terms of what it is not) applies to our efforts to appraise evolution theologically. One may not be able to join Hefner in such an explicitly theological interpretation of, say, the stages in stellar evolution that their spectra outline, but surely an appreciation of the immense energies and essential wonder of these physical processes must be everyone's reaction. Hence this subsection's heading includes the optional word *Divine* in parenthesis.

The Universe's Zest for Life

The formation of planets around stars is part and parcel of the story of the evolution of stars themselves. Already some 200 planets around other stars are known, and these form some 24 planetary systems.[2] Though these first planets found were the giant ones, like our familiar Jupiter, the trend of finding smaller ones is continuing, and so with the eventual expectation of more earthlike ones. At least in the case of our own Earth, this formation of planets is accompanied by the appearance of life. Others have outlined what we currently know of the fascinating geological and biological processes that took place on Earth, and these implicitly make a point similar to that of David Grumett (2007), that the universe shows not merely a survival instinct but a healthy "zest for life." The (Divine) energies are very fruitful, at least in the one instance that culminated in human consciousness. When we contemplate these processes, then we can understand the sentiment of Aileen O'Donoghue:

---

2   As of November 7, 2007. See <http://exoplanets.org> for an update.

It is in the unexpected, yet very ordinary wonders of nature
and people that call me to believe in God, and "God" is my
name for the creative source of the abundance of the universe that arises in the human soul as love (2007, 112).

A Patient, Nurturing Universe

Don't get the wrong idea. The universe has very violent aspects such as
supernovae and massive black holes; but it also has immense space and time
over which the primordial elements of the Big Bang, hydrogen and helium,
could build up gradually through nucleosynthesis in generations of stars into
sufficient abundance for the planets and life that we find today. So the universe
does also have aspects that echo patience and nurturing in humans. George
Coyne (2007) is one of those who discuss how the current end result can be
seen as a fertility of the universe, a fertility that gives meaning to the "chance
processes and necessary processes continuously interacting in a universe that is
13.7×10^9 years old and contains about 10^{22} stars" (172). Coyne ends with the
conclusion that "God lets the world be what it will be in its continuous evolution. He is not continually intervening, but rather allows, participates, loves"
(175). This perspective was also expressed by John Haught when he wrote,
"Creation and its evolutionary unfolding would less be the consequence of an
eternal divine plan than of God's humble and loving letting be" (1998, 234).
When one looks at the dramatic chaos of debris left over from the supernova
of AD 1054 that now appears as the Crab Nebula, one can only agree. This is
not the work of a dictator so much as that of a parent and artist.

Hope Amidst a Big Freeze or Big Rip

Lest we get carried away, misty eyed, by these beautiful pictures and
thoughts, we should address the ultimate fate of the universe. Observations
using supernovae in the most distant galaxies show, as the currently most
plausible conclusion, that we are in a universe that is not only expanding but
one in which the expansion rate started to accelerate about 6 billion years ago.
This leads to two possible scenarios for the end of everything: either matter
will continue to separate from each other particle of matter, thus resulting in
a universe that is too cold to sustain life, the *Big Freeze*; or the density of the
"dark energy," which is causing the acceleration of expansion, will increase in
time so that all life forms, no matter how small, will disintegrate into unbound
elementary particles and radiation, shooting apart from each other, the *Big
Rip*. Neither scenario seems to fit the drawing together of all matter, life, and
consciousness into Teilhard de Chardin's "Omega Point," which for him is
Christ. One might argue against a too "substantial" view of the universe in relation to God, but substance, or matter and energy, is of what we are made. One

might look to a "principle" of existence, more in the manner of Tillich.[3] But I think that the most important caution here is to avoid finding "contact points" between scientific scenarios and theological scenarios. This was a temptation for Pius XII with respect to finding a parallel between the "Let there be light" of Genesis and the Big Bang theory, a temptation he was warned against by one who had developed, from the initial concept of Alexander Friedmann, that very theory of the expanding universe, namely Abbé Georges Lemaître (Turek 1989). The hope that is centered in Christ, while *involving* our very matter just as did the Incarnation, is itself also *beyond* the material, as is God. The Book of Revelation (21:1) describes a new heaven and a new earth, and the emphasis needs to be on the *new*.

The Effect of an Astronomer's Faith

I have presented some ways in which an astronomer's understanding of the evolutionary nature of the universe "makes a difference to" or colors my faith in God. This is done to encourage you to use the "filters" from your own expertise to enhance *your* understanding of the evolutionary reality around you, i.e., to enhance your mindful reverence of what you experience and so to worship the Author of that reality. With that enhanced understanding I would also hope for an enhanced sense of responsibility in us all to hold precious everything that has been sustained so wondrously in its evolution so far.

Author's Note

Christopher Corbally is a vice director of the Vatican Observatory, about which further details can be found at <http://vaticanobservatory.org>.

References

Aquinas, T. 1920. *Summa Theologica*, 2nd and rev. ed. Fathers of the English Dominican Province, trans. Internet <http://www.op.org/summa/> accessed January 2008.

Carr, P. H. 2006. *Beauty in Science and Spirit*. Center Ossipee, NH: Beech River.

Coyne, G. V. 2007. God's chance creation. In *Faith and Knowledge: Towards a New Meeting of Science and Theology*, ed. G. Teres. Vatican: Liberia Editrice Vaticana.

García-Rivera, A. 2007. Endless forms most beautiful. *Theology and Science*, 5 (July), 125.

Grumett, D. 2007. Teilhard de Chardin's evolutionary natural theology. *Zygon*, 42 (July), 519.

---

3   Paul Carr (2006, 76) contrasts the thought of de Chardin and Tillich along these lines of substance and principle.

Haught, J. F. 1998. Evolution, tragedy, and hope. In *Science & Theology*, ed. T. Peters. Boulder, CO: Westview.

Hefner, P. 2007. Evolution: Life in the context of the energies of God. *Theology and Science*, 5 (July), 137.

Hopkins, G. M. 1967. St. Winifred's Well. In *The Leaden Echo and the Golden Echo: The Poems of Gerald Manley Hopkins*, 4th ed., eds. W. H. Gardner and N. H. Mackenzie. New York, NY: OUP.

O'Donoghue, A. 2007. *The Sky is Not a Ceiling*. Maryknoll, NY: Orbis.

Turek, J. 1989. Georges Lemaître and the Pontifical Academy of Sciences. *Vatican Observatory Publications*, 2 (13), 167.

Milkiy Way Courtesy NASA

Interlude

love letter to the milky way

I want to tell you about love
There are approximately 1 trillion galaxies
I want to tell you about
In the Milky Way there are about 100 billion stars
I want to tell you
Love is the breath of the cosmos

I want to write a love letter to the Milky Way

Everything is an expression of the galaxy
My 30 trillion cells
The four noble truths
The eight-fold path
The five precepts
The seven energy centers of the body
Everything is the Milky Way
including my lover,
and every kiss
of every lover that's ever
lived

The deep sky
The ubiquity of spirit
The DNA of dreams
The interlocking patterns of the cosmic constellations

"Cosmos" and "justice" are synonymous with beauty
but parts of the Milky Way don't give off light
Sometimes it feels like I've got Ground Zero in my heart

The dark sun bleeds shadows
The dark sun leaves shadows on everything
The forecast calls for scattered to broken skies

If there wasn't so much love there wouldn't be so much pain
It's like love is the nervous system of the universe
bringing us joy and sorrow

I inherit the
voice of the Milky Way in my dreams
The entire galaxy revolves around a single drop of wine

Your skin
the texture of the cosmos
the religion beyond religion
I want to know you like the wind knows the canyons
or the rain knows the rivulets
Lightning is continuously striking in 100 places every moment
The universe spills through our dreams
The future belongs to the most compelling story
Even the word "love"
is not adequate to define
the force that wove
the fabric of
space/time

If we could sense everything at once
like Krishna entering history with all the memory of his past incarnations
then I could tell you about love

Drew Dellinger

PART II

The Epic Explored from Diverse Perspectives

Cheryl Genet

Like all creation stories, the evolutionary epic contains within it-self great diversity, and can be received and appreciated and taught in many different ways, a bit like a complex crystal being slowly turned and turned and turned in front of many people, each of whom will see in it slightly different things.

David Christian

The epic story of science has had a great impact on a wide range of disci-plines and human endeavors and has found expression in history, literature, cosmology, art, and spirituality, not to mention poetry, as we see in the inter-ludes in this volume. In "The Evolutionary Epic and the Chronometric Rev-olution," the epic is considered by an historian who evaluates it through dis-tinctive historical features—that is, it embraces the entire past, it is scientific, and it is global. Also considered are critical changes in our capacity to build the historical story that have been brought about by our increasing ability to measure time more accurately back into the distant past.

> It is these changes that have made it possible to construct a chronologi-cally rigorous account of the past that links human history, the history of the biosphere and Earth, and the history of the universe, into a single account of the past.

Then, a narratologist examines the narrative nature of the epic story in "To Tell a Transformational Tale," comparing and contrasting it with literary forms, drawing out important considerations such as the ethical impera-tives found in the epic and the use of a labyrinth model to discover the epic's non-linear qualitative character. He also notes, with some amusement, the incompatibility of the terms "evolutionary" in relation to the idea of "epic," typically thought of as a completed tale of the past. "Epicers" however, will presumably remain undaunted by this technicality, as underscored by the title on the next page.

"The Epic of Cosmic Evolution" views our current human situation from the center of the universe. "It is turning out that the ancient human instinct to experience ourselves as central reflects something real about the universe—something independent of our viewpoint." The cosmic perspective may be essential to our progress and survival of our species.

But as cosmic as our perspective may need to be, we must also situate ourselves in our own time and place. "Bringing the Universe Story Home" is a performing artist's success in giving the evolutionary epic roots in the local history of a small island in British Columbia—through playacting and song. She also explores the role of sound in the telling of the epic story. The story, it is proposed, may not lead to the sustainability we desire "until our wonderful heady ideas [can] be warmed by the heart so they might stir people to action."

Finally, spiritual eyes are trained on the evolutionary epic in "Evolutionary Spirituality" to discover the importance of conscious evolution as humanity faces an unknown future:

> Evolutionary Spirituality is neither a new religion nor an organization. It is the offspring of the mystic experience of the great traditions of the world combined with the discoveries of science.... We place ourselves as pioneers standing in solidarity with the great self-creating events of the past, such as the forming of life, of animal life, of human life. This is our lineage. In our genes are all the generations.

> Our sense of the past was transformed and unified in the middle of the twentieth century by a second chronometric revolution.
>
> David Christian

The Evolutionary Epic
and the Chronometric Revolution

David Christian

This chapter raises a historian's question about the vision of the past described as "big history" or the "evolutionary epic": Why has that story emerged in the late twentieth century? Why now?[1]

Definitions

The evolutionary epic (a.k.a. "big history") can be defined as a particular way of thinking about, or imagining, or describing, the past. It is a historical genre. As a historical genre it has three distinctive features.

First, it embraces the entire past, from the earliest periods of which we have any knowledge, to the present day. In some versions, it even contemplates the future.[2] The large chronological scale of the evolutionary epic means that it can be regarded as a form of creation story because, like all creation stories (or cycles of creation stories), it tries to construct a complete map of the past, within which individuals and communities can find their place as part of a larger universe.

Second, the evolutionary epic is scientific. This is not the same as saying it is true. What it means is that the evolutionary epic, like modern science in general, stakes its reputation not on tradition or authority but on publicly available and publicly testable evidence, combined with the best and most up-to-date scientific theory. It expects to stand or fall on the evidence, and it is open to

---

1   This essay summarizes some of the ideas from a paper presented at the Evolutionary Epic conference, and develops arguments first discussed in "Historia, complejidad y revolución cronométrica" [History, Complexity and the Chronometric Revolution], *Revista de Occidente*, Abril 2008, No 323, 27-57.

2   In my own big history course, I began discussing the future after some of my best students persuaded me that it did not make sense to discuss history on a scale of 13 billion years, and then refuse to discuss whether any of the large trends they had studied might extend into the future. These discussions are reflected in the final chapter of my own book on big history, Christian (2004).

constant adjustment as new evidence appears or old evidence is discarded or refuted. In this respect, the evolutionary epic belongs to the same intellectual tradition as modern science and modern historiography.

Third, the evolutionary epic is global. It is true that modern science emerged in a particular part of the world (often loosely described as the "west") and within the cultural and religious traditions of Europe and the North Atlantic region. That is why much of its vocabulary can be traced to the intellectual and religious traditions of Europe. Nevertheless, the roots of modern science are multiple, and they spread out more widely than conventional accounts of the "scientific revolution" suggest. They can be found in Muslim scholarship and science, in Muslim translations of classical scholarship, in the scientific and philosophical traditions of classical Greece or Rome, in the archives of the great library of Alexandria, in the science of ancient Mesopotamia, and in the mathematical traditions of India. Rich scientific traditions also emerged in China and in Mesoamerica. So, it is far too simplistic to think of modern science as a "Western" invention. Just a millennium ago, it would have been perfectly reasonable to argue that the world's best "scientists" could be found in Bokhara or Baghdad.

Today's science, too, is much more than a Western tradition. This means that the evolutionary epic does not rest its truth-claims on the validity of a particular cultural tradition. It expects to survive rigorous testing in Tokyo or Beijing or Buenos Aires as well as in London or Paris or Los Alamos, because it has been constructed by scientists working in all parts of the world. So the evolutionary epic is global in its origins and building it has been a task for humanity as a whole. In fact, the evolutionary epic is the first creation story to be constructed and taught throughout the world. It is the first universal creation story.

When Did the Evolutionary Epic Appear?

Fred Spier has argued that one of the first works in "big history" was Erich Jantsch's (1980) *The Self-Organizing Universe*.[3] Since then, the evolutionary epic has appeared in versions written by historians, geologists, and astronomers. Earlier attempts at universal histories in the modern era, such as H.G. Wells' *Outline of History*, do not count because they were written before it was possible to construct a reliable scientific chronology for the whole of time. Wells himself regretted that he could assign no absolute dates to any event or change before the First Olympiad, in 776 BCE (Wells 1921, 1102). So, in general terms, we can say that the evolutionary epic appeared in the second half of the twentieth century.

---

3   For a fuller bibliography of contributions to the evolutionary epic, based on a preliminary list by Fred Spier, see Christian (2004, 12-14). See also Spier (1996).

Why Does the Evolutionary Epic Matter?

The evolutionary epic matters because its appearance marks a revolution in human understanding of the past. It is the first creation story based largely on the findings of modern science. It is also the first creation story to draw on intellectual resources from the entire world, and the first, therefore, that expects to appeal to societies throughout the world. As the first truly global creation story, it has the potential to unite rather than to divide humanity. Indeed, in an era when human beings possess weapons capable of destroying much of the biosphere in just a few hours, tribal accounts of the past are becoming dangerously anachronistic. H.G. Wells made the point well in a preface to the third edition of his *Outline of the World*, written just three years after the end of World War I:

> The need for a common knowledge of the general facts of human history throughout the world has become very evident during the tragic happenings of the last few years. Swifter means of communication have brought all men closer to one another for good or for evil. War becomes a universal disaster, blind and monstrously destructive; it bombs the baby in its cradle and sinks the food-ships that cater for the non-combatant and the neutral. There can be no peace now, we realize, but a common peace in all the world; no prosperity but a general prosperity. But *there can be no common peace and prosperity without common historical ideas*. Without such ideas to hold them together in harmonious co-operation, with nothing but narrow, selfish, and conflicting nationalist traditions, races and peoples are bound to drift towards conflict and destruction. This truth, which was apparent to that great philosopher Kant a century or more ago—it is the gist of his tract upon universal peace—is now plain to the man in the street. (Wells 1921, vi)

Why did the evolutionary epic emerge in the late twentieth century?

The appearance of the evolutionary epic is part of the larger cluster of changes usually referred to as globalization. A global creation story could be constructed in the late twentieth century because of the emergence of a global system of knowledge construction and exchange. Particularly since the end of the Cold War and the rise of the Internet, knowledge itself has been exchanged with an intensity and speed that is unparalleled. Scientific research is increasingly a global project. It draws on contributions from all parts of the world, and expects to be accepted by scientists and scholars throughout the world.

The study of human history remains more tribal both in its construction and its audiences, but the emergence of fields such as world history or international history show the extent to which even history is becoming a global discipline.

However, there were also more specific reasons for the appearance of the evolutionary epic, and it is these I will concentrate on in what follows. The most important was what I will call the "chronometric revolution": a series of technological innovations that transformed our ability to assign absolute dates to past events and, by doing so, helped transform our understanding of the past in general.

History before the Chronometric Revolution

By "chronometry" I mean the methods we use to assign absolute dates to past events. Absolute dates associate a past event with a specific moment in time; relative dates rank past events in order, but cannot specify when they occurred. To say that the age of dinosaurs preceeded the age of mammals is to give a relative date. We do not learn whether the age of dinosaurs ended 10 thousand or 10 billion years ago, though we do learn that it preceeded the age of mammals. To say that the age of dinosaurs ended 65 million years ago as the result of an asteroid impact is to give an absolute date.[4]

Historians often take chronometry for granted, because it is the most elementary level of historical analysis. Yet it is of fundamental importance. Without dates, our knowledge of the past consists of merely a random jumble of facts and events. Relative dates improve the situation but only to a limited degree. A rigorous understanding of the past requires not just evidence in general, but evidence *that can be ordered precisely in time*, because without a precise sense of temporal order, we cannot discuss causation. As the great English historiographer, R.G. Collingwood wrote, the historian's business is "to apprehend the past as a thing in itself, to say for example that so many years ago such-and-such events actually happened" (Collingwood 1994, 3). Without absolute dates, serious historical analysis is impossible.

In the course of human history, our ability to assign absolute dates to past events has passed through two major revolutions. In societies without writing, chronometry depended on the memory of individuals. Oral tradition can store large amounts of information, but it struggles with chronometry because chronological precision falls off rapidly within a few generations of the present day. This falling off of chronometric precision generates a distinctive chronological topology that was common in the historical thinking of many societies without writing. While the recent past consists of ordered events, within a few generations the past begins to lose chronological structure and shape, and

---

4   For a highly readable account of the science behind this particular date by the geologist who did more than anyone else to establish it, see Alvarez (1998).

time itself seems to lose coherence. The Aboriginal Australian notion of the dreamtime captures this distinctive perception of time well. As Edmund Leach has argued, in tribal societies there is often a sense of moving from a world of change to one of timelessness (Leach 1961; Eliade 1954). Collingwood treats this collapse of chronology in the deep past as a defining feature of "myth": Events "are conceived as having occurred in the past, indeed, but in a dateless past which is so remote that nobody knows when it was. It is outside all our time-reckonings and called 'the beginning of things'" (Collingwood 1994, 15).[5]

The first chronometric revolution was made possible by the appearance of writing and written records from about 5,000 years ago. Written documents made it possible to assign absolute dates with some confidence to events many centuries in the past. The Jewish historian, Josephus, writing in the first century CE, praised the "Egyptians, the Chaldeans and the Phoenicians" because they had "taken especial care to have nothing forgotten of what was done among them, but their history was esteemed sacred, and ever written in the public records by men of the greatest wisdom" (Toulmin and Goodfield 1965, 25-6). Eusebius of Caeserea (d. c. 340 CE) and his translator, St. Jerome (347-c. 420) used the uncertain illumination of Old Testament genealogies to estimate that God made the world about 4,000 years before the birth of Christ. In the Christian world, this chronology would survive for more than 1500 years.[6] Similar accounts of a more extensive past emerged within all literate societies, from China to Mesoamerica.

The vital role of written evidence to chronometry helps explain why history came to mean the study of the past on the basis of written records. "No documents, no history", wrote Charles Langlois and Charles Seignobos in a textbook published in English in 1898 (cited in Smail 2005, 1351). However, while writing extended our sense of the past, it also limited it in important ways. In the first place, a chronometry based on written records was bound to exclude most of the natural world. Such a history had to be almost exclusively about human beings. So it is not surprising that human history was increasingly portrayed in separation from the history of the biosphere. From the late

---

5   The flattened time of traditional creation stories is captured well in the Aboriginal Australian notion of a "dreamtime", but it also survives in personal memory, a sense that is captured well in T.S. Eliot's *Burnt Norton*: "Time present and time past / Are both perhaps present in time future, / And time future contained in time past./ If all time is eternally present / All time is unredeemable."

6   "In the *Universal History*, published by a syndicate of book-sellers in London in 1779, it is stated that the world was created in 4004 B.C. and (with a pleasant exactitude) at the autumnal equinox, and that the making of man crowned the work of creation at Eden, upon the Euphrates, exactly two days' journey above Basra." Wells (1971, 1:13-14).

nineteenth century, this chronometric limitation has contributed to a growing divide between history and the sciences. While the sciences dealt with regular, law-abiding processes such as the laws of motion, it seemed that history dealt with the contingent, the changeable, and the human. On the one side of this epistemological divide were what German writers referred to as the *Geisteswissenschaften*, disciplines such as history that dealt with the intentional actions of people; on the other side were the *Naturwissenschaften*, which concerned themselves with the much more predictable changes of natural phenomena.[7]

Second, as Leopold von Ranke pointed out, a chronology based on written records can never take us back to the beginning: "History cannot discuss the origin of society," wrote Ranke, despairingly, as he attempted a universal history, "for the art of writing, which is the basis of historical knowledge, is a comparatively late invention.... The province of History is limited by the means at her command, and the historian would be over-bold who should venture to unveil the mystery of the primeval world, the relation of mankind to God and nature" (Smail 2005, 1350).

Finally, a chronology based on written records cast an extremely selective and uneven light even on the human past. It could reconstruct only the pasts of literate societies; and within those societies, it could tell us little about the vast majority of people who were not literate, and who left no written records of their existence, their thoughts, and their lifeways. For all these reasons, even in the early twentieth century, "history" meant, essentially, a recounting of the deeds and thoughts of the great.

From the eighteenth century, geology and archaeology began to develop increasingly sophisticated methods for constructing relative chronologies, but neither discipline could assign reliable absolute dates to any of the periods they delineated in the past. When H.G. Wells attempted a universal history just after the first world war, he was acutely aware of the limitations he faced. "Chronology," he wrote, "only begins to be precise enough to specify the exact year of any event after the establishment of the eras of the First Olympiad [776] and the building of Rome [753]" (Wells 1921, 1102).

The Chronometric Revolution

Our sense of the past was transformed and unified in the middle of the twentieth century by a second chronometric revolution. In the decades after the second world war, there appeared new chronometric techniques that made it possible, for the first time, to assign absolute dates that were plausible and reasonably accurate, for events reaching back to the very origins of the universe. Suddenly, we could construct chronologies that went far beyond the written

---

7   There is a good discussion in Mazlish (1998, 86 ff.).

record, to embrace the pre-human past, and, eventually, the whole of time! The second chronometric revolution linked human history and the history of the natural world, the Earth and even the universe, within a single timeline.

At the heart of this revolution was the development of "radiometric" dating techniques. That the extreme regularity of radioactive breakdown might provide a way of dating events in the remote past had been realized within a decade of the discovery of radioactivity, early in the twentieth century, when Ernest Rutherford showed how it might be possible to date rocks containing uranium by estimating the extent of the radioactive breakdown of uranium to lead. But many practical difficulties had to be overcome before such techniques could be used routinely. Not until Willard Libby developed sophisticated methods for measuring the breakdown of Carbon 14 in the early 1950s did radiometric dating techniques begin to be used more widely. Carbon 14, with a half-life of about 5,730 years, can be used to date materials up to about 50,000 years old. Other elements, such as uranium, can date objects as old as the Earth itself. Indeed, using such methods to date a meteorite, Claire Paterson gave the first reliable date for the age of the Earth itself in 1953. His date, of about 4.5 billion years, still stands.

In the decades that followed, radiometric techniques were refined. In addition, other dating techniques were developed. These included dendrochronology (based on the counting of tree-rings, a technique that was used to calibrate Carbon 14 dates more precisely); genetic dating (based on comparisons of the DNA of different species to determine when they last shared a common ancestor); and a range of special techniques for dating the age of stars, galaxies and, eventually, the universe itself.

The Historicization of the Natural Sciences

Closely linked to the chronometric revolution were three major paradigm shifts that turned biology, geology, and cosmology into fully historical disciplines.[8]

Before the late eighteenth century, it was widely believed that most of the universe had changed little since its creation. Astronomers assumed that the stars and galaxies (which appeared to be stars) were much as they had always been. Geologists assumed that, even if landscapes had changed in minor ways, the Earth as a whole had changed little. And most biologists, including Carl Linnaeus (1707-78), the founder of modern taxonomy, assumed that today's living species were also much as they had always been. None of these disciplines concerned themselves seriously with the historical problem of change over time.

---

8   One of the few historians to appreciate the significance of these changes was the great world historian, William H. McNeill. See McNeill (1998).

As early as the late seventeenth century, however, evidence began to emerge that the natural world had changed significantly. Evidence from fossils demonstrated that living organisms had changed over time, and the appearance of fossils of marine organisms in mountain ranges such as the Alps showed that landscapes had also evolved. It became clear that in some sense both the Earth and the natural world had "histories". Yet without precise dates, it was impossible to reconstruct those histories with any precision. The result was that "history" continued to mean "human history" and "science" continued to be thought of as the study of those aspects of the world that did *not* change significantly over time.

Suddenly, in the two decades after the second world war, geology, astronomy, and biology all became historical disciplines. The chronometric revolution made it possible to construct precise timelines for the past of living organisms, of the Earth itself, and even of the universe. The discovery of DNA made it possible to explain and to track changes in the natural world with greatly increased precision. In geology, the new paradigm of "plate tectonics," which emerged during the 1960s, showed that the Earth's surface had changed fundamentally over time as continental plates floated on the semi-molten layers beneath them, colliding and rearranging the Earth's geography as they did so. Finally, also in the 1960s, astronomers became convinced that the universe itself had evolved over time, beginning in a huge "Big Bang" many billions of years ago.

Cosmology, geology, and biology now joined history as disciplines that studied the past, and did so with chronological rigor. It became clear that it was possible not just to construct the past of human societies, but also the past of the Earth, of life on Earth, and even of the entire universe. Our sense of what could be included in history was transformed.

The Chronometric Revolution and the Evolutionary Epic

It is these changes that have made it possible to construct a chronologically rigorous account of the past that links human history, the history of the biosphere and Earth, and the history of the universe, into a single account of the past. For the first time in human history, there now exists a rigorous, scientifically based account of origins that is largely culture-free. The evolutionary epic is the first creation story that can be shared by all of humanity. As such, it has the potential to unite humanity as a whole, as the great national histories once united entire nations. As H.G. Wells appreciated early in the twentieth century, such a sense of unity will be vital as humanity faces problems that can no longer be solved at the national level.

References

Alvarez, W. 1998. *T. Rex and the Crater of Doom*. New York: Vintage Books.

Christian, D. 2004. *Maps of Time: An Introduction to Big History*. Berkeley, CA: University of California Press.

Collingwood, R.G. 1994. *The Idea of History: With Lectures 1926 - 1928*, rev. ed. Ed., Jan van der Dussen. Oxford, UK: Oxford University Paperback.

Eliade, M. 1954. *The Myth of the Eternal Return*. W. R. Trask, trans. NY: Pantheon.

Jantsch, E. 1980. *The Self-organizing Universe: Scientific and Human Implications of the Emerging Paradigm of Evolution*. Oxford, UK: Pergamon Press.

Leach, E.R. 1961. *Rethinking Anthropology*. London, UK: Athlone Press. [9]

McNeill, W.H.1998. History and the scientific worldview. *History and Theory*, *37* (1), 1-13.

Mazlish, B. 1998. *The Uncertain Sciences*. New Haven, CN and London, UK: Yale University Press.

Smail, D. 2005. In the grip of sacred history. *American Historical Review, 110* (5), 1337-1361.

Spier, F. 1996. *The Structure of Big History: From the Big Bang until Today*. Amsterdam, The Netherlands: Amsterdam University Press.

Toulmin, S. and Goodfield, J. 1965. *The Discovery of Time*. Chicago, IL and London, UK: University of Chicago Press.

Wells, H.G. 1921. *An Outline of History*, 3rd ed. New York, NY: Macmillan.

Wells, H.G. 1971. *An Outline of History*, rev. and revised by R. Postgate and G. P. Wells, 2 vols. Garden City, NY: Doubleday.

---

9   See the two essays concerning the symbolic representation of time.

Considering that time is the real substance of the Evolutionary Epic, its formative medium, it seems ironic that the Evolutionary Epic, in measuring it out in spans, deprives it of its qualitative character.

Paul Harris

To Tell A Transformational Tale
The Evolutionary Epic as Narrative Genre

Paul A. Harris

The Evolutionary Epic is at its core a collective, interdisciplinary undertaking. In my view, there are two dimensions to interdisciplinary work. The first is *integration*: immersing oneself in unfamiliar fields, apprenticing oneself to new knowledge and discourses, and integrating them into a coherent understanding. The second is *intervention*: contributing to the interdisciplinary project from the standpoint of one's own expertise. The integrative work that informs this paper has been ongoing for some years now—reading several versions of the Evolutionary Epic, as well as more narrowly focused texts on specific segments of the great story. This paper constitutes my intervention in the Evolutionary Epic—I am a scholar of literature with interests that include narratology (the study of narrative forms), time, and ethics. Accordingly, I treat the Evolutionary Epic—as it manifests itself in many books and websites—as a literary genre, which I analyze in terms of its narrative form, its treatment of time, and its ethical purpose. I conclude by proposing a new narrative template for the Evolutionary Epic: a spiritual labyrinth.

In its extant forms, the Evolutionary Epic displays certain common features. First, it is told as a linear plot, where chronology of events corresponds to the order of telling them: it begins with the Big Bang and ends with the present, or a quick glance to the future. Second, the content of the Evolutionary Epic may be considered as a series of nested temporal scales or histories: human culture; life; planet Earth; the cosmic unfolding. Now, even though the linear plot seems the obvious logical choice from a narrative standpoint, I contend that a certain conflict exists between the linear plot and the Evolutionary Epic's content. The linear Evolutionary Epic begins at the point in time furthest removed from our present, and ends with us. Yet, content-wise, the Evolutionary Epic's nested temporalities ripple outwards from us to the distant horizon of the deep past. Perhaps it would be better pedagogy to consider starting the Evolutionary Epic with our present, moving back through the past, and then returning to the present with an eye to the future.

A third common—and intriguing—feature of the Evolutionary Epic is the admixture of hubris and humility that runs through different versions of it. On the one hand, even telling the truly epic story is an act of hubris. Moreover, *we*, humanity, are the species—perhaps the only species—that have evolved self-reflective consciousness and the ability to reflect on and shape the Story. On the other hand, the Evolutionary Epic expresses great humility: we are meant to feel wonder at our place in such a big story and realize that our typical individual aspirations are small and selfish in the face of such majestic beauty.

Now, if we analyze the Evolutionary Epic in terms of narrative time, we find that it is marked by a generative paradox: for a narratologist, its two terms have diametrically opposed meanings. The Epic is a genre whose purpose is to preserve a fixed, distant past; this past is a set of events that found a culture or tradition. The epic past is partitioned off from the present and privileged in relation to it. It has no interest in the future; its sole function is mnemonic. Consider, conversely, the term "Evolutionary": it entails tracing a continuous history that connects a deep past to the present with an open-ended arrow into the future. Interestingly, the name "Evolutionary Epic" indirectly connotes that the Evolutionary Epic itself will evolve—that it will change over time. In summary, for a narratologist, the Evolutionary Epic is an oxymoron!

The Evolutionary Epic's generative paradox underscores a significant tension at the heart of the genre. The Evolutionary Epic is an epic: a creation story and cosmology for the human species. It is a science-based tale whose reader, by mastering the knowledge presented, undertakes an epic journey from genesis to the present. Yet by virtue of being science-based, the Evolutionary Epic itself evolves. Scientific accounts, especially in the intriguing but often opaque realms of origin stories of the universe and life, are peppered with gaps, guesses, conjectures, qualified knowledge. As accepted scientific knowledge changes, the Evolutionary Epic thus evolves.

The narrative viewpoint of the Evolutionary Epic rests in the present of its author's dateline, but it takes a Janus-faced look into time. That is, from the present occasion of its being written, the Evolutionary Epic journeys back into deep time, but it also looks towards the future. The Evolutionary Epic *informs* us about the past through a series of narrative thought-experiments: imagine the Big Bang; imagine bacteria synergizing into multi-cellular organisms; imagine chipping a stone ax. Simultaneously, the Evolutionary Epic *inspires* us to act in the future through an implied ethos that arises as the story is told: act now to perpetuate humanity's role in the cosmic unfolding! Do more than read—become a steward of the Earth!

So, Evolutionary Epics transmit a global ethics; the Evolutionary Epic delivers a supplementary ethical imperative. The degree to which this dimension gets developed in particular Evolutionary Epics varies widely, but most Evolutionary Epics only broach ethics in a brief end section that speculates about various future scenarios. Because the Evolutionary Epic's intent is to transform readers, to induce those who complete the epic quest for knowing the cosmos to act to sustain the Earth, I contend that the Evolutionary Epic would best be served by integrating a more activist ethics from the outset. Ethics tends to function after the fact: some situation exists, and ethics weighs rules for guiding action. All too often, ethics amounts to a belated guide for "best practices," and its power to affect people is undercut by a normative tone ("you ought to do this because...").

In place of a relatively passive notion of ethics, I believe the Evolutionary Epic is best served by a *transformational ethics*.[1] In ethics so conceived, ethical subjects do not exist; one must become an ethical subject. One becomes an ethical subject by experiencing a demand to which one grants one's approval. Once the demand is approved, and one acts accordingly, the ethical subject continues to persist only through uncompromising fidelity to the demand. The ethical subject thus acts in constant excess of their "original" self—they are drawn forward by something greater than or outside themselves, and they internalize this force as the orienting ground of their being. In some sense, ethical subjects are always evolving, and always at some level strangers to themselves.

The foregoing remarks on the Evolutionary Epic as a narrative genre enable us to reflect on the way that we tell the story. It is by no means a necessity or natural choice that the Evolutionary Epic appears almost exclusively in linear form. In fact, if one accepts my analysis, the Evolutionary Epic's dominant form does not match its function. The Evolutionary Epic's generative paradox (fixed epic versus evolving science) demands that the Evolutionary Epic remain an open, supple form, able to accommodate changes to its script. One might in fact see the Evolutionary Epic as a virtual entity, something only defined generally, which is actualized anew with each telling. In literary terms, the Evolutionary Epic resembles an oral story more than a printed book: it changes with the tellings; the teller adapts it to context; it is dynamic, enactive and performative rather than fixed in content. The Evolutionary Epic's other salient characteristics in this analysis are its Janus-faced temporality and its ethical desire to transform its reader/listener.

In order to best fit the Evolutionary Epic's form to its function, I posit a narrative template for Evolutionary Epic tellers to contemplate: the spiritual labyrinth.

---

1   For a full exposition of transformational ethics, see Alain Badiou, *Ethics: An Essay on the Understanding of Evil* (translated by Peter Hallward; New York, NY: Verso, 2001).

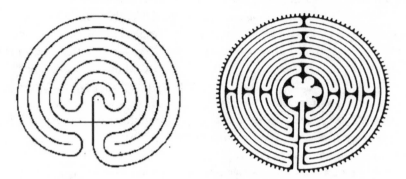

Pictured above are two shapes of spiritual labyrinths, known as the Cretan and Chartres labyrinths, respectively. Labyrinths, ubiquitous throughout the world for thousands of years, have enjoyed a resurgent popularity as tools for spiritual practice, psycho-therapeutic benefits, or general contemplation. Unlike mazes, which have forks in them, labyrinths are unicursal—there is a single path which one traverses from the outside inwards, and then back out again. While practices vary widely, labyrinth walking is generally marked out in three stages: the walk into the center is a journey inwards, to reflect deeply on something, or to shed away outside concerns; on reaching the center, one pauses to contemplate in the quiet of the womb, the origin; the walk back out opens one back to the world, the future, with a refreshed spirit.

The journey into and back out of the labyrinth comprises an integral part of the myth of Theseus slaying the Cretan Minotaur. The labyrinth, a setting for the tale, also may be seen as a map of the myth's narrative logic. Ariadne's thread, the "clew" that enables Theseus to find his way in and back out again, has long been treated by literary critics as a metaphor for narrative itself, for the story-line of plot.[2] Linking the telling of the Evolutionary Epic to the labyrinth walk thus has an inherent fit to it from the outset.

I proffer the labyrinth as a heuristic device, a template to use as an organizing principle for communicating the Evolutionary Epic. This template might be utilized in designing a course, a textbook, a collective experience, a print narrative, a film, a website ... or any other medium through which the Evolutionary Epic gets told. The labyrinth provides a fitting visual symbol or image for the Evolutionary Epic because in several cultural traditions, it is viewed as a map of the cosmos. The labyrinth walk may be neatly correlated to a new form of telling the Evolutionary Epic: begin in the present, move back through time to the origin, and then work back to the present into the future.

---

2   See for instance J. Hillis Miller, *Ariadne's Thread: Story Lines* (New Haven, CN: Yale University Press, 1992).

Beginning the Evolutionary Epic in the present grounds the teller and reader/ listener in a shared temporal context. The Evolutionary Epic then moves in concentric circles deeper back in time—familiar human historical scales are traversed before less intuitively accessible periods enter (geological, evolutionary, cosmological). At last, the Evolutionary Epic arrives at the mystical *aporia* of its origin, and pauses to let its reader/listener muse on the ever-elusive question of beginnings.[3] Then, the Evolutionary Epic moves forward from the beginning. This time, the emphasis shifts from informing the reader/listener to activating them: the story is unfolded under the aegis of attending to how things evolve, change, and what determines or shapes these vectors, directionalities, force fields in the great Evolutionary Epic saga. The reader/listener thus returns to the present ready to act on the world, to carry forward the line of the story. The story expresses a demand that they approve, and they emerge a transformed person.

It may be difficult to connect the labyrinth template to telling the Evolutionary Epic, whatever one's motive for doing so might be. Certainly, historians and many scientists would find the boomerang story arc (present/past/present) counterintuitive, if not illogical. But my aim here in treating the Evolutionary Epic as a narrative genre is foremost to make the form in which it is told visible—the presumptive default choice of linear form has left the issue invisible. I think that the tacit, utter acceptance of the Evolutionary Epic's being told in a linear form also may have the unintended or unforeseen consequence of reducing time to a timeline. Considering that time is the real substance of the Evolutionary Epic, its formative medium, it seems ironic that the Evolutionary Epic, in measuring it out in spans, deprives it of its qualitative character. Timelines mark out time but in doing so, they may unintentionally rob time of its dynamism, or smooth out time's textures: the eddies, backcurrents, and roiling pockets in its smooth flow.

Even if not adopted as narrative template for the Evolutionary Epic, the labyrinth may still stimulate us to reconsider how we tell the story, and what our aims are, especially in terms of how we affect our audience. The deliberate, step-by-step, pace of the labyrinth walk quiets the mind and opens the spirit to contemplation. If we design the Evolutionary Epic to produce a similar mood and atmosphere, we may well reach more people and reach them more effectively.

---

3   For a brilliant treatment of this theme, see Philip Kuberski, "Dark Matter: Thinking About Nothing," *Georgia Review*, Vol. LIV, No. 3 (Fall 2000): 431-41.

Like every earlier culture, we need to know our place in the universe, and where we are in time, space, and size is part of situating ourselves in the epic of cosmic evolution.

Nancy Abrams and Joel Primack

The Epic of Cosmic Evolution

Nancy E. Abrams and Joel R. Primack

Every culture known to anthropology has had a shared creation story that helped bind the community together. But not us. We in the contemporary West have many creation stories left over from earlier cultures—poetic indigenous tales, the two creation stories in Genesis and more from other religions, New Age speculations—and the scientific approach represented by the theories of the Big Bang and biological evolution. None of these, including the scientific, satisfactorily explains to the average person where the world we actually live in came from and how we fit in. Is this a problem? Do people still need a believable creation story? Our answer is yes, and modern scientific cosmology is providing the first creation story in the history of humanity that might actually be true and could provide a unifying basis for a global community.

Scientific cosmology studies the origin and nature of the universe-as-a-whole, and it is in the midst of a scientific revolution. Until recently, cosmology was mocked by other scientists as the data-less fantasizing of theorists, but today we have massive amounts of data and a reliable theory that has been tested against the entire visible universe. We are seeing a face of the universe no earlier culture ever imagined. We need to make sense of it and of our lives in their full cosmic context.

Anthropologists use the word "cosmology" differently: to them it means a culture's shared understanding of what is real, how the cosmos (as that culture envisions it) works, how humans fit in, and what the gods expect of them. An anthropological cosmology grounds people in a meaningful context, even though until now such pictures have been scientifically inaccurate. But people today, who now have the scientific ability to see so much more deeply into the universe than any earlier culture could, experience the universe much less and connect with it almost not at all. We have no shared understanding. We have libraries full of creation stories and a culture of skepticism. Without a believable story that explains the high-tech, fast-paced, and dangerous world we are actually living in, there is no way to conceptualize the big picture, thus no way to see it. *Without a big picture, we are very small people.* Indifference to the universe is a staggering fact of our time and a mental handicap that can prevent even very smart people from understanding, let alone solving, global-scale problems. The immense possibilities of a cosmic-scale future may hinge

on a seemingly mundane path of choices that our society is stumbling along
almost blindly today. Scientific cosmology is not about human beings; we
modern people need to go a step beyond it toward a meaningful cosmology
of the kind that earlier cultures created for themselves, but ours will be built
on the foundation of science. Such a meaningful cosmology could be the most
valuable, practical knowledge of our time, letting us make sense both of the
threats and the opportunities of our time.

The last time Western culture shared a coherent understanding of the
universe was in the Middle Ages. For a thousand years, Christians, Jews, and
Muslims believed that the earth was the immovable center of the universe,
and all the planets and stars revolved on crystal spheres around it. The cosmic
order descended into everyday life: God had created a place for every person,
animal, and inanimate thing in a great chain of being. This medieval picture of
the cosmos made sense of the rigid social hierarchy of that time, and the whole
gave meaning to people's inescapable roles in life. But the medieval certainty
was shattered by early scientists like Galileo and Newton. Ruled out by observations, the cosmic hierarchy of the spheres lost its credibility as the organizing principle of the universe. Newtonian physics was phenomenally successful,
so scientists extrapolated it throughout the universe, which led to a picture
of Earth orbiting an average star among other stars (maybe with planetary
systems) scattered throughout endless emptiness. The modern world has so
deeply absorbed this 400 year-old image that it seems like reality itself—but
now we know it is not an accurate picture. The universe has a fascinating
structure in both space and time.

Until the late twentieth century, there was virtually no reliable information about the distant, early universe. Today astronomers can observe every
bright galaxy in the visible universe. Because of the finite speed of light, looking out into space is the same as looking back in time—so we can actually see
with our telescopes the history of the universe. Peering beyond the cosmic
"Dark Ages" before galaxies had begun to form, we can study in detail the
heat radiation from the Big Bang. And from these snapshots, we have pieced
together the great movie of the evolution of the universe: throughout expanding space, vast clouds of invisible, mysterious non-atomic particles called "dark
matter" collapsed under the force of their own gravity, pulling ordinary matter
together to form the galaxies. Galaxy clusters, long filaments of galaxies, and
huge sheet-like superclusters built of galaxies have formed along wrinkles in
spacetime, which were apparently generated during a brief episode of cosmic
inflation at the earliest moments of the Big Bang and etched into our universe
forever. Inside the galaxies, generations of stars arose, whose explosive deaths
spewed complex atoms—stardust—from which planets would form around
new stars, eventually providing a home for life such as ours to evolve.

Most of us have grown up thinking that there is no basis for humans to feel central or even important to the physical cosmos. But with the new evidence, it turns out that this is just a prejudice. While there is no geographic center to our expanding universe, intelligent creatures (including those on other worlds, if they exist) are cosmically special or central in multiple ways that derive directly from fundamental principles of physics and cosmology. We are made of the rarest material in the universe, and our size scale is at the center of all possible sizes. We also live in the middle of time, on the scales of the universe, our solar system, and our planet. These are only some of the ways we are central that are discussed in our book, *The View from the Center of the Universe: Discovering Our Extraordinary Place in the Cosmos* (Riverhead/Penguin, 2006). Each form of centrality has been a scientific discovery, not, as one might assume, an anthropocentric way of reading the data. It is turning out that the ancient human instinct to experience ourselves as central reflects something real about the universe—something independent of our viewpoint.

We Are Made of the Rarest Material

We and our planet are made almost entirely of stardust. A first step toward conceptualizing our place in the cosmos is to understand what stardust is, how exceedingly rare it is, and how special that makes us in the context of the universe as a whole. Except for hydrogen, which makes up about a tenth of a person's weight, the rest of our bodies are made of stardust. Hydrogen and helium, the two lightest kinds of atoms, came straight out of the Big Bang, while a little more helium and essentially all other atoms were created later by stars. The iron atoms in our blood carrying oxygen to our cells came largely from exploding white dwarf stars, while the oxygen itself came mainly from exploding supernovas that ended the lives of massive stars. Most of the carbon in the carbon dioxide we exhale on every breath came from planetary nebulas, the death clouds of middle-size stars a little bigger than the Sun. We are a pastiche of materials created and ejected into our Galaxy by the violence of earlier stars and which underwent tremendous space journeys before coming together to incarnate us.

How rare is stardust? It is about $1/100^{th}$ of one percent of the universe. All the stars, planets, gas, comets, dust, and galaxies that we see—all forms of visible matter, both stardust and the primordial hydrogen and helium—total only about half a percent of what is out there. An additional four percent of the content of the universe is invisible atoms, mostly hydrogen and helium between the galaxies, not in stars or illuminated by stars. But most of the matter in the universe, it turns out, is neither atomic nor visible. It is not even made of the protons, neutrons, and electrons that compose atoms. It is an utterly strange substance called "cold dark matter," and its existence was only established late in the 20th century. It accounts for about 25% of the universe. Dark matter neither emits, reflects, nor absorbs light or any other kind of radiation, but its immense gravity holds the spinning galaxies together. But 70% of the density of the universe is not even matter—it's "dark energy." Dark energy powers the expansion of the universe. It causes space to repel space. The more space there is—and increasing amounts of space are inevitable in an expanding universe—the more repulsion. The more repulsion, the faster space expands, and this leads to an exponentially accelerating expansion, possibly forever. Heavy atoms seem ordinary to us only because our planet represents a tremendous concentration of them. But from a cosmic perspective, they are phenomenally rare.

The story of our universe is founded on the now well-supported "Double Dark" theory, which explains how dark matter plus dark energy have interacted to form the cosmic structures we observe. Dark energy may be a property of space itself. In the early universe there was relatively little dark energy because there was relatively little space—the universe had not had time to expand very much, but there was the same amount of dark matter then as now. For the first nine billion years, the gravitational attraction of the dark matter slowed the rate of expansion. The dark matter thinned out as the universe expanded, but since dark energy is a characteristic of space, it never thins out; instead its relative importance has tremendously increased with the amount of space. Now the repulsive effect of all that dark energy has surpassed the gravitational attraction of dark matter as the dominant effect on large scales in the universe, and expansion is no longer slowing down but accelerating. The turning point was about four and a half billion years ago—coincidentally just when our solar system was forming.

Symbolic images and stories have shaped and given meaning to all earlier cosmologies. We too need to visualize *our* universe—not just random fragments of it, which is all that even the most stunning astronomical photos give us, but the *whole*—so that we can see where we fit. Since over 99% of the universe is invisible, the only way to visualize the whole is symbolically. The following symbols are taken from our book, *The View from the Center of the Universe*.

The Pyramid of All Visible Matter (Fig. 1) borrows an image everyone in the United States possesses: the pyramid topped by the eye of Providence, which appears on the back of the dollar bill. The pyramid's capstone is separated and floating above it, blazing with light. This symbol—reinterpreted—can represent all the visible matter in the universe, i.e., all the matter that people until the late twentieth century thought existed. The volume of each section of the pyramid is proportional to the contribution of that particular ingredient to the density of the universe. The large bottom section of the pyramid represents the lightest atoms, hydrogen and helium, which are so plentiful that they far outweigh all the heavy atoms. The floating capstone represents the stardust, which composes not only living things but also Earth and all rocky planets in the universe. Within the stardust capstone, the fraction associated just with living things is very tiny. Within that very tiny fraction, the matter associated specifically with *intelligent* life is vanishingly small—yet it is only *that* which looks at and grasps this pyramid. The eye in the capstone represents the trace bit of stardust associated with intelligent life—which includes intelligent aliens, if they exist, since they also must be made of stardust. The eye is the only part of the pyramid not drawn to scale, since if it were to scale, we couldn't see it. Intelligence bursts out only from tiny bits of stardust. As the Latin motto at the bottom of the figure says, this really is "the new order of the ages."

Figure 1. The Pyramid of All Visible Matter

The Pyramid of all Visible Matter stands on the solid ground of Earth with a few plants for emphasis. But now we know that there is a hidden base extending deep underground. This is shown in the second figure, which we call the Cosmic Density Pyramid (Fig. 2 - next page).

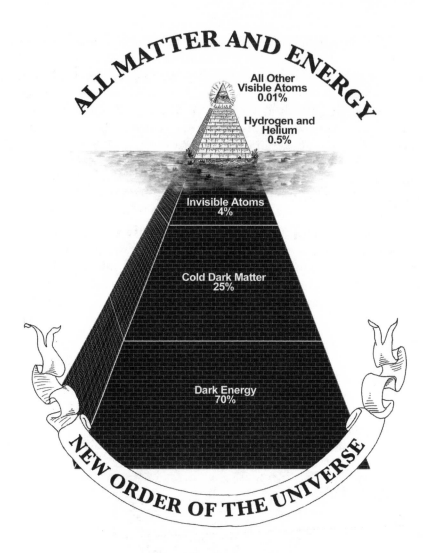

Figure 2: The Cosmic Density Pyramid

Our rare kind of matter does not take up much space or contribute much to the total density of the universe, but it contributes out of all proportion to the complexity and thus potential of the universe. Ordinary matter interacts with itself: particles interact to form atoms, atoms interact to form molecules, and under at least some circumstances molecules can form living cells and eventually evolve into higher forms of life. But dark matter does none of this.

When dark matter is viewed in computer simulations that make it visible, it behaves like nothing anyone has ever seen before. Gravity swings clumps of it around in the presence of other clumps, but they can pass right through each other. Dark matter can only make galaxies and larger things such as galaxy clusters, but all the interesting events inside galaxies are due to atoms. We intelligent beings sit at the peak of the pyramid not only because our atoms are so rare but also because we are supported by the immense base below us responsible for the expansion of the universe and the evolution of galaxies.

We are at the Center of All Possible Sizes

We intelligent beings are at the center of all possible sizes. How can there be a central size? In mathematics numbers go on infinitely in both directions, but in physics there is a largest size and a smallest size. The interplay of relativity and quantum mechanics sets the smallest size. General relativity tells us that there can not be more than a certain amount of mass squeezed into a region of any given size. If more mass is packed in than the region can hold, gravity there becomes so intense that the region itself—the space—collapses to no size at all: a black hole. Any object compressed enough will hit this limit and suddenly become a black hole. Meanwhile, quantum mechanics also sets a minimum size limit but in a very peculiar way. The "size" of a particle is actually the size of the region in which you can confidently locate it. The smaller the region in which the particle is confined, the more energy it takes to locate it, and more energy is equivalent to larger mass ($E=mc^2$). There turns out to be a unique, very small size where the *maximum* mass that relativity allows to be crammed in without the region collapsing into a black hole is also the *minimum* mass that quantum mechanics allows to be confined in so tiny a region. That size, about 10^{-33} cm, is called the Planck length. We have no way to talk or even think about anything smaller in our current understanding of physics.

The largest size we can see is that of the entire visible universe; the distance to our cosmic horizon is about 10^{29} cm. From the Planck length to the cosmic horizon is a difference of about 60 orders of magnitude. The number 10^{60} is extremely big, but it's not infinite. It is comprehensible. With it, we have something to compare our size to.

Adapting an idea due to Sheldon Glashow, a 1979 Nobel laureate in physics, we borrow the ancient symbol of the uroboros (a serpent swallowing its tail) to represent all possible sizes. Tail-swallowing represents the possibility that gravity unites the largest and smallest scales, but also the fact that the universe unites them all.

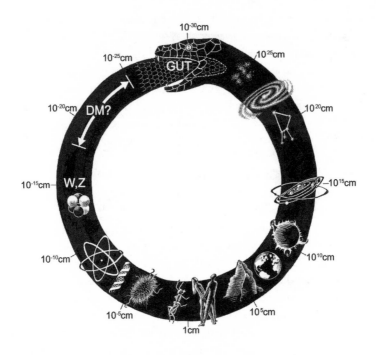

Figure 3: The Cosmic Uroboros

The Cosmic Uroboros (Fig. 3) represents the universe as a continuity of vastly different size scales. The tip of the serpent's tail corresponds to the Planck length (10^{-33} cm), and its head to the size of the visible universe (10^{29} cm). Traveling clockwise around the serpent from head to tail, the icons represent the size of a supercluster of galaxies (10^{25} cm), a single galaxy, the distance from Earth to the Great Nebula in Orion, the Solar System, the Sun, the Earth, a mountain, humans, an ant, a single-celled creature such as the E. coli bacterium, a strand of DNA, an atom, a nucleus, the scale of the weak interactions (carried by the W and Z particles), and approaching the tail the extremely small size scales that may be associated with massive dark matter (DM) particles, and on even smaller scales a Grand Unified Theory (GUT).

What does symbolizing the range of size scales do for us? It allows us to take a second step toward finding our place in the universe. Intelligent beings like us, including aliens if they exist, must be close to the center of the Cosmic Uroboros: much smaller creatures would not have enough atoms to be sufficiently complex, while much larger ones would suffer from slow internal communication (limited by the speed of light)—which would mean that they would effectively be communities rather than individuals, like groups of communicating people, or supercomputers made up of many smaller processors. The central size of intelligent life has nothing to do with the choice of units.

The laws of physics set the tail size, and the speed of light and age of the universe set the head size. We would still be central if the units of length were light years or nanometers.

Not only does the Cosmic Uroboros reveal our place in the universe—it reveals two essential ideas: First, that emergent phenomena are inevitable between widely differing size scales, and second, that on different size scales, completely different physical laws can control events. For example, gravity is all-powerful on the scale of planets, stars, and galaxies, but on the sub-atomic scale, gravity is utterly irrelevant, and the weak and strong forces control. On neither of these size scales is electromagnetism dominant, yet on the human scale it is what makes chemistry work and what makes our bodies function. Thus, size matters. This is a useful and widely applicable principle.

The jurisdiction of most physical laws is limited to a range of size scales, and this is the reason we can never extrapolate from what is true on Earth to what is true in the universe. The fundamental flaw of the Newtonian picture of the universe was that physics accurate for Earth and the Solar System was extrapolated to the entire universe. Human intuition only works across a narrow range of size scales, approximately from the size of a flea to the size of the Sun. This range is humanity's mental homeland. Developing the symbol a little further, we can name this central range of size scales "Midgard" (Fig. 4).

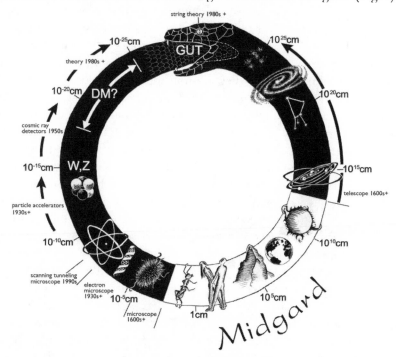

Figure 4: Midgard

Midgard spans about fourteen orders of magnitude, from 10^{-2} cm to 10^{12} cm, holding everything for which people have intuition. The figure also shows the approximate decade and technology by which scientists discovered the rest of the Cosmic Uroboros.

Midgard is everywhere in the universe. It is not a place but a setting of the intellectual zoom lens. In the old Norse mythological cosmos, Midgard was the human world. It was an island representing stability and civilized society in the middle of the "world-sea," the Norse universe, and elsewhere in the world-sea lay the land of the giants and the land of the gods. This is an excellent description—metaphorically, of course—of Midgard as the center of the expanding universe. Our modern Midgard is the island of size scales that are familiar and comprehensible to human beings. But beyond Midgard in one direction—outward—into the expanding universe is the land of incomprehensibly giant beings, like black holes a million times the mass of the Sun and galaxies made of hundreds of billions of stars. In the other direction from Midgard—inward, toward the small—lies a living cellular world, and beyond that the quantum world, and these microlands are the evolutionary and physical sources of everything we are. That may not make them gods, but compared to us they are more prolific, more ancient, universal, and omnipresent. Midgard is not isolated from these other lands but bridges them.

The range of size scales we call Midgard is what people generally think of as "physical" reality. Very large and very small structures on the Cosmic Uroboros are not physical in the common sense use of the term. Superclusters of galaxies are expanding apart and in billions of years will disperse. Unlike galaxies and galaxy clusters, they are not bound together by gravity. In the opposite direction from Midgard toward the very small, there are elementary particles that are not really "physical" particles but rather quantum mechanical ones that are routinely in two or more places at once. The strange truth is that what we usually think of as "physical" is a property of Midgard, perhaps the defining property, and the further from Midgard a phenomenon is, the more metaphorical all verbal description of it must be. Such phenomena can only be known through science and only experienced, if at all, via the educated imagination. This includes most of the universe. The Cosmic Uroboros thus presents a scientific context for those exotic size scales of the universe that no human tradition ever had a connection with before.

Is this practical knowledge? Modern science has led to practical technologies that tap into the powers of the universe—nuclear energy, for example, or genetic engineering—but until now science has provided no context in which these powers make sense. There are major threats to human survival today—world environmental degradation, extinction of species, destabilization of the climate, nuclear war, terrorists with weapons of mass destruction. All these threats result, at least in part, from the unrestrained use of such new technologies without a meaningful cosmology that makes sense of the nature and scale of these powers. People whose actions could damage the Earth for thousands and possibly millions of years are thinking on minuscule time scales and only see short term costs and benefits as *real*. "Size matters" is a universal law, and therefore we cannot extrapolate safely in any context when the numbers or sizes we are dealing with differ by many orders of magnitude. We court disaster whenever policy-makers extrapolate their traditional values and intuitive sense of time to global-scale decisions. This is a reason why cosmic perspective can be valuable in human affairs. It is almost impossible to recognize a threat that does not make sense in your cosmology. We humans are exploiting the powers of a universe to which we are blind. But we need no longer be.

When we open our eyes to the view from the center of the universe, we see that intelligent beings exist on multiple levels at once, and now we can scientifically understand how this is so. Vast amounts of information, fantastic strokes of luck, and billions of years to work them out are invested in us, and we need concepts by which to value those inputs accurately.

Like every earlier culture, we need to know our place in the universe, and where we are in time, space, and size is part of situating ourselves in the epic of cosmic evolution. But unlike all traditional stories, ours cannot start "In the beginning," because no one really understands the beginning, although we now have a well-tested scientific theory from about a thousandth of a second after the Big Bang, forward. Creation stories of the future therefore should explicitly start at the earliest point we actually understand, in the expectation that that point will move earlier as scientific knowledge progresses. Big changes are happening on our planet, and shepherding ourselves through them successfully is going to require tremendous confidence, creativity, and knowledge. An essential ingredient may be the first cosmic story to be solidly based on scientific evidence—and such a story is just becoming available. Not a moment too soon!

Editors Note

This paper was adapted by Nancy Abrams and Joel Primack from their conference presentation and their DVD, *The View from the Center of the Universe*. The illustrations in this chapter first appeared in their book: *The View from the Center of the Universe: Discovering Our Extraordinary Place in the Cosmos* (2006). Their DVD and book can be ordered from their website at <http://viewfromthecenter.com> where interviews with the authors can also be found.

I envisioned a deeper role for theatre, one that echoed back to its ancient roots as a vehicle for catharsis and discovery. Each story I wrote was its own vivid world, with its own intelligence and wisdom.

Pauline Le Bel

Bringing the Universe Story Home
Engaged Cosmology and the Role of the Artist

Pauline Le Bel

ACT 1: How the Universe Story Sang Itself into My Heart

Scene 1: Science's New Creation Story

Physicist Richard Feynman, in *What Do You Care What Other People Think*, concluded, "This is not yet a scientific age." "Is no one inspired by our present picture of the universe?" he asks. "This value of science remains unsung by singers: you are reduced to hearing not a story or poem, but an evening lecture about it" (Feynman 1998, 244).

One could draw a parallel between artist and scientist. Both are obsessed with the truth; both are willing to sit in the dark for a long time before they stumble across it. I had been sitting in the dark for years, disturbed by the increasing commodification and trivialization of art, the use of theatre as distraction.

I've been a storyteller for over 30 years, as a singer, an actor, and as a writer of songs, novels, screenplays, and musicals. As a young actress, weary of being cast in meaningless roles, I had started writing my own plays. I envisioned a deeper role for theatre, one that echoed back to its ancient roots as a vehicle for catharsis and discovery. Each story I wrote was its own vivid world, with its own intelligence and wisdom. Each story transformed me in some way.

Eight years ago, I heard for the first time Brian Swimme's *Canticle to the Cosmos*. This eloquent science-based creation story, this cosmic womb of a story, was the one I had been waiting to hear all my life. A path for heart and soul, it would give me the courage to act upon my deepest knowing. At last, science was asking the questions I was seeking answers to, while honoring my desire for intimacy with the natural world.

Every culture has its creation stories through which individuals discover and shape their sense of self and their knowledge of others. Here I was, discovering a new shape for myself and for my world. I began to dream how I might work with the story, how it might be enriched with poetry and music to reach deeper into people's hearts. I would find a way to sing the scientific story of the universe, to make the Universe Story accessible and irresistible to everyone.

"Every single atom in your body, every single note of music was once inside a star."

(All scene quotes in this chapter taken from Le Bel 2005).

Scene 2: Trouble in Paradise

Around the same time, I moved to a small rural island on Canada's west coast. I was invited to be co-founder of the Bowen Island Life Long Learning Society, to deal with issues of sustainability on the island. I was reluctant at first, not convinced that as an artist I had enough expertise. It soon became clear that all the planning and expert talk would not lead to sustainability until it was connected to spirit, until our wonderful heady ideas could be warmed by the heart so they might stir people to take action. I knew I had a job to do.

The island, a rural paradise 20 minutes on the ferry from Vancouver, had been experiencing intense development pressure. Many islanders were concerned that our municipal council was beginning to look like a developer's rubber stamp. Letters to the editor were getting crankier, and public meetings sometimes turned into brawls. We needed a better picture of where we were and who we were.

I decided to write a full-length musical to tell the story of the island, weaving the Universe Story into the bioregional story. In poetic and musical language, I would tell the deep time story of an old volcanic rock, a rock that dreamed of becoming an island, a beautiful green island with ferns and cedars. And every plant, every animal, every person living on the island was part of this dream. We would sing the galactic history, the natural and the human history, sing songs of praise for the beauty here, and lamentations for what we had carelessly destroyed.

"*She dreamed us all, every voice, every song, and in our hearts her dream goes on. And now that we're here, now that we're here, what is the island dreaming now?*"

Scene 3: The Singing Universe

I set aside time to research and write, to find the rhythm and lilt of this rocky, watery landscape, and learn the tales that longed to be told. Since I'm a musician I would tell the story through sound, calling the play *Voices in the Sound*. Partly because Bowen Island is cradled in the waters of Howe Sound, but especially because it is the sound of a thing that makes it what it is, just as a person's voice tells us about the nature of their soul.

I imagined the music of stars and galaxies and wondered about the first sound of the universe. Through the Internet, I was introduced to astronomer Mark Whittle at the University of Virginia. Seems the universe was singing right from the beginning. And it didn't bang. It roared, and hissed, and hummed.

I became obsessed by the sounds of the island and how they had changed over the years since human habitation. I kept a sound journal, noting the call of herons, the clatter of gravel trucks, the whistle of the ferry, the whine of chainsaws, and the winter wind howling through the Sound.

"*Though Bowen Island change and grow, and many other voices come and go, I'll walk upon this holy ground, and hear the ancient voices in the sound.*"

ACT II: *Voices in the Sound* – From My Heart to Their Hearts

Scene 1: Setting the Stage

We needed a suitable setting for the musical. Outdoors, of course, with the audience on the grass, as close to the skin of the land as possible, that they might hear the heartbeat of the island.

I surveyed the island for months, calling and singing as I went, waiting for the song to return. There were several majestic groves of cedars but they didn't make music or they were too far from the village. I wanted to make it possible for people to walk to the "theater." I settled on a grove of alder trees in a meadow with a powerful echo. Alders are considered the "junk trees" here because they do not serve humans in the same way as do the hardwoods. But alders are the healing trees: they nourish and renew the soil for the next generation of big trees. I saw this as a suitable metaphor for a play whose mission was to heal and nourish the cultural and spiritual soil of the island.

No need to spend money on set design. Mother Nature had taken care of that beautifully, thousands of years in the making. I could hear the actors and singers breathing with the trees, energized by the vast sky above, accompanied by western tanagers and tree frogs.

"We are always walking this island, we are always wearing her dream like a green cloak. We are always walking this island, we are always singing her dream."

Scene 2: Gathering the Voices

Although my work had been in professional theatre, it was clear this play wanted to belong to the community. I approached everyone I knew to take part – the electrician, the choir director, the art gallery curator, the stonemason, the carpenter, the retired gynecologist. Enough of them said yes.

Never one to do things in half-measures, I organized a three-day festival, also called *Voices in the Sound*, so other essential voices could be heard: nature walks to listen to the voices of plants and rocks; storytelling so the old timers could share their experiences; and the "bull kelp orchestra workshop" for children to make musical instruments from kelp, bamboo, and seashells found on the island. The festival would build community through the telling of our stories. It would deepen our knowledge and respect for the land and for each other. It would honor the past and dream the future.

I invited the Squamish Nation, whose ancestors used the island for over 5,000 year as a meeting place. They no longer have a presence on the island, and there has been little contact between our cultures even though their reserves are just across the waters.

They graciously accepted and brought storytellers, dancers, their hand-carved 45-foot cedar dugout canoe, and their deep connection to the ancestors. It was a thrill to have them watch the musical and to see how they resonated with the Universe Story.

"This is our home, this is our destiny, here in the web of life."

ACT III –Island Dream

Scene 1: The Spectacle

Islanders came with lawn chairs and blankets, with little ones and old ones. They all cheered as the actors stepped out of the forest to weave the strands of history, cosmology, spirit and nature. They experienced the stardust in their bones, the magic of the singing meadow, and were proud to learn that they were children of the greatest love story we have ever known, the enduring love affair between Earth and Sun. And we all thanked the heavens it didn't rain.

Within a few weeks, attitudes had shifted. Islanders began to see and hear the island in a new way. The old, ineffectual municipal council was soon replaced by a "green" council ready to stand up for the preservation of the precious green spaces on the island. Our cosmological musical as the centerpiece of the festival had served as a bridge, bringing together those who had previously found it difficult to talk to each other.

"We are the dreamers, the actors who choose the plot, who shape this island in the Salish Sea. May we dream wisely. May we sing a worthy song."

Epilogue

It's been two years since the last performance of *Voices in the Sound*, now embedded in the cultural DNA of the island. The community continues to respond to the power of the story:

> *Your musical will do more to shape the future of Bowen Island than all those who are planning and arguing. It will percolate in the groundwater and shift people's perceptions. So many people focus on our differences. Your musical focused on what we have in common, our shared history, our shared cosmic origins, the primordial wisdom handed down from grandparent to grandchild.* (Anthony Ocana, M.D.)

> *Pauline is on to something big with Voices in the Sound. She has created a mirror for our community and held it in front of us, inviting us to be a part of the evolving history of the island.* (Chris Corrigan, Open Space Facilitator)

> *The musical is fabulous. So moving! And humor punctuated throughout. It is the most magnificent wedding of the Universe Story and bioregionalism that I have ever witnessed. It seems to me that you should be able to keep busy for the rest of your life using the Bowen Island play as a template, working in collaboration*

> *with bioregionalists all over the continent to produce similar plays*
> *for each and every one.*
> (Connie Barlow, science writer, www.thegreatstory.org)

Playwright's Note:
Many thanks to Brian Swimme and Thomas Berry for opening my mind and heart to the magnificent story of the universe; to the forests and waters of Bowen Island for ongoing nourishment and inspiration; and to all those who generously gave financial and artistic support. May the *Voices in the Sound* musical inspire other communities to take the Universe Story down from the stars and bring it home. Please contact me if you would like more information, or to order a DVD of the musical or a CD of the soundtrack:
Email: songspinner@shaw.ca
Website: www.suncoastarts.com/paulinelebel.html

References

Feynman, R. P. 1998. *What Do You Care what Other People Think?* New York, NY: Norton and Company.

Le Bel, P. 2005. *Voices in the Sound, the Musical.* Unpublished manuscript of a play performed in Bowen Island, Canada.

No one on Earth has been trained in how to evolve a planet from its high tech, over-populating, polluting, and warring state to a future equal to our full potential. None of the existing authorities can lead us through this transition—not heads of nation states, or organized religions, or global corporations.

Barbara Marx Hubbard

Evolutionary Spirituality
The Soul of Evolution

Barbara Marx Hubbard

What Is Evolutionary Spirituality?

Evolutionary Spirituality is the *Impulse of Evolution*, unfolding now as our own passionate yearning to create and participate in self and social evolution. It is the soul of evolution. It is experienced subjectively as an unfolding, directional pattern toward higher consciousness, greater freedom through more complex and synergistic order. Through evolutionary spirituality we sense that we *are* evolution. We are nature evolving. As the crises on Earth deepen, this "soul" is becoming self aware in many of us. It is felt as a resonance with the deeper patterns of evolution, often called Spirit, with one another and with nature.

Evolutionary spirituality is neither a new religion nor an organization. It is the offspring of the mystic experience of the great traditions of the world combined with the discoveries of science. It comes forth as an evolving human, one who seeks to fulfill the ethical and spiritual insights of great visionaries of the past as co-creators of our world. It is giving birth to a global "communion of pioneering souls," spontaneously arising among people from every race, nation, and religion who experience within ourselves the emergence of a more universal, empathetic, spiritually-awakened human, a co-creator of new worlds.

Evolutionary spirituality seems to attract people Teilhard de Chardin (1964, 137-138) described as "*Homo progressivus*," those in whom a "flame of expectation burns," those who sense the future as an organism progressing toward the unknown. It is a type of human sensitive to and attracted by what is emergent within themselves and the world. I read with admiration the brilliant works of scientists who express awe and reverence for the laws and splendor of the universe objectively, but who do not also feel this universal intelligence subjectively, within themselves. I wonder if they have a slightly different genetic code or a "missing gene" that is not sensitive to transcendent experience, like being tone deaf or color blind.

The Experience of Evolutionary Spirituality

Evolutionary spirituality is founded on a continuing inquiry to understand the laws and processes of the physical universe with a concurrent deepening

awareness of unfolding patterns of evolution within. Evolutionary spirituality
feels like love at the core of our being, reaching out to all life. Empathy expands.
Comprehensive compassion grows. Our own passion to create appears to us as
part of a larger design of creation. We are propelled forward as vital elements
of that design through our own choice and intention.

We place ourselves as pioneers standing in solidarity with the great self-
creating events of the past, such as the formation of life, of animal life, of human life. This is our lineage. In our genes are all the generations.

We are unique aspects of the universe in the process of evolution toward a
more complex order. We are not simply one with an eternal deity, or living in a
pointless universe going down to an inevitable heat death. We are bringing "the
gods" home as our own developmental potential to co-create our futures.

The New Field of Conscious Evolution

Evolutionary spirituality springs from radically new conditions facing us
on Earth. Through science and technology we have gained powers we used to
attribute to our gods. We can destroy our world or create a future of literally
infinite potentialities. This new condition is acting as an evolutionary driver
requiring us to learn how to evolve consciously, or to render ourselves extinct
through misuse of our powers. I call this new potential the advent of *conscious
evolution*, the evolution of evolution from unconscious to conscious choice
(Hubbard 1998). In retrospect I believe we will discover that conscious evolution is as important as the invention of language or DNA. We will become a
self-evolving species. We are facing an unknown.

No one on Earth has been trained in how to evolve a planet from its
high tech, over-populating, polluting, and warring state to a future equal to
our full potential. None of the existing authorities can lead us through this
transition—not heads of nation states, or organized religions, or global corporations. In our academic institutions there is not even a subject, field, or
department on humanity's requirement to learn to evolve consciously. Science
alone, as science, cannot guide us, for it is often not imbued with a sense of
direction, progress, or pattern for the future.

This vacuum of evolutionary leadership in the existing system is stimulating a large global movement of spiritually-based personal growth, social
change, technological inventions, noetic sciences, health breakthroughs, developing and networking innovations in all fields, fostering new methods of co-
intelligence, social synergy, sacred activism, etc., usually underneath the radar
of the "news," outside of academic disciplines or religions, ignored by current
politics, yet instigating what Paul Hawken (2007) describes in the title of his
book *Blessed Unrest: How the Largest Movement in the World Came into Being
and Why No One Saw it Coming*. This movement of civil society is inspired by
some form of evolutionary spirituality, by whatever name it is called.

A New Image of "God"

Evolutionary spirituality brings forth an evolving image of God from a paternalistic deity external to us, or an internal field where only the changeless is real, as in some Eastern traditions, to an image of God as what Sidney Lanier (unpublished journal) calls the "Great Creating Process," what Aurobindo (1972, 735) calls the "Consciousness Force," David Bohm (1980) refers to as the "Implicate Order," Ken Wilber (1996, 66) calls "Spirit in action," and Beatrice Bruteau (1997) calls "Cosmogestation... animating every atom, molecule and cell from within" (174).

Evolutionary spirituality arises out of the subjective intuition that the fundamental Reality is Consciousness, Creative Intelligence, Unified Field, or Mind. Consciousness is not seen as the epiphenomenon of matter, but as the Creative Intelligence out of which matter, life, and human life have evolved. The universe does not appear as mindless, purposeless, or directionless, as posited by some, such as Nobel physicist Steven Weinberg (1977) who said "the more the universe seems comprehensible, the more it also seems pointless." Rather, we witness a continuous process of transformation toward higher consciousness and greater freedom through more complex order.

This explanation proposes that "what Darwin termed natural selection is an intelligently guided process that promotes the creative expression and evolution of ever more complex and interconnected systems: the operation of intelligent evolution," as Gary Schwartz (2006, 12) puts it. It respects and deepens the scientific inquiry into the nature of creative evolution, probing into the anomalies that reductionist science cannot fully explain, such as the perfect fine-tuning of the first three seconds after the Big Bang or the origin of the universe itself (Laszlo 1996). It goes beyond the dogmas of Creationism or Evolutionism to open an inquiry into the nature of universal creative intelligence, subjectively, and objectively at "all levels and all quadrants," as Ken Wilber (2000, 70) puts it.

Neither the point of view of a contingent universe or an intelligent universe can be proven or dis-proven at this stage of human intelligence. Those experiencing evolutionary spirituality *choose* by deep attraction, metaphysical preference, intuition, and subjective experience, the world view that Consciousness is prime, that there is a fundamental designing universal intelligence at work in the universe, experienced as our own oneness with IT.

Evolutionary Spirituality Fosters a Three-Fold *Evolutionary* Consciousness

Evolutionary spirituality looks *inward* to the Mystery, the Void, the Unified Field, the Mind of the Cosmos out of which everything is arising. It does not see that Mystery as a personal deity or a Being outside of the Field, but as the ground of being itself which is sensitive to our own intention since we are IT in human form. It is a non-dual, unitive awareness, not of the supernatural, but of expanded nature, including human nature, which is, at its source, a profound mystery. It draws from the new revelations of quantum physics that the universe is a unified whole, that it displays non-locality, entanglement, connectivity, and coherence throughout the whole. It finds that Mystery is animating the source of our own being, the center of supreme reality within ourselves.

Evolutionary consciousness looks *backward* in time, discovering that cosmogenesis, the whole story of creation, is alive in us now. We are the universe in person. The intelligence of the life force has broken into our consciousness as our own impulse to evolve, to create, and to expand to fulfill life's potential. In expanded evolutionary consciousness we can imagine, for ecstatic moments, tuning into the trillions of cells and the billions of miles of DNA within that are encoded with the universe story.

While experiencing inner oneness with supreme reality and feeling the active presence of the evolutionary story alive in our own being, when we are in evolutionary consciousness, we concurrently move *forward* to express our potential through action and self expression in the world. We find ourselves awakened from within by a passionate desire to realize our innate creativity, to join with others, to find our life purpose so that we are not left out of the story. We become authors of our own story, co-creators with the process of creation.

The Path of the Co-creator

Co-creation means aligning with the Creative Intelligence of the universe and cooperating consciously with it in our own lives and in partnership with others doing the same. Co-creation is a developmental path that fosters an exploration of the art and practice of conscious evolution, inspired by evolutionary spirituality.

The Path of the Co-creator focuses on the weaving self and social evolution leading toward wholeness. In brief, the Self Path works toward an expansion of identity from the egoic self, to the essential or higher self, to the universal self, the highest frequency of our being, until finally we expand our identity to include the Great Creating Process, the prime agency of evolution as the source and momentum of our being.

In the Social Path of the Co-creator we start with resonant circles of two or more individuals who affirm the essential self as our true being, cultivating a field of non-judgment and love. This field allows the essential self to become stabilized as the center of our being. From there we move toward co-creative circles. These are little "multi-celled organisms," clusters of people joining center with center, heart with heart to fulfill their life purpose in a way that models the change we would like to see in the world (Anderson and Roske 2001).

A Meta-Religio?

I believe that evolutionary spirituality can foster the maturation of the human species. It offers a context for the unique contribution of every great faith to the conscious evolution of humanity. It is child of all the traditions, born into the next stage of human evolution. This convergence into what Sidney Lanier (unpublished journal) calls a "meta-religio" will form a new body of spiritual experience and practices, transcending yet including the best of the traditions, affirming and connecting what truly works to mature us through peer validation. In such a meta-religio, we move beyond dogma and cultural limitations, allowing that which does not work, that which imposes on us by "faith" unbelievable and destructive scriptural stories, freeing us to fulfill our potential as co-creative, coevolving, universal humans (a model that I sense has not yet fully evolved on this Earth.)

Our spiritual ancestors paved the way for us not only through direct experience of supreme reality, but also in their mystical visions of the future. They foresaw a radical new stage of being – a new heaven and a new earth; a New Jerusalem beyond sorrow, beyond death, the former things passed away; a paradise beyond this life through surrender to God; nirvana, the extinction of the separated self through union with the Field out of which all is arising.

These visions of the future that have attracted pre-scientific humanity to go beyond the current limits of human life, are actually becoming real through our capacity for conscious evolution. Through the maturation of evolutionary spirituality we can experience ever more direct contact with Source, not only as Pure Awareness of the Eternal, but also as the evolving aspect of the creation. We can, through the harmonious use of our new technological capacities, transcend the limits of the creature human condition, extending our lives, exploring the universe – becoming a universal co-creative species. The mystical visions of the future can be reached for, not as life after death, but as life after this stage of life.

Religions are now being "evolutionized" as Sri Aurobindo evolutionized Hinduism and Teilhard de Chardin evolutionized Catholicism. In my work as an evolutionary futurist, for example, I was inspired by a personal experience to write an evolutionary interpretation of the New Testament (Hubbard 1993). I discovered that much of the New Testament is coded evolution that could not be decoded until the human species could begin to attain actual powers of "gods." For example, St. Paul writes:

> Behold, I show you a mystery: We shall not all sleep; but we shall all be changed in a moment, in the twinkling of an eye. At the last trumpet, for the trumpet shall sound and the dead shall be raised incorruptible, and we shall be changed. (1 Corinthians 15:51-55).

I wrote:

> Behold, the mystery will soon be revealed. The time of trans-
> formation is at hand. The twinkling of an eye, the trumpet's
> last blare, come for the person when the planet has reached
> its limits and is ready like an egg to give birth to its child. We
> humans, bodily children of Earth, will become universal as
> we carry Earth's body into the universe. In that environment,
> mammalian bodies will soon perish. The new bodies will be
> formed by the intention to survive and grow in the new en-
> vironments of a universe of infinite variety, magnificence and
> surprises..." (69).

I saw the life of Jesus as that of a future human, a quantum jump toward what I am calling a universal human. We can do the works that he did, and far greater works, when we learn ethical conscious evolution. We can produce in abundance; we can heal; we can resurrect simple organisms from the "dead," that is, from DNA; we can perform virgin births; we can create holograms that appear real; we are studying the possibility of teleportation; we can leave this Earth and return alive, etc. Our technologies are actually inventing real capacities to do what appeared to a pre-scientific age as "miracles." Since the whole process of the rise of the physical universe out of No Thing at All, is a mystery, a "miracle," is it possible that the apparently mythical stories are evo-lutionary forecasts and visions of what is actually to happen when we combine heart, mind, and spirit with radical evolutionary technologies that transform the physical world? As we once believed, so it can in fact become!

Revelation unfolds as evolution, not as some future heaven or a Utopia, but as breakthroughs toward genuine newness, as once life was new, or hu-mans were new.

All our religions were born before the threat of environmental collapse or nuclear holocaust. They all emerged before humanity gained its unprecedented powers. None of them can tell us what to do about cloning, stem cell research, non-human intelligence, space settlement, overcoming aging, and many other such radical breakthroughs. The spiritual texts of the past have prepared us, but we now can update the covenants.

New sacred scriptures will emerge from the experience of *being* co-cre-ators as we learn to restore this Earth, free ourselves from poverty and disease, co-design new synergistic systems, transform "a terrible love of war" (Hillman 2004) to the passionate love of evolving ourselves and exploring the vast untapped domains of inner and outer space. These new writings will be the sacred scriptures of the early phases of universal conscious evolution. They are being written now as the new covenants, coming through higher guidance, and through discoveries at the forefront of the new physics, biology, psychology, and social innovations at the growing edge of human endeavor.

From the perspective of evolutionary spirituality, we are at the threshold of the emergence of a universal humanity. We can become capable of conscious ethical evolution, first on this planet, then in the solar system, and finally throughout the universe. We can reach ever-deeper understanding of and participation with the processes of creation until we become co-creators on a universal scale. This is the promise of evolutionary spirituality.

References

Anderson, C. and Roske, K. 2001. *The Co-Creator's Handbook: An Experiential Guide for Discovering Your Life Purpose and Building a Co-creative Society.* Nevada City, CA: Global Family.

Aurobindo. 1972. *The Life Divine.* Vol. 18 & 19 of the Sri Aurobindo Birth Centenary Library Twin Lakes, WI: Lotus Press. (Original work published 1939 from serial appearance in the *Arya* from August 1914 to January 1919.)

Bohm, D. 2000. *Wholeness and the Implicate Order* UK: Routledge.

Bruteau, B. 1997. *God's Ecstasy: The Creation of a Self-Creating Universe.* New York, NY: A Crossroads Book.

Hillman, J. 2004. *A Terrible Love of War.* New York, NY: The Penguin Press.

Hubbard, B. M. 1993. *The Revelation: Our Crisis Is a Birth.* Santa Barbara, CA: The Foundation for Conscious Evolution.

Hubbard, B. M. 1998. *Conscious Evolution: Awakening the Power of Our Social Potential.* Novato, CA: New World Library.

Lanier, S. *The Sovereign Person.* Manuscript to be published from his journal.

Laszlo, E. 1996. *The Whispering Pond: A Personal Guide to the Emerging Vision of Science.* Rockport, MA: Element.

Schwartz, G. and Simon, W. 2006. *The G.O.D. Experiments: How Science Is Discovering God In Everything, Including Us.*

Teilhard de Chardin, P. 1964. *The Future of Man.* New York, NY: Harper & Row.

Weinberg, S. 1977. *The First Three Seconds: A Modern View of the Origin of the Universe.* New York, NY: Basic Books.

Wilber, K. 2000. *A Brief History of Everything.* Boston, MA and London, UK: Shambahala.

PART III

The Epic Engages Education and Big History

Cheryl Genet

The strange thing…is that the evolutionary epic is not taught in every school in every country in the world!

David Christian

As far-seeing educators implement teaching the full sweep of the evolutionary epic as big history, inevitable successes occur and challenges arise. "Implications of the Evolutionary Epic for the Study of Human History" delineates some of these challenges, including the problem of running "head-on into the traditional religious teachings and [doing] so in ways that offer little room for accommodation because the scenarios characteristically rest on highly secular views of reality."

"The Convergence of Logic, Faith, and Values in the Modern Creation Myth" continues the discussion of some of the hands-on challenges inherent in the teaching of big history and the extent of the students' search for meaning. "Ironically then, it turns out that the modern creation story, utterly devoid of gods and spirits as it is, is a powerful tool to engage and challenge undergraduates at the highest level of both their cognitive and spiritual consciousness."

There are technical challenges to teaching big history as well. "Why Aren't More People Teaching Big History" lists among these challenges the size of the task, the lack of textbooks and other resources, and the simple fear of looking ridiculous. "[Educators] have never imagined or thought about the complete story from the beginning to now, the whole idea is likely to seem preposterous." But value is found in turning the tide against academic fragmentation, full use of constantly accumulating scientific knowledge, and responding to global challenges. "Learning the whole story has the potential to change our students' sense of their very identity as well as their relationship to to their studies, to the environment, and to the world."

Education and students are both impacted by the vast amount of information that must be processed, during which the capacity for deep intimacy with the material is often diminished. "Contemplatio ad Amorem Natura" finds that "[i]ntegrating contemplative practice into our courses provides students with specific ways to enter reflectively into their education. Perhaps more importantly, it embodies the message that we must work to become wise in our endeavors—especially considering the potential global cost of not doing so."

"Big History as Global Systems History" explores complex and non-linear ways of looking at our evolutionary history and our place in it—encorporating evolving wisdom as well as knowledge.

> The benefit of a term that includes "global," "systems,"and "history," all in one, is that it draws attention to the reciprocal relationships of parts within a larger whole, thereby including even the internal relationship of mind and heart.

"A Consilient Curriculum" addresses the question of how we organize what we know and the lack of diversity in core curriculum.

> If we do not understand how social systems work and how they contribute to making whole persons out of mere humans, then we cannot claim to have an adequate grasp of human nature.

It concludes that the evolutionary epic, the biggest of all pictures of reality, must "be recognized as the new centerpiece of core curriculum of American higher education if it is to remain relevant."

> If the contemplation of timeframes—or the size and location of objects—seems to diminish our significance dramatically, attention to the pervasive connectedness of the universe begins to restore it, for what we discover everywhere we look are webs of relationships whose very existence suggests meaningful responses to questions about how we fit into the ultimate scheme of things.
>
> John Meares

Implications of the Evolutionary Epic for the Study of Human History

John A. Mears

I first became interested in what David Christian has recently taught us to call big history in the 1970s.[1] A range of factors drew me to this grand view of reality. I had always been attracted to sweeping treatments of the past, so when I decided as a junior in high school—a moment quite early in my life—that I would teach history at the college level, I immediately followed up my decision by reading H. G. Well's *Outline of History* cover to cover. Thereafter, I perused the two-volume abridgement of Arnold J. Toynbee's *A Study of History* as time permitted or whenever such topics as the comparability of civilizations or the idea of "challenge and response" caught my attention. Despite my persistent interest in broad historical perspectives, I completed my graduate training in a conventional fashion, concentrating in early modern Europe and then settling into what I anticipated would be a typical academic career.

By the mid-1970s, however, having taught for about a decade, I found myself bristling at what I experienced as the increasing intellectual fragmentation of the academy, and I initially expressed my frustration with a determined defense of general education. A series of conference papers led to the publication in 1985 of a journal article entitled "Evolutionary Process: An Organizing Principle for General Education," in which I stressed our ability to establish connections between our respective disciplines. "Every discipline," I argued, "embraces an element of historicity; every discipline is connected in one way or another with how the relationship patterns between apparently disparate phenomena alter over time.... And whatever our disciplines, we discover—when we observe the evolutionary process over long time spans—a persistent direction in the order and sequence shaped

---

1   Three books provided the initial impetus for my thinking: Preston Cloud, *Cosmos, Earth, and Man: A Short History of the Universe* (New Haven: Yale University Press, 1978); Ilya Prigogine, *From Being to Becoming: Time and Complexity in the Physical Sciences* (San Francisco: W. H. Freeman and Company, 1980); and Eric J. Chaisson, *Cosmic Dawn: The Origins of Matter and Life* (Boston: Little, Brown and Company, 1980). David Christian presented his concept to the wider profession in "The Case for Big History," *Journal of World History*, Vol. 2, No. 2 (Fall 1991), 223-38.

by our minds, a direction that moves things from the singular to the plural, from the homogeneous to the heterogeneous, from the simple to the complex, from isolation to integration" (Mears 1986, 315).

By 1985, I had joined the fledgling World History Association. Soon I was moved to develop my own world history survey, and understandably, given my previous interests, I began my year-long introductory course with a series of topics starting with the Big Bang and ending with the onset of the Holocene that consumed about half of the fall semester. Steady avocational reading in the sciences with a heavy emphasis on the work of paleoanthropologists enabled me to handle this material, more or less satisfactorily, by myself. My purpose was somewhat different than the goals of Brian Swimme and Thomas Berry in *The Universe Story*, Eric Chaisson in *Epic of Evolution*, or David Christian in *Maps of Time*. Using big history as my framework, I wanted to set the stage and establish a context for my own extended analysis of the unfolding of humanity's past considered as a totality, a project that I am laboriously turning into a book I have tentatively entitled *To Be Human: A Perspective on Our Common History*.

Committed to this agenda, I have served in recent years on a variety of conference panels designed to orient other academics to the primary themes of world history and the nature of big history. Academic audiences have invariably found the presentations stimulating and occasionally even intriguing. Responding to the idea of big history, they have perceptively raised questions about significant problems that remain unresolved: How do cosmologists explain the origins of galaxies in the early universe, how do chemists understand the emergence of life forms out of matter, and how do historians integrate what we once called prehistory with what has happened to humankind in the last five millennia? But again and again, individuals have introduced more basic quandaries into the discussions. For the most part, devotees of big history have moved beyond the concerns of those being exposed to this concept for the first time, having already addressed a range of difficult questions to their own satisfaction. Hence, my fellow panelists have occasionally been surprised when they encountered colleagues who are not prepared to accept what they have learned to take for granted. Although advocates of big history have sometimes shown frustration by the concerns of panel audiences, the very persistence with which critics have raised their points means, I think, that we are compelled to respond.

Skepticism about big history has been articulated at different times and in different ways. But in my experience expressions of doubt tend to cluster together into three groups. We can understand the first set of frequently asked questions in terms of uncertainty over why big history makes any difference.

Even if we can muster the breadth of knowledge necessary to write a book or give a course on big history (and frankly, many of my inquisitors, having been trained to write monographs, remain doubtful), why should we take the trouble? What have we accomplished once we have completed our task? How does anything that happened prior to the Holocene, including hominid evolution, significantly affect our approaches to human history? At least with these concerns we are prepared to respond with relative ease, since the queries are obviously fundamental and essentially intellectual in nature.

The second set of reactions is more difficult to handle. The questions arise less frequently, but are invariably interjected into the conversation with a vehemence that in an age of political correctness makes them impossible to ignore. This group focuses on the charge that world history represents an insidious kind of Western intellectual imperialism since its methods and outcomes tend to rest on Western assumptions, values, and modes of investigation. In addition these methods and outcomes often fail to consider non-Western societies on their own terms, and are inclined to orient the entire historical process, especially the last five hundred years, around what William H. McNeill (1963) called in the title of his magnum opus "the rise of the West."[2] In my experience, critics apply a somewhat different version of such charges to big history as well, in large measure because it relies so heavily on the fruits of Western science, a point that leads me to the third set of common reactions.

I have learned that this third group of concerns can become particularly contentious because the questions are grounded in people's religious beliefs, and given the conservative mood of contemporary society, are often highly charged emotionally. After all, big history, or cosmic evolution, if you prefer, challenges head-on traditional religious teachings and does so in ways that offer little room for accommodation because the scenarios characteristically rest on highly secular views of reality. For their part, when advocates of big history are challenged by individuals, including at least some trained academics, who reject conclusions about the human condition derived largely from modern science, they typically respond by reciting the obvious differences between science and religion, which operate in different realms with different assumptions and purposes. So far as I can determine, these ready responses seldom resolve the issue. If that is the case, what are we to make of the resulting standoff? How can we respond more effectively? Is it possible that our current methods are incomplete, that we might enrich our own understandings of big history if we folded into our own thinking at least some of the concerns of this third set of critics? Having ruminated over these various problems at considerable

---

2   See the argument set forth in Chapter XIII of McNeill (1963).

length, I want to share a few ideas about each in turn, beginning with the direct implications of our enterprise for the study of human history.

As esoteric and distant as the ideas of big history may seem, we have learned that theories taking us from the Big Bang to the emergence of our kind on planet Earth do have a direct bearing on our understanding of human history when we consider it as a totality. As we are inclined to tell our students, we are invariably startled by the brevity of the human experience when we place it against a cosmic backdrop. The Sun, our life-giving source of heat and light, may appear to us permanent in its being; yet it has glowed in the heavens for less than a third of the time that has passed since the Big Bang and is destined to burn itself out in another few billion years. Our earliest hominid ancestors seem so far removed from current affairs as to be beyond the range of our imagination; yet the Earth had turned on its axis billions of times before the first apelike hominids made their appearance between six and seven million years ago—a reminder, incidentally, of what a young species humans actually are. Societies we call civilized have existed for five thousand years, most of which for us—and certainly for our students—represent a distant, hazy past; yet the time span appears to be virtually nothing when compared to the 3.8 billion years since the oldest known terrestrial rocks solidified. The history of the United States becomes a blink of the eye in eternity's presence, while the Biblical three score years and ten accorded to an individual human can scarcely be recorded at all on a cosmic timeline. Big history, we remind our critics, encourages us to think about the human experience and its possibilities in much longer intervals of time instead of the very short periods we normally consider.

If the contemplation of timeframes—or the size and location of objects—seems to diminish our significance dramatically, attention to the pervasive connectedness of the universe begins to restore it, for what we discover everywhere we look are webs of relationships whose very existence suggests meaningful responses to questions about how we fit into the ultimate scheme of things. The achievements of modern science allow us to delineate clear lines of development, tracing the formation of simple atoms out of energy, galaxies out of shapeless matter, heavy elements out of stars, and, under the right combination of circumstances, the molecular building blocks of life out of heavy elements. Relativity theory points toward a shared beginning for all energy and matter—a modern creation myth as we like to call it—just as our explanations of chemical evolution indicate a common origin for the physical bodies that make up the solar system, and our ideas about biological evolution underscore the kindred nature of every living organism on the face of the Earth. We possess sound evidence that many of the atoms essential for the existence of our planet and our own bodies were forged deep in the interior of the earliest stars. It is the natural unfolding of the universe that has produced the wonders of life, and as offspring of the stars we surely do not stand apart from the cosmic realities that surround us. As Charles Darwin (1898) asserted so eloquently:

> We may be excused for feeling some pride at having risen, though not through our own exertions, to the very summit of the organic scale; and the fact of [our] having thus risen, instead of having been simply placed there, may give [us] hope for a still higher destiny in the distant future. (Darwin 1898, 634)

The assurance we receive from a recognition of all-embracing interrelationships is fortified by our sense that everything changes continuously throughout the universe in accordance with certain recurring tendencies. When we observe any chain of events over long periods of time, we do discover a persistent direction in the order and sequence shaped by our minds. Such self-organizing propensities appear to be embodied in the universe, giving it intrinsic power to generate ever more differentiated forms out of what already exists.

We should take care to disassociate these pervasive tendencies from the idea that cosmic events advance inexorably toward predetermined goals. Instead of undeviating progress, we find evolutionary processes replete with false starts and blind alleys. But we may still reasonably conclude that major developments do not occur in an entirely accidental or random fashion. Irrespective of the variations we find in discrete structures, the universe does seem nearly the same wherever we look. The basic qualities of matter and energy are always constant; fundamental evolutionary dynamics apparently never vary. We can therefore infer that similar causes yield similar effects. Should conditions that transformed the Earth into a living planet be replicated in other parts of the universe, the predictable results would be something close (although not identical) to life as we know it. Our existence, in other words, is not an improbable fluke. The potential for our being may have been contained within the solar system from the very outset, as the presence of such indispensable components of life as amino acids prior to the formation of the Earth readily demonstrates.

Cynics might argue that the overriding order we see in the universe is actually imposed on a discordant reality by the structured operations of the human intellect. Our yearning for structure is undoubtedly very strong. Darwin's celebration notwithstanding, many of us have lost our compelling sense of purpose and learned to our dismay that scientific analysis of natural phenomena does little to penetrate the most profound mysteries of existence. Striving to comprehend a perplexing world, we can find modest comfort and reassurance in the tidy design of the solar system or the precise arrangement of the periodic table. Driven to ask the question "why," we are wont to believe that the elaboration of the universe, like the course of human history or the progression of our individual lives, assumes meaningful contours and directions when examined retrospectively. In each case, an element of chance is always present. But spontaneous happenings invariably encounter responses dictated by what we call scientific laws or dominant cultural values or deeply engrained personality traits.

Hence, viewed over the long term, apparent coincidences do not look entirely accidental, in large measure because through the pursuit of big history we are able to explain cause and effect rationally and establish connections between seemingly unrelated episodes. By integrating all available information into a consistent whole, we comprehend an underlying order to otherwise random events in the universe, in the human experience, in our personal lives. Complete or final explanations invariably elude us, but as we broaden and deepen our understanding of what we can know, we are better able to tie together particular details into sequences of events that tell a story about cosmic evolution, human development, or a life in progress. And when we grasp the links between those unfolding patterns through general conclusions potentially applicable to a wider variety of situations, we truly make our knowledge meaningful and usable for human purposes. This is why, we tell our skeptical colleagues, a history of humankind should be set within the broadest possible evolutionary context.

But even if these familiar arguments are greeted with a modicum of satisfaction, what about the charge of intellectual imperialism? My response to this challenge can be brief. As Russian historian E. H. Carr put the matter in his enduring reflections on historiography, "We can view the past, and achieve our understanding of the past, only through the eyes of the present. The historian is of his own age, and is bound to it by the conditions of human existence" (Carr 1962, 19). We know that the power and pervasive influence of the West have been an inescapable reality during the last several hundred years. Granted, the science we use to assemble an understanding of the evolutionary epic has largely been a product of Western creativity. The concept of big history, like recent approaches to world history, has been devised mostly by Western scholars. As Carr has suggested, however, those historians who remain self-consciously aware of their particular situations enhance their capacity to transcend their time and place: "The serious historian is the one who recognizes the historically conditioned character of all values...." (Carr 1962, 38, 78). Perhaps that level of self-awareness is our best safeguard against the possibility of intellectual imperialism.

Nonetheless, having addressed two of our persistent challenges, the third and most difficult still looms before us. If our view of the evolutionary epic is inescapably grounded in the achievements of modern science, what can we say to those who view the past from more traditional, and in particular, more religiously-oriented perspectives? How can we bridge the gap between our science-based explanations and widely held religious views? Here, we might find modest comfort in reminding ourselves that some of the greatest scientists in the modern age have not viewed science and religion as irreconcilable. Isaac Newton, who yearned to be known first and foremost as a theologian, devoted space in his renowned *Mathematical Principles of Natural Philosophy* to the religious issues raised by his view of the cosmos.[3] More convincing, perhaps, to the twenty-first-century reader is the thinking of Albert Einstein, who developed an interpretation of religion that implied "a dependence of science on the religious attitude.... While it is true," he asserted, "that scientific results are entirely independent from religious or moral considerations, those individuals to whom we owe the great creative achievements of science were all of them imbued with the truly religious conviction that this universe of ours is something perfect and susceptible to the rational striving for knowledge.... Individual existence [impressed them] as a sort of prison and [they wanted] to experience the universe as a single significant whole" (Einstein 1982, 38, 52).

If the thinking of Albert Einstein begins to reassure us, many of the critiques of modern science, which stress its limitations, can be disquieting. One of the most penetrating of those critiques came from the pen of Fyodor Dostoevsky, who examined the human predicament amidst secular modernity from a conservative and religiously based point of view. In *The Brothers Karamazov*, Father Paissy tells Alyosha that "the [scientists] of this world...have examined the parts and missed the whole, and their blindness is even worthy of wonder." The prevailing consequence for Alyosha's mentor, Father Zosima, is

> the period of human isolation.... For everyone now strives most of all to separate his person, wishing to experience the fullness of life within himself.... For all men in our age are separated into units, each seeks seclusion in his own hole, each withdraws from the others, hides himself, and hides what he has, and ends by pushing himself away from people and pushing people away from himself.... They have science, and in science only that which is subject to the senses. But the spiritual world, the higher half of man's being, is altogether rejected.... Taking freedom to mean the in-

---

3   See the selections from his *Principia* published in T. V. Smith and Marjorie Grene, *Philosophers Speak for Themselves: From Descartes to Locke* (Chicago and London: The University of Chicago Press, 1957), pp. 335-38.

crease and prompt satisfaction of needs, they distort their own nature, for they generate many meaningless and foolish desires, habits, and the most absurd fancies in themselves. They live only for mutual envy, for pleasure-seeking and self-display. (Dostoevsky 1991, 171, 303, 313-14)

Whatever we may conclude about Dostoevsky's diagnosis of the human condition, we surely must agree that scientists succeed in their tasks by harnessing careful observation and experimentation to mathematical (or at least rational) analysis. Their method requires them to focus on a particular natural phenomenon and to break that phenomenon down into its component parts. It has been an extraordinarily fruitful means of expanding human understanding of our physical environment; it is much less powerful as a means of grasping ultimate reality, providing insights into our present situation, or guiding us toward a better comprehension of such crucial aspects of our being as consciousness. As practitioners of big history, we stress the contextual character of meaning and assume that little about particular cosmic patterns can be understood without examining how they are encompassed by larger patterns, indeed without examining the whole of the cosmic order. We seek the more inclusive understandings to be achieved through the study of interrelated, interacting systems and relationships of the parts within the wholes. As we enlarge our perspective, our knowledge becomes more comprehensive, and for us that means grappling with the history of the universe considered in its entirety, or at least in as much of its entirety as the human mind can currently understand and grasp.

Given our presuppositions and objectives as practitioners of big history, we are surely positioned to transcend the most obvious limitations of the scientific enterprise at the same time that we are drawing on its achievements. But can we do so in ways that bridge the gap between the theories of science and the teachings of religion without blurring the critical differences between the two? Can we constructively build upon both kinds of knowing to grasp more firmly the implications of the evolutionary epic for the study of human history? My answer is a cautious "yes," and I base my position largely on what I learned from a Unitarian Universalist minister named Dwight Brown more than thirty years ago. Unexpectedly, the sermons I heard him deliver in the early 1970s played a major role in shaping my ideas about big history. A brief summary of a few key principles will hardly do justice to his rich theology, but it can provide some indication of how we might respond to the religious anxieties provoked by our scholarship.

Dwight Brown dedicated two decades of his career to the task of convincing his parishioners that venerable religious teachings and practices, while replete with wisdom we must not lose, no longer provided adequate guidance and support amidst the tumult of the twentieth century. A transformation of belief systems, value structures, and modes of spiritual expression, more in keeping with current realities, had already begun, he insisted, and one of the greatest resources we have at our disposal to participate in that transformation involved the fundamental changes being wrought by the recent revolution in physics, since those changes have manifold implications for our religious lives. The scientific method encourages us to take things apart, break them into their components. It is a very powerful mode of analysis, he affirmed, if our aim is to learn how to manipulate our environment (Brown, 1975). But if we want to understand what is ultimately real, especially with regard to the nature of humanness, we must examine the interacting systems of the larger whole, ultimately the whole of the universe, the entire cosmic drama whose patterns, taken together, reveal the most comprehensive truth about existence (Brown 1984).

The chief preoccupation of religion, after all, has always been a grappling with the pattern of the whole. Our word "religion" in its medieval Latin form originally meant "that which binds things together." Religion has persistently sought the largest and most inclusive cosmic patterns that humans can discover, patterns which they have persistently embodied in the familiar religious name God, the ancient symbol of the power and majesty of being. Religion, the essence of which involves "the ancient search for the meaning of human existence," thus strives relentlessly to bind together more and more of what is known, "trying to lift our gaze from the grubby details of the daily round to the transcendent and beautiful in which we live and move and have our being" (Brown 1982). To connect with this realm of the spirit, this domain of the divine, in which the "why" of existence is the insistent central question, becomes then the overriding object of religious striving (Brown 1985). From such a perspective, we can imagine how the creative powers of the universe are incorporated in our humanness and how, through the unfolding of our awareness, meaning in the cosmos is defined. Through the development of our human potential, we are active agents in the creative process, giving significance to the cosmos as we impart, through our personal growth, significance to our own lives. In other words, the goal of evolution's creative energy, which in this view becomes simply another way of saying the purpose of God the creator, is personhood, "personality not only as we now know it, but the process of personal development extended as far onward and upward as we can conceive it" (Brown 1975).

Now, in my own efforts to grapple with the third set of objections to our understanding of big history, I am not trying to imply that the views of one Unitarian Universalist minister alone have the potential to bring modern science and contemporary religion into happy harmony. I am certainly not suggesting that we accept this mode of thinking *in toto*. I do not believe for a moment that every Big Historian will find these arguments convincing. What

I am trying to say is that these ideas do give us hope that the tensions scholarship raises between science and religion might be eased, that responses to the objections of the religiously concerned are actually implicit in the story of big history, and that by following an approach which places theology within the context of cosmic evolution, we might be able to impart greater meaning and purpose to the on-going human adventure. At least that is my earnest desire.

References

Brown, D. 1975. The transient and the permanent in Christianity. An unpublished sermon series delivered at the First Unitarian Church of Dallas, January 1975.

Brown, D. 1982. Impersonating the Divine: An essay in theological anthropology. An unpublished sermon delivered at Shaker Heights Unitarian Church, June 21, 1982.

Brown, D. 1984. God and the new physics. An unpublished sermon delivered at the Shaker Heights Unitarian Church, March 25, 1984.

Brown, D. 1985. The realm of the spirit. An unpublished sermon delivered at Shaker Heights Unitarian Church, January 20, 1985.

Carr, E. H. 1962. *What is History?* London, UK: Macmillan.

Darwin, C., 1898. *The Descent of Man and Selection in Relationship to Sex*, 2nd ed., rev. New York, NY: D. Appleton.

Dostoevsky, F. 1991 (1880). *The Brothers Karamazov.* New York, NY: Vintage Books.

Einstein, A. 1982. *Ideas and Opinions.* New York, NY: Three Rivers Press.

McNeill, W. H. 1963. *The Rise of the West: A History of the Human Community.* Chicago & London: The University of Chicago Press.

Mears, J. A. 1986. Evolutionary process: An organizing principle for general education. *JGE: The Journal of General Education, 37* (4), 315-325.

Our students do have the ability to move to a more nuanced worldview, but only if we facilitate this, only if we provide an appropriate environment in our classrooms for the sort of complex conversations this will demand. We can go even further and create a climate of awe and wonder inside the walls of the academy.

Craig Benjamin

The Convergence of Logic, Faith, and Values in the Modern Creation Story

Craig G. R. Benjamin

From the moment I started teaching big history I was struck by its impact on students. Here was a course that in a single semester explained the origins and evolution of virtually everything, and did so in a way that provided context for all of the apparently random events of history. Students were swept up into the epic recounting of the evolution of the universe from a tiny sub-atomic seed into an unimaginably vast entity of billions of galaxies. Yet, just as the scale threatened to reduce humans to insignificance, big history began to hint at the possibility of a crucial role for *Homo sapiens* as the most complex entity that we are thus far aware of in the cosmos. As that possibility took shape—the idea that, rather than unmasking our species as a meaningless speck, big history offers a tentative argument for our fundamental significance—students achieved a moment of orientational enlightenment that many of them described as life-changing.

David Christian (2004) emphasizes the potential for big history to provide meaning and context by describing it as a modern creation myth (modern in the context of this essay means a contemporary or scientific story rather than a historical period) and comparing it to the traditional creation stories of earlier cultures. "Who am I? Where do I belong? What is the totality of which I am a part?" are questions he poses in the introduction to *Maps of Time* (Christian 2004). He reminds us that: "In some form, all human communities have asked these questions .... Often the answers have been embedded in cycles of creation myths" (Christian 2004, 1-2). In the 21st century, however, many of us believe that we have outgrown the need for creation stories, particularly if they are associated with the word "myth." Indeed the word "myth" makes professional historians most uncomfortable, because myth and history are seen as antithetical.

Post-modernists like Jean-Françoise Lyotard (1984) have argued against the representation of any phenomena in the form of a metanarrative, arguing that the recounting of the history of *anything* as a coherent story (a story which is not natural but humanly constructed) will turn history and science into dangerous mythologies that will serve only to reinforce the power of the myth spinners. An even greater danger in articulating a sense of continuity between past and present is that this disguises an existential reality of chaos, fragmentation, and meaninglessness.

The response of big historians to this charge is that humans, as much today as at any time in the past, need the sense of orientational security that creation myths once provided. As Christian (2004, 2) puts it, creation stories "speak to our deep spiritual, psychic, and social need for a sense of place and a sense of belonging." Furthermore, the lack of a modern creation myth is actually harmful to our species because without it we are left only with an overwhelming sense of disorientation and purposelessness that Durkheim (1947) referred to as "anomie." This is hardly a danger for the post-modernist however, who believes that it is much better to embrace a naturalized state of disorientation than to seek false comfort in an artificially constructed paradigm that has been developed for the purpose of reinforcing the power of its authors.

My experience in the college classroom has shown, however, that as the big history version of creation unfolds across a semester, any power engendered in the myth-teller (the professor) is matched by the sense of empowerment that the tale generates in the listener, undergraduate students only recently embarked upon their great college adventures. With very little warning of the disorientation that is about to occur, at the age of eighteen these students leave their homes to live in large residences in the midst of their peers, away for the first time from the daily, personal influence of their parents and the other champions of the creation stories of their childhood. The contrast is even more pronounced for the unsuspecting big history student who walks into a classroom on the first day of her new life to be ambushed by an elegant creation myth articulating an alternative explanation of origins and purpose for existence. Even more unsettling, of course, is the immediate realization of the one really profound difference between the myths of yesterday and this new account—there are no gods in it!

Now, for anyone raised, as I was, in a liberal humanist tradition, the idea that the universe can be entirely explained without reference to a creator deity is hardly Earth shattering stuff. But this meant that I was completely unprepared for the reaction of so many students during my first semester of teaching big history. As much as I tried to steer the conversation in another direction, the central issue for many was the absence of a creator in the creation myth. In fact, it became impossible to make progress in tutorials without confronting the question head on. And the discussions that ensued were disturbing enough that students found their entire belief system, even their previously understood purpose for existence, being challenged.

What I could not see at first was that, when my students moved from their homes and high schools to a university dedicated to providing a secular, liberal education, they found themselves confronted by a far more nuanced view of the world than the paradigm that had sustained their lives thus far. For undergraduate students embarking on this journey from a dualistic to a more nuanced worldview, the first crisis they have to face is a crisis of faith. Once this realization dawned, it was I who had an epiphany: I am ignoring my obligation to these students if I ignore their faith, if I try to pretend that it is not the elephant sitting in the room. If I am genuinely committed to the task of fusing intellectual development with character and ethical development, surely a central goal of liberal education, I need to concentrate on all of the functions in my students and help them make the connections. And a core function for most of them is their faith.

That this all came as something of a revelation to me demonstrates how much I had been ignoring the increasing significance of religion worldwide. It also unmasked my ivory-tower smugness in assuming that most rational people thought the same way I did! But this is a view widely prevalent in the academy, I think. Joel Tishken reminds us of this when he writes:

> Our academic definition of religion, as an abstraction separate from the rest of life, is not one shared by most peoples past and present, but is an invention of modernity... Religion does matter to most humans, and we must find ways to represent the power of religion by remembering that the academy's views on religion are not the global norm. (2007, 5)

The number of students in the United States who enter university convinced that Darwinian evolutionary theory is just plain wrong and that God created the universe 6,000 years ago is astonishing. How should historians handle the persistence of debates between creationists and evolutionists when every fiber of our souls is offended that anyone could still doubt natural selection in the 21st century? Should we ignore it? In our classrooms, we boldly address all manner of controversial topics, but rarely attempt to seriously engage the religious beliefs of the majority of our students. In so many spheres of public and pedagogical life, we academics praise ourselves for our ability to raise the level of intellectual discourse, but few of us seem comfortable taking the same approach to religion despite our core pedagogical commitment to developing critical thinking skills in our students.

It is in this context that big history can make an important contribution. By offering a coherent scientific account of the origins of the universe and life, the modern creation story becomes a powerful rationalist argument in favor of the scientific paradigms. For a surprising number of students, a big history classroom is the first context in which these theories and their evidence have been explained. And what a splendid environment it is for this to occur in!

Most big historians are not trained scientists, and we have developed ways to explain this scientific material in lay terms. Many younger college students have only a basic scientific knowledge anyway, so an explanation that is in the form of historical narrative works better than one laden with jargon.

Providing a clear overview of the paradigms is just the first level of engagement, however. Students, unsettled by the compelling logic of these paradigms, immediately try to reconcile this modern creation story with their own religious accounts, and having been warned that liberal professors will try and take them away from their faith, the first response is to fall back upon a dualistic paradigm in which only one account can be correct. This tension can only be resolved through a frank and mutual consideration of the inner conflict, and in the context of intensive, systematic, student-led class discussion, this frank and mutual consideration must take place. In my course, small teams of students lead the weekly discussion sessions; it is their responsibility to frame questions and facilitate the full-class conversation, seeking commonalities and the accommodation of apparently mutually exclusive accounts rather than further division along entrenched cultural lines. The professor's role becomes that of teacher-student in a classroom full of student-teachers. In every big history class I have ever taught, these discussions have quickly become the most valued part of the course.

As students begin to see the college classroom as a representation of wider society, they realize that there has to be a way of reconciling seemingly irreconcilable positions if the destructive national cultural divide is to be bridged. Our students are future leaders whose responsibility it will be to lead their society away from the chasm and seek out commonalities rather than divisions, but how can we expect this when many members of the academy seem to have a difficult time of it once we move beyond the cognitive level to matters of the heart and soul? Yet surveys show that students *want* to associate themselves with faculty who can help them in a search for meaning. Students are asking "who am I and how can I make a difference?" If we ignore our students' questions and argue that our job is simply to teach the subject matter of our discipline, we are abdicating one of our core responsibilities, which is to teach the "good life." The good life is not about individual success but about doing good for others, making a difference, changing the world for the better. We ignore this central component of liberal education at our peril.

Ironically then, it turns out that the modern creation story, utterly devoid of gods and spirits as it is, is a powerful tool to engage and challenge undergraduates at the highest level of both their cognitive and spiritual consciousness. Even as we educators present, as persuasively as possible, a modern creation story founded on scientific principles, we need to understand that students will be hearing this from a very different perspective. The greatest error we can make is to dismiss their perspective as simplistic and naïve, stemming from an ignorant past, as something that we now demand our students simply leave behind and shed like an old skin.

Our students do have the ability to move to a more nuanced worldview, but only if we facilitate this, only if we provide an appropriate environment in our classrooms for the sort of complex conversations this will demand. We can go even further and create a climate of awe and wonder inside the walls of the academy. The big history story is ideal for this, because at every level it raises profound questions about origins, what it means to be human, the reason and purpose for existence. This is an *awesome* story, yet how can we encourage our students to enter into the imaginative consideration of these questions if we teachers are not prepared to also give up the sort of control and narrative power that Lyotard (1984) argues is embedded in the recounting of all coherent stories? We are teachers *and* mentors, and a crucial role of the mentor is to challenge *and* support. Our job is to teach students *how* to think, not *what* to think, to focus on student development, not mechanical subject knowledge and bland methodology. Big history provides an elegant, awe-inspiring, multi-disciplinary account that connects all facets of reality in a modern creation story of extraordinary sweep. Despite the fact that it is a creation myth with no gods in it, it also turns out to be a powerful way of engaging faith and rationality and offering ways of reconciling both. For this reason, it deserves to be at the heart of every general education program at every university that is genuinely dedicated to providing their students with a liberal education.

Author's Note

Australian-born Craig Benjamin, Ph.D., is a professor in the History Department at Grand Valley State University in Michigan. He is the author of numerous published articles, chapters, and books on ancient Central Asian history and world history historiography. He is currently working on three textbooks for major US publishers, including a big history textbook for Mc-Graw-Hill with co-authors David Christian and Cynthia Brown.

References

Christian, D. 2004. *Maps of Time*. Los Angeles, CA: University of California Press.

Durkheim, E. 1947. *The Division of Labour in Society*. G. Simpson, trans. New York, NY: The Free Press.

Lyotard, J-F. 1984. *The Post-Modern Condition: A Report on Knowledge (Theory and History of Literature, vol. 10)*. G. Bennington and B. Massumi, trans. Minneapolis, MN: University of Minnesota Press.

Tishken, J. 2007. Religion and world history. *World History Bulletin*, 23 (spring).

To become whole adults, students must emerge from adolescence with a clear comprehension of their relationship and orientation to the world and the cosmos. In hunting/gathering times people achieved this through oral history and wilderness experience; today they must achieve it through classes and written history. We need to impart the scientific creation myth as clearly as possible for students to achieve their orientation to the universe.

Cynthia Brown

Why Aren't More People Teaching Big History?

Cynthia Stokes Brown

It has been almost twenty years since David Christian began saying to his colleagues in the history department at Macquarie University in Sydney that they needed to provide an introductory history course that started at the beginning of time—at the Big Bang itself. After some resistance, his colleagues eventually encouraged Christian to construct and teach such a course, which he did by inviting specialists in astronomy, physics, geology, and biology to cover the material that he could not yet handle.

Now, almost twenty years later, how many courses that start with the Big Bang and go to the present are being taught in the world? David Christian has indefatigably written and spoken about the need for big history courses and the rewards of teaching them, but as far as I know there are still no more than about a dozen such courses at the college/university level. Fred Spier holds the world's only appointment in big history at the University of Amsterdam. Marnie Hughes-Warrington teaches big history courses at Macquarie University; David Christian teaches them at San Diego State University. Their former student, Craig Benjamin, teaches big history at Grand Valley State University in Michigan, while John Mears has pioneered it at Southern Methodist University. Other big history instructors include Walter Alvarez (geology) at University of California, Berkeley; Eric Chaisson (astronomy) at Tufts University; Loyal Rue (philosophy/religion) at Luther College, Jonathan Markly at California State University, Fullerton, and myself at Dominican University of California.

Many of those teaching big history share my own experience of teaching under the radar. We have often not asked permission, but simply used the names of world history courses on the books and transformed them into big history courses, informing the students of our intentions as we give out the syllabus. This strategy has enabled us to gain experience and to demonstrate the rewards of such courses, particularly the overwhelmingly positive response from students.

Now, however, it seems time to go more public and engage our faculty colleagues across the disciplines in a dialogue about why big history needs to be widely taught and where it might fit into the curriculum, comprising as it does the whole curriculum.

To stimulate this discussion, I want to analyze some of the reasons that big history has been building slowly. Then I will state as clearly as possible the reasons why big history needs to be widely taught and suggest some ways to overcome the difficulties. This may seem a bit abstract to those who have not yet taken a plunge into the waters of big history; perhaps you could get into the mood by imagining yourself constructing a syllabus for big history.

One reason so few people teach big history is our natural fear of looking ridiculous. Big history covers too many fields for comfort and ignores the great divide between science and the humanities. How could one person possibly know enough about so many fields to face classes of students without fearing embarrassment from their questions?

Another reason for the slow development of big history is that very few faculty or students even recognize the term "big history." They have never imagined or thought about the complete story from beginning to now; the whole idea is likely to seem preposterous. Furthermore, there is not even common agreement about the term "big history." Scientists tend to call it the "evolutionary epic;" some call it the "cosmic epic" or the "universe story." "Big history" may seem a bit flip for so awesome a story, but historians have not yet come up with another term as appealing.

A third reason for the slow start of big history is that it does not fit into the departmental structure of colleges and universities. It seems to fit most easily into history, but only if history is expanded from its traditional sense of recorded history into including all other fields. Our twentieth-century understanding that the universe itself is expanding, even accelerating its expansion, means that the universe itself has a history, and astronomy has become a historical field. But this is not yet widely recognized by the general public. Geology and biology have been historical fields only since the nineteenth century, and this, too, is still contested.

Perhaps the most obvious, practical obstacle preventing professors from rushing to teach big history lies in the lack of a conventional textbook. There is not one yet, but McGraw-Hill has recently contracted with three of us (David Christian, Craig Benjamin, and Cynthia Brown) to complete one by 2010. There are, however, several appropriate and accessible books already available, cited at the end of this paper.

Finally, history professors who might want to teach big history have to deal with the rewards and expectations built into their departments. Tenure and promotion traditionally are rewards for examining some topic closely and extensively, rather than for distilling large-scale meaning from history. Teaching big history has been seen so far as rather an extra activity, optional to the basic required ones.

Now, however, these difficulties no longer seem sufficient to keep big history out of the curriculum. The time is right for big history courses to fill the need created both in the world and within higher education. Why is McGraw-Hill willing to bet that big history courses are going to proliferate in the coming years? Because many history professors are telling them that they want to teach big history if only they had a textbook.

Here is my analysis of why more professors want to initiate courses in big history. I believe that professors are responding to the global environmental issues, particularly climate crisis, that confront us. Just as history professors constructed Western civilization courses in the context of World War II and world history courses in the context of globalization, so they realize that students need the framework of at least planetary history in order to understand the current challenges.

In addition, professors are responding to the current fragmentation of the prevailing curriculum. They feel a need for a common core that all students would take, that would give coherence to the curriculum and provide a framework for future learning. A big history course fills that bill precisely.

A third reason is that the facts of the whole story are now known with enough confidence that the narrative can be put together without too much hesitation. This has only been true for twenty or thirty years, perhaps a short time as far as curricular change goes. But now that the facts are known, withholding this information, or expecting students to assemble it on their own, seems an outright dereliction of a teacher's duty.

Finally, students need the whole story to understand themselves as human beings. To become whole adults, students must emerge from adolescence with a clear comprehension of their relationship and orientation to the world and the cosmos. In hunting/gathering times people achieved this through oral history and wilderness experience; today they must achieve it through classes and written history. We need to impart the scientific creation myth as clearly as possible for students to achieve their orientation to the universe.

Now for some suggestions about how to overcome the challenges of teaching big history. No one wants to look ridiculous in the classroom; the preventive would seem to be some additional learning by history professors in fields adjacent to theirs. This can take place by inviting colleagues from astronomy, physics, chemistry, geology and biology and/or by reading the books listed at the end. The excitement of seeing the whole narrative unfold without being dissected into disciplines can carry most of us through this additional work. Then, instead of appearing ridiculous, we can seem ever more on the leading edge.

Where to place big history in the curriculum will have to be discussed by faculties in colleges and universities until some consensus is reached. The three of us working on the first textbook believe that the ideal place in the curriculum is a General Education (GE) requirement for all students in the freshman year. Based in the history department, the big history courses would be managed by historians but could include professors from several departments. Would a one-semester big history course replace other required history courses? We would hope not, but GE committees will have to work that out. Meanwhile, as things unfold, world history teachers could revise their courses to add big history ideas and extend the time period back to the big bang, sacrificing only a few sessions of other material.

Another way to introduce a big history course is through interdisciplinary programs; big history combines well with any other course. At my university every graduate must take one colloquium, which consists of three courses from separate departments around a common theme. I designed a colloquium called "The Universe Story," consisting of the history course, called "Whole Earth History," a science course called "Life on Earth," and a philosophy/religion course called "The World's Religions." Students take the first two courses simultaneously, followed by the third in the next semester. My course gives students the overall framework, while the other two courses provide detail on the evolution of life and religion. We have taught this colloquium two times and have scheduled it for a third time, due to unusual student enthusiasm.

Of course, another place in the curriculum for big history is in any department, where some professor wants to offer it. Examples already mentioned would be Eric Chaisson in astronomy, Loyal Rue in philosophy/religion, and Walter Alvarez in geology.

On the matter of what materials to use, I believe there already exists an excellent choice: *Maps of Time* and *This Fleeting Life* by David Christian or *Big History* by me. These three vary by length and complexity, but they vary little in overall structure and content. They can be matched to other course content and the skill level of students. Additional materials for a professors' own background or for use with students are listed in my bibliography.

Finally, on the question of history department expectations, I find I have little to say. With my Ph.D. in the history of education, I was based in a school of education rather than in a history department. My promotion and tenure depended on my work in education; my teaching in the history department was considered a sidelight. Probably this helped enable me to develop my ideas and courses about big history; I did not need to specialize for tenure in history. When my students responded positively, the department of history was pleased. I am confident that, as big history courses expand, the expectations of history departments will change and pioneering professors will not be punished.

In conclusion, I look forward to discussions about what to call big history and where to install it in the curriculum. I see this as the most exciting development in university education since Harvard began expanding the classical curriculum a century ago. Learning the whole story has the potential to change our students' sense of their very identity, as well as their relationship to their studies, to the environment, and to the world.

References: Big Histories/Evolutionary Epics

By Historians

Brown, Cynthia Stokes. 2007. *Big History: From the Big Bang to the Present.* New York, NY: New Press, 304 pp.

Christian, David. 2004. *Maps of Time: An Introduction to Big History.* Berkeley, CA: University of California Press, 642 pp.

Christian, David. 2007. *This Fleeting Life: A Short History of Humanity.* Berkshire Encyclopedia, 105 p.

Other Perspectives

Chaisson, Eric. 2006. *Evolutionary Epic: Seven Ages of the Cosmos.* New York: Columbia University Press, 478 pp. (astrophysicist)

Genet, Russell M. 2007. *Humanity: The Chimpanzees Who Would Be Ants.* Santa Margarita, CA: Collins Foundation Press, 215 pp. (astronomer)

Rue, Loyal. 2000. *Everybody's Story: Wising Up to the Epic of Evolution.* Albany, NY: State University of New York Press, 146 pp. (philosopher)

Spier, Fred. 1996. *The Structure of Big History: From the Big Bang Until Today.* Amsterdam: Amsterdam University Press, 113 pp. (biochemist, anthropologist, historical sociologist)

Swimme, Brian, and Thomas Berry. 1992. *The Universe Story.* San Francisco: Harper San Francisco, 305 pp. (natural scientist and cultural historian)

Humorists

Gonick, Larry. 1990. *A Cartoon History of the Universe: From the Big Bang to Alexander the Great.* New York: Doubleday, 358 pp. (cartoon educator)

Schulman, Eric. 1999. *A Briefer History of Time: From the Big Bang to the Big Mac.* New York: W. H. Freeman & Co., 171 pp. (astronomer and science educator)

Supporting Material

Alvarez, Walter. 1997. *T. Rex and the Crater of Doom.* Princeton: Princeton University Press, 185 pp. (geologist)

Carroll, Sean B. and David M. Kingsley. 2006. *Evolution: Constant Change and Common Threads.* Chevy Chase, MD: Howard Hughes Medical Institute. DVD, from <biointeractive.org>. (evolutional development biologists)

De Waal, Frans. 2005. *Our Inner Ape: A Leading Primatologist Explains Why We Are Who We Are.* New York: Riverhead Books, 274 pp. (primatologist)

McNeill, J. R. and William McNeill. 2003. *The Human Web: A Bird's-Eye View of World History.* New York: Norton, 347 pp. (historians)

Smith, Cameron M. and Charles Sullivan. 2007. *The Top 10 Myths About Evolution.* Amherst, NY: Prometheus Books. (anthropologist and writing teacher)

When we, and more recently our students, came to nature as children, we came with open arms and eyes and ears and the capacity for deep intimacy. We spent hours outdoors exploring, musing, thinking. We soaked up information with eagerness and embraced the universe with our full selves.

Trileigh Tucker

Contemplatio ad Amorem Naturae
Contemplative Practice in Ecozoic Education

Trileigh Tucker

We who teach about the natural world, and who want to contribute to healing our current environmental crisis, face three time-related problems.

First: a problem of historical time. One of the beauties of teaching the origins of our natural world is that our work has a deep historical context. We can tell the story of the universe's creation; the workings of evolution over billions of years; the slow erosion that carved the Grand Canyon.

However, this gives us a lot to cover.

Which brings up our second time problem: it is getting late. Remember what you were doing ten minutes ago? Since then, 600 acres of tropical rainforest have been logged, and yet another species forever eliminated from our planetary ecosystem. By the time you reach the end of this paper, two thousand additional rainforest acres will have been cut, and three more species will be gone, irrecoverably—taking with them all the future species that might have evolved from these sacrificed ones. To slow down this staggering loss, we must act quickly.

But we have so much else to do.

We are more scheduled than ever. We teach about critical subjects, participate in important meetings, prepare papers, travel to conferences, evaluate student work—not to mention family life, driving the kids to soccer, sleeping fewer hours, exercising. When will we have time to work on the other environmental problems as well? This is our third "time" problem.

A typical faculty approach to these time problems is to cover more material in our courses; we do not want to leave anything out, and we have so little time with our students: ten, fifteen weeks in a course. The very love of nature that brought us into our scientific careers can lead us to switch on the fire hose that threatens to drown our students. We want them to know as much as possible about the fascinating complexity of chemistry, geology, biology, or physics. We could talk for longer than our students can listen about critical problems or beautiful insights from our disciplines—but we are pressured by these time problems, and so we end up feeling busy, drained, frustrated, and, deep inside, afraid.

When we, and more recently our students, came to nature as children, we came with open arms and eyes and ears and the capacity for deep intimacy. We spent hours outdoors exploring, musing, thinking. We soaked up information with eagerness and embraced the universe with our full selves.

By the time we get to college, though, "learning" has acquired a very different image. For so many students in our college science courses—often their last formal encounter with nature—learning means trying to swallow the fire hose of required facts and concepts that we, in our desire to heal our endangered environment, turn on them. They often feel they can never catch up and that they are just trying to pass tests toward graduation. Students in our classes often feel busy, drained, frustrated, and, deep inside, afraid.

Educators and students both, then, end up entangled in an academic system that becomes consumerist: we grab as much as possible as quickly as possible, then discard it onto the growing pile of unwanted "stuff" with one hand as we reach for our next helping with the other. Our attention span is limited; in our grasping at muchness, we do not take time to understand deeply.

We thus betray our very humanness as we also harm the rest of our Earth community; David Orr notes most of the damage to Earth's ecosystems has been managed by highly educated people (Orr 1994, 7). How can we re-envision college education about our natural world so as to embrace our deepest human selves, to develop knowledge required for healing our planet, and to recover and enhance our love for our natural home? Thomas Berry has coined the term "Ecozoic" for the time beyond the Cenozoic, "when humans would dwell upon the Earth in a mutually enhancing manner" (Berry 1991). What kind of education can help bring us healthfully into the Ecozoic? I call it Natural Presence.

Natural Presence and Contemplative Practice

Natural Presence integrates two ancient ways of encountering the natural world: natural history and contemplative practice. Through natural history, we learn about the world through personal observation, using our physical senses *in situ* in nature and over time, interpreting our observations with multidisciplinary intellectual inquiry. A contemplative approach allows us to integrate our intellect with our whole intuitive, affective, creative selves as we develop our relationship with a whole natural Other.

Parker Palmer has characterized teaching as "creating a space in which the community of truth is practiced" (Palmer 1983, 1998). In Natural Presence education, the space includes inner space, and our community includes the immense and immanent natural world.

But how can we make the space for contemplative practice in our classes? We've got so much important material to cover, and it is so late, and we already do not have enough time.

Mahatma Gandhi was informed by his harried advisors one morning that he would be meeting with three world leaders that day. His response? "Ah, then I had better meditate for twice as long." *The more important our tasks, and the more urgently we have to do them, the more critical it becomes to take the time to reflect on what we are doing.*

Integrating contemplative practice into our courses provides students with specific ways to enter reflectively into their education. Perhaps more importantly, it embodies the message that we must work to become wise in our endeavors—especially considering the potential global cost of not doing so.

Contemplative Practice in College Environmental Education

In the sixteenth century, Ignatius of Loyola, founder of the Jesuit order, developed "Spiritual Exercises" that invite those on retreat into a deeper awareness of their belovedness and how to respond. One of his most beautiful exercises is the *Contemplatio ad Amorem,* or "Contemplation to Attain Love."

Ignatius begins by reminding us that love is a reciprocal exchange between the lover and the beloved, who both give and receive. Asking us to recognize what we have been given through creation, he invites us to likewise examine ourselves, with our particular gifts, and to ask how we can gratefully respond.

How can we bring Ignatius's wisdom to bear on the difficult situation of creation today? This paper's title, *Contemplatio ad Amorem Naturae,* refers to the contemplative dimension of an educational approach that can help us deepen our college environmental teaching, so that it becomes education toward a love of nature rather than against the intimacy to which we are born.

Contemplation and Science

Contemplative practice is already an integral, but often unrecognized, aspect of scientific research. After intense analytical work, the brain needs time and space to digest new inputs, allowing it to reach new insights. The "three B's" of scientific discovery—bed, bath, and bus—encapsulate this need; of course, other forms can also provide the contemplative encounter that generates new insights. Einstein's wife, Elsa, described his work habits:

> "Music helps him when he is thinking about his theories. He goes to his study, comes back, strikes a few chords on the piano, jots something down, returns to his study."(Pais 1982, 301)

In a related example, mathematician Poincaré, who had been working hard on a particular mathematical function, took some time off to go on a geological field excursion:

> We entered an omnibus to go some place or other. At the moment when I put my foot on the step, the idea came to me, without anything in my

former thoughts seeming to have paved the way for [an important in-sight]. (Hadamard 1945, 13)

As we teach students what it is to do science, to come to know our natural environment, we can invite them into this critical aspect of scientific research through integrating contemplative space in our courses.

Forms of Contemplative Practice

Contemplative practice may be defined as a practice whose intention is cultivating awareness or connection/communion. A wealth of contemplative forms available to us is suggested in Figure 1, from the Center for Contempla-tive Mind in Society. Of course, we may embrace other forms as well; several are described below.

In environmental courses, our students may engage with the natural world in several ways: in the classroom, in field-based activities, and in indi-vidual or collaborative projects. Each of these is amenable to integration of contemplative spaces.

In the Classroom

Freewriting. I often begin class by asking students to simply write for five minutes "to get the chatter from your mind onto the page." Sometimes I sug-gest a word or theme, but often just encourage students to write whatever they are thinking about. The room becomes astonishingly quiet after their freewrit-ing; we have now created an open space in which "the community of truth" can actually be practiced.

Working with an image. This practice is adapted from Joanna Ziegler, Professor of Art History at Holy Names College, whose students return to the same painting repeatedly during the semester, deepening their un-derstanding of and relationship with it (Dustin and Ziegler 2005). For my geology classes, I choose an image (painting, drawing, or photograph) that depicts many geological processes. I invite students to mentally sit in a comfortable place in the image, becoming present to it; then to look around from that location, noticing what they notice. I may suggest that they attend to both the physical sensations and the emotions they have or imagine in that place.

Depending on the particular topic for that part of the course, I may draw their attention to a particular geological feature and tell them to imagine it in the future or past; or as if they were looking through a microscope.

In the Field

Sitting Students tend to look quickly at natural phenomena (outcrops, plants, streams) and then move on, assuming that they have seen what there is to see. As with the image-based exercise described above, I assign students to simply sit and observe (touch, listen to) the site for several minutes, without writing or photographing.

Figure 1. (Reprinted with permision)

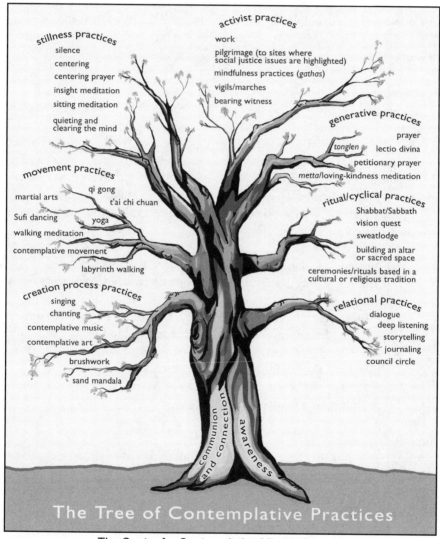

The Center for Contemplative Mind in Society
www.contemplativemind.org

<u>Sketching</u>. After a period of simply observing, students may draw or paint some aspect of the object of their study: a bat's "view", for example, or light green

things. These exercises help them to understand nature from different senses and perspectives—allowing the holistic interaction with nature that is our genetic inheritance. Sketching focuses and trains the eye and builds the habit of close observation and intense concentration, important forms of contemplative awareness.

Natural-history journal. Keeping a journal allows students to integrate their scientific observations and analyses with poetry, photographs, and memories. With the traditional, structured format of Joseph Grinnell (Herman 1986), journals include a distinct space for the intuition that both promotes new insights and reveals potential meaning in students' learning.

In Projects

In my geology course, students may choose a contemplative project in place of the usual research project. For this project, they are required to spend 90 minutes per week in meditation or other contemplative activity related to the natural world. This practice must take the same form for at least four weeks to allow development of a reliable rhythm to their contemplation; then they may experiment with different forms. They turn in weekly descriptions of their practice.

Students have chosen a variety of different contemplative forms, suggested by me or created on their own; for instance:

- Sitting at a shoreline twice weekly, observing and sketching.
- Contemplating a painting, and each week creating a new story from the painting, from the point of view of a child; an animal; a stone.
- Working each week on a continuing drawing of a view from the student's home and noticing how it changes, and how the student's experience of it changed, during the term.
- Meditation on an inner image of a beach, exploring different aspects of the beach each week. The beach becomes an increasingly complex inner landscape.

Student Response

Student comments on contemplative dimensions of environment-related science courses have been overwhelmingly positive:

> "Throughout the process of contemplative meditation, I definitely felt like my scientific learning was enriched. ... I kept 'finding' things out that I had not previously known.... They were like my own little discoveries, as a scientist unearths archaeological artifacts...."

> *"I think that I became more attentive to everything from having to be so attentive to a single image. I learned to look deeper because ... as I looked longer I noticed things that I had previously overlooked. Additionally it helped to reinforce what I was learning in the class because I began to look for examples... in the image that I was examining."*

> *"Every day I went was a new beginning to something peaceful and momentous that captured my attention... I almost smile every time I think of how peaceful it was to observe my surroundings and just remain in a state of peace... It so became evident of how much more I noticed the geological features while at the park."*

> *"Having been analyzing something like an image that was dear to my heart, I noticed that the subject matter was more accessible to me."*

These students have expanded their capacities for presence, observation, reflection, and insight. They have allowed what they study to become "dear to their hearts." This is the promise that *Contemplatio ad Amorem Naturae* holds: knowledge, embedded in love. This is what we need to help heal our planet: taking time, just in time.

Author's Note

This project was made possible through research support from Seattle University: a sabbatical release, a Summer Faculty Fellowship, and the Writing Retreat for the Scholarship of Teaching and Learning sponsored by the Seattle University Center for Excellence in Teaching and Learning (Therese Huston and David Green, conveners). I am indebted to the Center for Contemplative Mind in Society for its 2006 Summer Session on Contemplative Curriculum Development (Arthur Zajonc and Mirabai Bush, conveners) and for use of the graphic from their website (Figure 1 of this chapter). Conversations with Joanna Ziegler at the summer session particularly contributed to development of this project. I am grateful to David Green and Rob Duisberg for their helpful reviews. Author contact information: Environmental Studies Program, Seattle University, 901-12th Avenue, Seattle WA 98122; tri@seattleu.edu.

References

Berry, T. 1991. The Ecozoic Era. *Center for Ecozoic Studies.* Internet <http://ecozoicstudies.org/EcozoicEra.pdf> accessed 3 February 2008.

Center for Contemplative Mind in Society. 2007. Tree of Contemplative Practices. Internet <http://contemplativemind.org/practices/tree.html> accessed 3 February 2008.

Dustin, C. A. and Ziegler, J. E. 2005. *Practicing Mortality: Art, Philosophy, and Contemplative Seeing.* New York, NY: Palgrave Macmillan.

Hadamard, J. 1945. *The Psychology of Invention in the Mathematical Field.* Princeton, NJ: Princeton University Press.

Herman, S. G. 1986. *The Naturalist's Field Journal: A Manual of Instruction Based on a System Established by Joseph Grinnell.* Vermillion, SD: Buteo Books.

Orr, D. 1994. *Earth in Mind: On Education, Environment, and the Human Prospect.* Washington, DC: Island Press.

Pais, A. 1982. *The Science and Life of Albert Einstein.* Oxford, UK: Oxford University Press.

Palmer, P. 1983. *To Know As We Are Known.* New York, NY: Harper Collins.

Palmer, P. 1998. *The Courage to Teach.* San Francisco, CA: Jossey-Bass.

In short, we need to develop a strategy for action that takes into account a full understanding of the complexity of the human personality as well as a full understanding of the complexity of the natural world around us. But the ideologies we have inherited from the past—most of them growing out of the rationalist, reductionist, mechanistic, and materialist views of the late eighteenth century—are not up to the task at hand, at least not by themselves.

Alan Wood

Big History as Global Systems History

Alan T. Wood

I often marvel, even as I grow long in tooth and short of hair, at how much our adult outlook on life is shaped by childhood experiences. Perhaps that seems obvious. And yet I am continually struck by its truth. I grew up in the 1950s. I can still remember, as if it were yesterday, peering up at the night sky on a cool fall evening in 1957 to watch Sputnik twinkle its way across the dome of stars. As a 12-year-old, I was mesmerized. I decided to be an astronaut right then and there. At the time, that decision might have posed a bit of a problem, since I was also planning to play first base for the Boston Red Sox. Fortunately, I saw no incompatibility between those aspirations. I was sure some way could be found to arrange my space flights between games.

As luck would have it, I never played baseball in Fenway Park. Alas, I never made it into space either. But I did go around the world a few times, having been lucky enough to have a history professor as a father. We spent his sabbaticals in the Philippines and India, and we always traveled by ship because in those days sea passage was far less expensive than airline flights. To be sure, the vessels we traveled on were not spaceships, and they went only 15 miles an hour. Nevertheless, circumnavigating the world—whether as an astronaut or an argonaut—permanently rewires the brain. Before, one sees differences; afterwards, one sees commonalities. Before, one sees parts; afterwards, one sees the whole. From that point on, no matter what subject I ended up studying, I always wanted to put it into the widest possible context.

So it should probably come as no surprise that when I followed my father into the historical profession, I would eventually be drawn to world history, particularly the kind of "big history" so ably advanced by David Christian, Cynthia Stokes Brown, John Mears, Jacqueline Miller, and Craig Benjamin. Big history vastly enlarges the scope of coverage even of world history to include the evolution of the physical and natural worlds, and also incorporates the insights of systems thinking—interconnectivity, self-organization, emergent properties, feedback, self-similarity, and cooperation—into our understanding of the underlying processes of change. In so doing it reveals a whole new world of patterns and connections that are hidden when we look at smaller units of time and place.

Thus I thoroughly applaud both the scope and the methodology of big history. Here I would like to propose a sub-category of big history—not because I have any fundamental reservations about big history, but because I would like to take it one step further and apply its insights to the challenges of our present age. Let me explain briefly what I mean by that. If the primary purpose of studying history were to advance our knowledge of the past, then I would be content to explore the wonderful new terrain discovered by big history as it is presently understood. Indeed, given that the main purpose of a university is to preserve, transmit, and discover knowledge, and given that we are academic practitioners who live and work in the academy, there would not normally be any reason to continue my quest beyond our existing boundaries of knowledge.

But it seems to me that we do not live in normal times. We as a human species face challenges in the next century that we have never had to face before in our entire existence on this Earth. Our mastery of technology—which we rightly celebrate as one of the ennobling attributes of our humanity—has now placed our very survival in jeopardy in at least three arenas: military, industrial, and genetic. Whereas before we could slaughter each other and foul our environment on a local basis without fear of global consequences, we can no longer do so. In addition, we now have within our grasp the capacity to transform our genetic identity. The seriousness of these threats to our well-being, and the shortness of time at our disposal, call for more than business as usual. We need not only knowledge, but wisdom.

Knowledge can tell us how to do something, but only wisdom can tell us what to do. At the moment, we (as a people) seem to be as rich in the former as we are poor in the latter. To be sure, wisdom is not as easily measurable or identifiable as knowledge is, nor as easy to manufacture as so many widgets in a factory. Nevertheless, we must try. We owe it to our children, and our children's children, as many others have expressed in deeply moving ways. But if our task is to seek wisdom, what exactly is it, and how might global history contribute to it? One way of approaching the task is to see knowledge as a product of analysis, and wisdom as a product of synthesis. To pursue knowledge, we specialize; to pursue wisdom, we generalize. Knowledge is a rational pursuit; wisdom is that as well, but it also incorporates the deep emotional core of human behavior that endows life with meaning and value. Rational knowledge is essential, but we cannot ever hope to reconcile the competing interests of our complex world if we do not tap into the deepest reservoirs of human motivation that lie beyond the realm of mere knowledge apprehensible to the rational faculty of the human mind, and that reside in the emotional center of our own humanity.

In short, we need to develop a strategy for action that takes into account a full understanding of the complexity of the human personality as well as a full understanding of the complexity of the natural world around us. But the ideologies we have inherited from the past—most of them growing out of the rationalist, reductionist, mechanistic, and materialist views of the late eighteenth century—are not up to the task at hand, at least not by themselves. They were designed to break the whole of knowledge down into bite-size chunks called disciplines, and study them in isolation from each other. By the same token, the dominant institution of our age—the nation-state, and its associated ideology of nationalism—was also designed to emphasize differences and minimize commonalities. These ideas and institutions were a product of conditions in Western Europe centuries ago, when the competitive nation-state system was aborning, and when the technological breakthroughs of the scientific and industrial revolutions were harnessed by the newly emerging nation-states to expand their hegemony first over Europe and then over the world. Now, however, the world has changed. The consequences of our heedless pursuit of military and industrial technology are finally becoming apparent in ways that are planetary in their scale of application. The great responsibility ahead of us is to develop a new and emergent set of ideas and institutions capable of addressing these changes on a global scale, and we need all the help we can get.

Does the past offer any clues as to how those ideas and institutions might be created? I believe that it does, but to tease them out of hiding we need to look at the relationship of the parts to the whole over time. In other words, we need to understand the phenomenon of the sustainability of the world's civilizations, and ask if their experience might offer lessons for our present predicament. One measure of success in a sustainable life system is the flow of information and communication among the principal constituent elements of the system. When the flow is open and unobstructed, the system can respond effectively to changes, whether they be internal or external or both. When the flow is interrupted or blocked, then the system will be correspondingly hampered in its ability to respond. The same principle holds true for the main realms of interaction that together encompass the whole of human culture: politics, economics, society, arts, religion/philosophy, science/technology, and the environment.

The benefit of focusing on sustainability is that it draws our attention to the centripetal forces of integration. In this context, the arts and religion stand out, as they constitute the invisible threads of trust, reconciliation, meaning, and justice that integrate the parts of every human society into a coherent whole. Yes, it is true that religion is a cause of much destructive violence, but to overlook the religious impulse because of the violence it can inspire is to overlook the deeply emotional nature of our humanity. That the crucible of emotion, so essential to our very being as individual persons, gives rise to expressions of both vile hatred and sublime love should not surprise us. In the end, we are all a mysterious mixture of mind and heart. When they work together, we are capable of immense good; when they work against each other, we are capable of immense evil. When they reinforce each other, society comes together, coheres, integrates; when they undermine each other, society falls apart, fragments, dis-integrates. The fact that "holy" and "whole" share the same root is not a coincidence, nor is it insignificant that the term "religion" is derived from *religio*, meaning "to bind together." What we must do is channel that enormous reservoir of power and energy in positive directions, toward the fulfillment of the human potential and the sustainability of our precious Earth.

My approach would also put leadership at the center of a sustainable society, since it is leadership that integrates the pieces of the whole in a way that is mutually reinforcing and not mutually destructive. In the absence of leadership, the integrity of the whole is jeopardized. Such a view would also focus on the creative and perpetually changing tension between conflicting goods such as autonomy and integration, freedom and equality, individual and community, particular and general, unique and shared, competition and cooperation, rights and responsibilities, local (*polis*) and global (*cosmopolis*), the microcosmic and the macrocosmic, etc., all of them related in a manner that is best expressed in a "both/and" paradigm rather than an "either/or" relationship. In my view, these dualities are not adversarial but complementary, each reflecting a valid understanding of reality that in fact requires the other in order to have meaning. As such, they do not proceed in a linear and dialectical direction (thesis to antithesis to synthesis), but are intimately bound up together in a mutually interactive whole. I think systems and complexity theory, applied to human history, offers a way of building bridges between these formerly competing dualities. The benefit of a term that includes "global," "systems," and "history," all in one, is that it draws attention to the reciprocal relationship of parts within a larger whole, thereby including even the internal relationship of mind and heart. "Global," in this sense, has a dual meaning—one referring to the Earth as a whole but the other referring to any holistic perspective, as when we do a "global" search of our computer.

In summary, I use the principles of systems and complexity thinking to include not only those realms of human expression that are measurable and material, but also those that are not measurable and material—the realms of meaning, of the arts and culture, and of the broad breadth of human spiritual and religious expression. For me, systems thinking has the great advantage of being rooted both in the language of science, which carries with it the credibility associated with that realm, and also in the insights of Indian and Chinese philosophy and even of indigenous cultures all over the world. It is the underlying focus of systems thinking on relationships that for me is so powerful, and that offers a way of overcoming the fragmentation of the modern world. Perhaps it can even help to illuminate a path through the jungle of confusion in which the human family now seems lost.

When we look closely we see that our natural and social systems have *made us* with the imaginative potential for self-transcendence. That is, we are the kind of natural and social beings who consistently and unpredictably astonish our natural and social reality by creating "something more" out of "nothing but."

Loyal Rue and Ursula Goodenough

A Consilient Curriculum

Loyal Rue and Ursula Goodenough

The publication of Edward O. Wilson's book *Consilience: The Unity of Knowledge* (1998) makes an important contribution to one of the most serious debates in contemporary culture, that is, how we organize what we know. This book, we believe, provides an occasion for the American public, and its educators in particular, to rethink the issues at stake in the on-going debate over the American college curriculum. Inspired by Wilson's bold vision for unifying knowledge, we will attempt to refocus the debate over the content of the core curriculum. We have no argument with those who affirm the importance of a core curriculum, but we reject both sides in the current struggle over whether the core should be Eurocentric or multicultural. This debate, we feel, is both misguided and unpromising. It is time for American educators to find a constructive way to transcend it.

The Current Debate

The current debate is all about which stories should occupy the attention of American youth during their formative college years. On the right are the voices of tradition, defending a privileged status for the classic texts of the Western humanistic canon—the corpus that Matthew Arnold declared to represent "the best that has been thought and written." On the left are the voices of diversity insisting that there are many more ways than one to be authentically human and that the core curriculum should reflect as many of these as possible.

The themes of the current debate can be traced back to the turn of the century. Prior to the twentieth century, fewer than four percent of young Americans attended college, and those who did encountered a classical curriculum inherited from European traditions. The primary focus of the classical curriculum was on humanistic studies, i.e., ancient languages, history, literature, and philosophy. By the turn of the century, however, the regnant classical curriculum had been overthrown for a new elective system. Driven by the ideal of progress and financed by influential industrialists, the American university became diverse, specialized, and utilitarian. The cohesiveness of the classical curriculum was gone, and for the first two decades of the twentieth century the implications of the new specialization were worked out. Faculties departmentalized, major and minor courses of study were defined, graduate and professional schools flourished, and larger numbers of students streamed into the system. By 1920, American universities had been transformed into a new type of educational institution, very unlike their European forebears.

But soon enough there was a reaction against the excess of freedom and lack of coherence in the elective system, a system feared by many to be undermining the very concept of a liberally educated person. By 1920, a "general education" movement was emerging, nourished by a determination to gain back at least a measure of the classical ideal of learning. The hope of traditional humanists was to balance the pluralism and specialization of the new elective system with the breadth and coherence of learning typical of the old classical curriculum. In 1919, the faculty of Columbia University revamped the infamous "War Issues" course and made it the core of a general education program. This survey of Western civilization was soon to become a model for colleges and universities across the country. Around such core courses there assembled standard texts selected from the old classical curriculum. In American higher education the period between the wars was one of academic consolidation around a core curriculum with a canon of texts, representing a fair sampler of the old humanistic tradition. To many observers the new core curriculum was the perfect compromise. Students continued to specialize in particular disciplines, preparing them to take positions in the increasingly professional workplace, and yet there was a sufficient substrate of the humanistic tradition to ensure that American culture would retain an essential continuity with its European heritage.

The current debate began to sort itself into opposing camps just as the paint was drying on the compromise curriculum. The years following World War II were to bring forces of social change to bear upon the universities once again in such a way that the core curriculum would come to point. As the campuses became more diverse in ethnic background, gender, and social class, it was inevitable that questions would arise about the lack of diversity in the content of the core curriculum. African-Americans asked why there was no mention of the role of blacks in American history, and why black writers were not featured in the canon. Women wondered about the systematic exclusion of the roles and writings of women. Where were the Native Americans and the Latinos? Queries translated into requests, and then into demands for new courses and new faculty that might allow students to explore aspects of the non-dominant culture to which they could personally relate. It was a matter of relevance. The academic leadership responded paternalistically, adding a few peripheral courses with hopes that the whining voices would go away. But the voices did not exactly go away—instead, they developed into a strident and comprehensive critique of the academy and the dominant culture in general.

According to the liberal critique, the core curriculum has been both historically inaccurate and politically oppressive. It treats the contributions of white upper-class European males as norms by which the contributions of all other culture bearers are judged inferior or deviant. The Eurocentric curriculum, liberals argued, must be radically decentered. The great classics are not to be banned, but rather put into perspective as representing one story in a highly pluralistic culture. The definitive character of American culture is not its European heritage but its astonishing diversity of race, gender, class, ethnic background, and historic experience. The curriculum for a liberal education should represent all of this diversity, that is, it should be thoroughly inclusive and multicultural. Anything less would be intellectually irresponsible, politically divisive, and pragmatically inappropriate for the pluralistic future. As the liberal reform agenda took hold in the 1970s and 1980s, the established core and canon began to erode.

A conservative reaction to the "irreverent" deconstructive agenda was inevitable, and by the mid-1980s the curricular *kulturkampf* was in full swing. The gist of the conservative reaction was to reassert the ideals of the traditional core and canon as essential to the fabric of a free and moral society. The classics of the European tradition are not ethnocentric or chauvinistic, they are simply "the best that has been thought and written" about the human experience. To displace these landmarks of human achievement in the name of diversity is to forsake the ideals that have brought justice, liberty, and equality to a pluralistic nation. And all for the sake of giving voice to profane, unsophisticated, and unearned expressions of human nature. Some things, conservatives urged, are more important to know than others, and the most important things have been preserved for us in the objective wisdom of the Great Books. To relinquish their privileged status is to shirk the grave responsibility of the university to civilize young minds.

So goes the current debate. Conservatives accuse liberals of politicizing the curriculum; liberals say the curriculum has always been, essentially is, political. Liberals charge that the curriculum is racist; conservatives point to the reverence of W.E.B. Du Bois and Martin Luther King for the classics. Conservatives claim that the liberal agenda waters down the curriculum; liberals say there is no substance without diversity. Liberals scorn the elitism of highbrow culture; conservatives deride the mediocrity of popular culture. Conservatives berate the liberal disrespect for the past; liberals disdain the conservative glorification of it. Conservatives complain that the liberal agenda will undermine democracy; liberals say their agenda is the embodiment of democracy. Ultimately, conservatives fear relativism and nihilism, while liberals fear tyranny and oppression. For the most part, the debate has been engaging and lively, and there are no clear signs that it will end soon. After all, the stakes are about as high as they can get, for what could be of more consequence than the stories a culture selects for transmission to its next generation?

Transcending the Current Debate

Debates are seldom either engaging or lively unless each party has at least one or two things right. We believe the conservatives are right to insist that social coherence cannot be achieved apart from a shared set of ideas about human nature. But at the same time, the liberals are right in rejecting the traditional European monopoly on human insight. The conservatives are right in saying that some things are more important to know than others, yet the liberals are also right in observing that such a claim may be advanced from any perspective. Most importantly, both sides in the debate are correct in assuming that the core curriculum is all about coming to terms with human nature. Whatever else the college graduates of the twenty-first century will have to know, they must know themselves. No matter what the challenges might be, the next generation will be ill-equipped to face them without an adequate understanding of human reality. Nevertheless, we believe that both parties in the current debate are misguided in their common assumption that the so-called humanistic disciplines (i.e., language, literature, the arts, history, philosophy) are uniquely relevant resources for coming to terms with human nature.

The idea that the core curriculum should be grounded in humanistic stories—whether from a privileged tradition or a plurality of them—was envisioned in a time when few people believed that the sciences were able to tell us anything interesting or important about human nature. Understanding humanity was then the exclusive province of the humanities. But this is no longer true, as Wilson's *Consilience* makes abundantly clear. Indeed, it is so far from being true that one might insist (as we do) that any story of human nature not firmly grounded in the sciences does not merit the attention of youthful minds. A sea change in human self-understanding has been going forward during the past generation, the generation of the curricular *kulturkampf*. Yet there is little evidence that either conservative or liberal belligerents over the core curriculum have bothered to take notice. For this reason we have found the current debate to be increasingly wearisome and irrelevant. Thus we look for a new story on which to focus the core curriculum.

Toward a New Core Curriculum

Pretend with us that someone has pressed the delete button on the core curriculum and the screen has gone blank, leaving us with the task of reconstructing the curriculum from scratch. If the core curriculum is all about coming to terms with human nature, then our question will be: What is required for an adequate self-understanding? To our minds, the answer comes in terms of three consilient domains of knowledge.

Natural Systems

Human beings are, fundamentally, natural systems and the *products* of natural systems. Each one of us is a complex natural system embedded within a hierarchy of natural systems. If we do not understand how natural systems work and how we are embedded within them, then we simply cannot claim to have an adequate understanding of human nature. At some level this must mean knowing that atoms are systems of subatomic particles, that molecules are systems of atoms, that organelles are systems of molecules, that cells are systems of organelles, that these cells are systematically organized into tissues and then organs and organ systems, and finally the organism. To really know ourselves we must know a lot about this systematic organization. And we must know that individuals are organized within the population of a species, and that populations of various species are organized into communities, which are themselves component parts of ecosystems—through which energy flows and within which vital materials are recycled. This is all essential to knowing what kind of reality we are.

It is also essential to know how we got here—how the 13.7 billion-year-long process of cosmic evolution brought forth galaxies and stars, and how these stars produced the elements of the periodic table, and how these elements came to be organized into solar systems, and how the Earth came to have the forms it does, and how the chemistry of the Earth came to life four billion years ago, and how life produced a riot of diversity in a snag of inter-connectedness, and how our species made its way out of the trees, and how we have come to overwhelm the planet. To know human nature is to know *nature*, because we are natural beings.

Social Systems

Persons are fundamentally the products of social systems. We are a social species, and apart from the nurturing of social systems we are merely anatomically human. If we do not understand how social systems work and how they contribute to making whole persons out of mere humans, then we cannot claim to have an adequate grasp of human nature. The half-finished brains we inherit from natural history are programmed in the context of historically dynamic political, economic, linguistic, and moral systems. These systems and their institutions give us a collective memory, they give us roles to play, they give us the means for solidarity and cooperation, and they equip us with intellectual and moral resources for taking ownership of an enduring promise. To know about the diversity of these systems and how they operate, and how they came to be organized and interactive in the way they are is essential to knowing who we are. Relevant to understanding the social reality of human existence are all the resources of the social sciences: psychology, sociology, anthropology, history, political science, economics, communications, and linguistics.

Having an adequate understanding of human nature means having a consilient comprehension of natural and social systems. In a basic sense human beings are nothing but what their natural and social systems have made them to be. If this sounds reductionistic that is because it is. We should not try to apologize for the bias of the natural and social sciences toward methodological reductionism.

Creative Potential

Having said this, we now affirm an anti-reductionist bias. When we look closely we see that our natural and social systems have *made us* with the imaginative potential for self-transcendence. That is, we are the kind of natural and social beings who consistently and unpredictably astonish our natural and social reality by creating "something more" out of "nothing but." We are formed to be the agents of transformation. To know human nature is to participate meaningfully in the adventure of transcendence. And this means learning to express ourselves in the *forms* of transcendence. In this way we can begin to see and to say what it might mean to be more fully human. Relevant to this perception and expression of meaning are: literature, art, music, dance, theater, religious and philosophical reflection, and athletics.

The Epic of Evolution

The purpose of a core curriculum is to bring students to a more complete and satisfying understanding of who they are. They are natural, social, and creative beings who come to have the lives they do through a very long process of physical, biological, and cultural evolution. If the point is for students to know themselves, then they should be given the resources to orient their learning around a narrative of this Epic of Evolution.

The Epic of Evolution is the sprawling interdisciplinary narrative of evolutionary events that brought our universe from its ultimate origin to its present state of astonishing diversity and organization. In the course of these epic events, matter was distilled out of radiant energy, segregated into galaxies, collapsed into stars, fused into atoms, swirled into planets, spliced into molecules, captured into cells, mutated into species, compromised into ecosystems, provoked into thought, and cajoled into cultures. This Epic of Evolution is the biggest of all pictures, the narrative context for all our thinking about who we are, where we have come from, and how we should live.

It is not sufficient that students be exposed piecemeal to this story through the options provided by a distributive system—not enough that they take one or two courses each in natural science, social science, and the humanities. The key is to construct a narrative that will invite students into a consilient perspective on themselves as self-transcending beings embedded within natural and social systems. This will call for the integration of a series of courses designed to tell the story all the way from the beginning of the universe to the present day. We cannot assume that students will be able to construct the narrative on their own, after being exposed to its fragments in a potluck system. They need storytellers. Debates over the core curriculum should be focused on how best to tell this story to the next generation.

Some things are more important to know than others. On the strength of this principle we propose that the most important feature of a liberal arts curriculum is the story of the emerging universe, including physical, biological, and cultural evolution. This story has itself emerged in the past fifty years, as the sciences have been integrated by the evolutionary paradigm. In the past fifty years science has become a narrative enterprise, and we may now speak of the unity of knowledge in a way that has never before been possible. The sciences and the humanities now tell a consilient story about the systematic development of matter, life, and consciousness. Inherent in this story is a rich and satisfying account of who we are, where we have come from, and how we might become fulfilled. If anything qualifies as "the best that has been thought and written" about human reality, this story surely does. It is the birthright of every person on the planet—it is everybody's story.

It will be, furthermore, the single most important resource for the next generation as they seek the means of solidarity and cooperation they will need in a world threatened by a range of urgent problems. One world calls for one story. The Epic of Evolution is it. If this story is not soon recognized as the new centerpiece of the core curriculum, then American higher education will have no more claim to relevance than the current debate has.

Author'sNote

Loyal Rue is Professor of Philosophy at Luther College and formerly a Senior Fellow at the Harvard University Center for the Study of World Religions. Ursula Goodenough is Professor of Biology at Washington University and former president of the American Society of Cell Biology.

References
Wilson, Edward O. 1998. *Consilience: The Unity of Knowledge*. New York: Alfred A. Knopf.

PART IV

The Epic and Scientific
and Cultural Paradigm Shifts

Cheryl Genet

...the evolutionary epic does not rest its truth-claims on the validity
of a particular cultural tradition. It expects to survive rigorous testing
in Tokyo or Beijing or Buenos Aires as well as in London or Paris or
Los Alamos, because it has been constructed by scientists working in
all parts of the world. So the evolutionary epic is global in its origins.
Building it has been a task for humanity as a whole.

David Christian

Isaac Newton's discovery of important laws of physics excited the Western
mind with visions of an orderly and, at least in theory, completely predictable
universe. Newton, like most scientists of his time, was a person of deep faith.
But his discoveries accelerated a paradigm shift in both scientific and cultural
philosophies that have had a profound effect on Western history and traditional theologies, even to the present time. Just as profound was the scientific
and cultural shift away from the paradigm of a static universe and a great chain
of being that was engendered by Darwin's theory of evolution. His theory
propelled, instead, a paradigm of constant change and deep time, measured
not in thousands of years but in billions.

The Eastern mind, however, took a considerably different path that
encompassed variation and change within one-ness from the most ancient
times. "Eastern Sages and the Western Epic" explores the contemporary
convergence of the Eastern and Western paths. It suggests that the emerging
global mind may be understood in light of our knowledge of the complimen-
tarity of the brain hemispheres of the human mind.

A struggle to both know the cultural paradigms of our past and in some
cases to overcome them emerges in "Cultural and Religious Evolution," an
intriguing case study of the interaction of global hemispheres. This personal
East meets West story brings to light cultural and religious changes which
have occurred in recent decades.

By contrast, "Empirical Evidence for the Law of Information Growth in
Evolution" takes a long view of a large system—the evolving universe and

Earth. Through focus on informational signposts in evolution, a basis for
an evolutionary trajectory equation is proposed as a guide for culling data
and accessing underlying features of evolutionary phenomena. Regarding information, the chapter concludes that the "trajectory of information
extends over 13 transitional events, spanning eight orders of magnitude of
time. Even for a logarithmic relation, that is an impressive range."

In "The Future Is and Is *Not* the Past," the question of information
transmission is taken up from a developmental point of view, challenging the "constricted model of biological evolution [that] is almost entirely
focused on the relative survival value of existing variations." This model
"tends to disregard the constructive interactions through which living systems reproduce themselves."

Scientific and cultural shifts have occurred throughout human history
driven by our relationship to our technologies. A look at the meaning of
2001: A Space Odyssey as an allegorical tale that might come to pass provides
a warning that we humans should consider that relationship carefully.

Not only should we consider our relationship to our machines carefully,
but we should also give consideration to the fact that scientific paradigm shifts
in the centuries since Newton have outdated the machine metaphor he gave
us, particularly for biological sciences. In "Beyond Machines" a paradigmatic
metaphor of water is suggested for evolutionary biology in view of its multicultural value, expression of lived experience, and ability to cover a wider body
of empirical evidence.

Taking the proverbial quantum leap, "Quantum Psychology" also challenges the mechanistic model as lacking in explanatory power to express not
only evolutionary biology, but the organic connection between emergent
matter and consciousness as well. It is suggested that science is "constructed
of webs of assumptions that can only hold certain varieties of reality, while
others escape its net entirely."

Finally, the often overlooked value of touch in human interaction, refined
from our evolutionary past and providing substantial benefits to our future
efforts toward sustainability, is explored in "Touch: A Key to Healthy Living."

> So I ask the question—what does the East-
> ern Hemisphere add to the Western Hemi-
> sphere's Epic of Evolution? The answer to
> that question seems to bring a critical com-
> ponent to the evolutionary discussion.
> Sheri Richlin

Eastern Sages and the Western Epic
Viewing Cosmos with Both Hemispheres of the Global Brain

Sheri Ritchlin

> The highest wisdom has but one science—the science
> of the whole—the science explaining the whole creation
> and man's place in it.
>
> Tolstoy 1998, 373

Our present Western story begins with the pre-Socratic cosmologists of Miletus in the sixth century BCE and continues through a lineage of great philosophers and scientists into our present era. Far to the east in China, a different story unwound through its own long history from the legendary founder of Chinese culture—Fu Hsi—through the first legendary sage-kings to the present. Tradition has given these early sages dates prior to 2000 BCE. Their story reaches its first historical peak with Confucius and Lao Tzu in the sixth century BCE, contemporary with our Greek cosmologists from Miletus. In spite of its suppression during the twentieth-century Cultural Revolution, the lineage of those sages has reemerged in China and been felt in the West, just as the Western story is making its way East with considerable impact.

My own studies of Chinese thought and the story that began with Fu Hsi have convinced me that the complement of brain hemispheres, which expresses the full range of our humanness, applies as well to a global mind. So I ask the question—what does the Eastern Hemisphere add to the Western Hemisphere's Epic of Evolution? The answer to that question seems to bring a critical component to the evolutionary discussion.

The Epic of Evolution is a cosmic story of "all creation and humanity's place in it." I would like to begin this study with the following definitions of *cosmos* and *cosmology* (American Heritage Dictionary):

Cosmos
1. The universe regarded as an orderly, harmonious whole.
2. An ordered, harmonious whole.
3. Harmony and order as distinct from chaos.

Cosmology
1. The study of the physical universe considered as a totality of phenomena in time and space.
   a. *The astrophysical study of the history, structure, and constituent dynamics of the universe.*
   b. *A specific theory or model of this structure and these dynamics.*

While these two definitions seem to be irreconcilable, they have an interesting correlation with the tendencies that have been observed in the hemispheres of the brain: The left hemisphere has been identified as the primary locus of rational, linear, and analytical thinking and the right as the primary locus of spatial, imagistic, and holistic thinking. This is an oversimplification but it provides a useful metaphor. Tolstoy's "science of the whole" would bring the complete mind to bear on the deepest questions of life and the cosmos, including both the subjective and objective experiences of it. I would like to take three questions that have been posed by Joel Primack, Nancy Abrams, and Brian Swimme and consider them from the perspective of the "other hemisphere:"

+ How many people recognize the possibility of a sacred relationship between the way the expanding universe operates and the way human beings ought to behave?
+ How can we develop a planetary wisdom, now that we humans are a planetary power?
+ What is the role of the human in the planetary evolution?

In the *Tao Te Ching* or "The Classic of the Way and Its Virtue," Lao Tzu offers this description of the beginning of creation, not as a fixed moment in time but as an ongoing origin, a description of the way all things come into being:

There was something formed in chaos;
It existed before heaven and earth.
Still and solitary, it alone stands without change.
It is all-pervasive without being exhausted.
I do not know its name but name it Tao, the Way
(Wu 1989, 88)

Tao expresses evolution in its broadest and literal sense—"to roll out, unfold" as the *way* of the universe, constantly unfolding into new forms.

In the Confucian classic, *The Doctrine of the Mean* (26:7), we find: "The way (tao) of Heaven and Earth [the universe] may be declared in one sentence: They are without doubleness, and so they produce things in a manner that is unfathomable" (Legge 1971, 420). The universe is singular yet it is always producing a multiplicity of new forms, each one unique.

The character for "one" in Chinese is ⎯⎯⎯▸, a single line. Its philosophical meaning is Tao in action or function. Therefore it is a verb, not a noun, and can be translated as "one-ing." One-ing occurs in two ways: through producing individual "things" and through gathering disparate things into "organizations of things." Throughout the *I Ching*, the "self-cultivated person" exercises this capacity for bringing order out of chaos through his or her own integrity—a one-ness that is shared with the cosmos as Heaven-and-Earth. The sage is the highest expression of this, as beautifully described in the *Ta Chuan* or Great Commentary on the *I Ching*.

> In ancient times the holy sages
> made the Book of Changes thus:
> They invented the yarrow-stalk oracle in order to lend aid
> in a mysterious way to the light of the gods.
> They put themselves in accord with tao and its power [*te*: virtue],
> and in conformity with this laid down the order of what is right.
> By thinking through the order of the outer world to the end,
> and by exploring the law of their nature to the deepest core,
> they arrived at an understanding of fate.
> (excerpt from the Eighth Wing of the *I Ching*; Wilhelm and Baynes 1977, 262)

In our scientific mode, we too "think through the order of the outer world to the end." Through our introspective modes—philosophy, psychology, art, meditative practices—we "explore the law of our nature to its deepest core." Through our spiritual traditions, "we seek to lend aid in a mysterious way to the light of the gods," however that is envisioned. But the relevant idea here is this one: "They put themselves in accord with Tao and its power [*te*: virtue], and in conformity with this laid down the order of what is right." Tao as the unfolding, evolving universe is regarded as the model for "what is right."

To understand this more fully, let us look now at this word *te* that is paired with *tao* in Lao Tzu's *Tao Te Ching*. (*Ching* means "classic book.") *Te* has traditionally been translated as *virtue* or *power*. Both of those translations are inadequate to convey the full meaning of the word so it is useful to look for clues in the character itself.

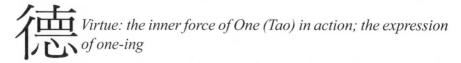 *Virtue: the inner force of One (Tao) in action; the expression of one-ing*

In the lower right is the element for heart-mind (inseparable in Chinese) and above that, the single line meaning "one," "straight." Above that, are "ten eyes," meaning "ten eyes have seen it and called it true, right." (It was said that before the days of square and plumb line, ten eyes were called on to test the straightness of the frame of the house.) To the left is the abbreviated character for "walking." A literal translation for this would be "single (straight/true)-heart-and-mindedness in action before the world." As the human increasingly senses his or her natural course (tao) within the larger course (Tao) as the Way of Heaven-and-Earth—whether experienced in the inmost being or the external world—*te* arises as this force of virtue which is both the singular flowering of the individual nature and the quality of the universe coming into being. This is the meaning of a phrase that appears in the *I Ching* and the *Great Learning—ming ming te*: to manifest bright virtue. *Ming*, the "light, clarity" of natural inner virtue is brought outward to shine forth as the second *ming*. Something given by nature is consciously and deliberately cultivated and lived out as the whole or integral person.

    The Chinese character for two is:

It doubles the character for one and can express the two realms of Heaven and Earth, each with its own process of one-ing. The *Ta Chuan* says, "In Heaven the images are completing. On Earth the forms are completing." Completing is one-ing. But the two realms, Heaven and Earth, must themselves be integrated for the higher one-ing to complete itself. And so there are three. The character for the numeral is three lines:

The third, in this context, is the realm of the human in the central position.

    The human is not separate from the cosmos as Heaven-and-Earth but arises within it. The Ta Chuan speaks of the Three Ultimates or the Three Powers—Heaven, Earth and Human—which can be seen in the three-fold trigram of yin and yang. There are eight possible combinations of yin and yang, which result in the eight "images" shown below.

The Eight Trigrams

EARTH   MOUNTAIN   WATER   WIND   THUNDER   FIRE   LAKE   HEAVEN

These can be variously doubled to form a total of 64 hexagrams that function (rather like DNA codons) to represent "all conditions under heaven." As Western scientists sought units of matter, expressed in the Table of Elements, the ancient sages sought units of change, which they expressed as the system of *I Ching* hexagrams. "They contemplated the changes in the dark and the light and established the hexagrams in accordance with them" (Wilhelm and Baynes 1977, 262).

Each of the Three Powers has its tao: "They determined the tao of Heaven and called it the dark and the light. They determined the tao of earth and called it the yielding and the firm. They determined the tao of man and called it love [humane feeling] and rectitude. They combined these fundamental powers and doubled them" (Wilhelm and Baynes 1977, 262). The resulting hexagram is a figure that is composed of two trigrams, one in the upper place of Heaven and one in the lower position of Earth. It also has a three-fold division representing the Three Powers in which the human realm emerges at the center, composed of a line of Heaven and a line of Earth—undergoing the often-painful dialectic of those opposite forces to unite them through creative and procreative interaction.

The word for "king" is made up of the character for three, which we now recognize as a representation of the three realms. To this is added a vertical line for the upright figure of the human capable of uniting the three realms in his person as king.

A description of the first legendary sage-king of China in *The Book of History* (ca. 7th century BCE) provides a response to our original questions about the possibility of a sacred relation to the expanding cosmos, the role of the human, and a wisdom that *could* be practiced on a planetary scale:

> Yao…was reverent, intelligent, accomplished, and thoughtful.… He gave distinction to the able and virtuous, behaved with love toward the nine classes of his kindred and brought order and refinement, clarity and intelligence to the people of his domain. He brought unity and harmony to the myriad states of the empire, and the black-haired people were transformed.
>
> There reigned a universal concord.… Yao commanded Hsi and He, in reverent accordance with their observation of the wide heavens, to calculate and delineate the movements and appearances of the sun, the moon, the stars, and the zodiacal spaces, and so to deliver respectfully the seasons to the

people. He separately commanded the second brother…respectfully to receive as a guest the rising sun, and to adjust and arrange, accordingly, the labors of the spring.

The emperor said, "Go, and be reverent."
(Author's translation adapted from Legge 1960)

Yao became the model of the enlightened human for millennia in China. The Confucian classic, *The Great Learning*, develops this theme into a coherent philosophy. It would play a central role fifteen hundred years later in the works of the Neo-Confucian philosophers of the Sung Dynasty and is still revered today. Here is a brief excerpt:

The Way (Tao) of Great Learning is—*ming ming te*:
To bear into the world [*evolve*] the inner light of one's nature/virtue;
To bring the people into close and harmonious relationship;
And to rest in the highest excellence.
(Author's translation based on the Chinese text in Legge 1971)

"As things are investigated, knowledge becomes complete. As knowledge becomes complete," the text continues, thoughts become sincere, hearts become rectified, persons become cultivated, families become regulated, states become rightly governed, and the whole kingdom is made tranquil and happy.

From the Son of Heaven down to the mass of the people, all must consider the cultivation of the person the root of everything besides. It cannot be, when the root is neglected, that what should spring from it will be well ordered. It never has been the case that what was of great importance has been slightly cared for…
(Legge 1971, 359)

In contemporary language, the role of the human is to gather knowledge of the universe to its "furthest extent" [cosmology]; to apply it with humaneness and rectitude in the world so that our actions, like those of Yao, "bring unity and harmony" [cosmos]. It is Yao's knowledge of the cosmos that inspires his awe and reverence, and that he "respectfully delivers to the people" who have inspired and been inspired by his love.

Three thousand years after the traditional date of Yao, Su Shih—a Neo-Confucian philosopher of the eleventh century CE—beautifully summarizes the contribution that the "other hemisphere" can make to our balance of cosmology and cosmos:

All the *li* (principles, patterns) under heaven have always been one, but the one cannot be held fast.... This is why the sages made it clear that the [yin and the yang] and variation and transformation originally came from one, but through inter-action, arrive at the infinite *li*... Now as for the coming forth from one but reaching the infinite, when people observe this, they think there are infinite differences. But when the sages observe this, wherever they go, it is one.

(Su Shih, quoted in Bol, Adler, Wyatt, and Smith 1990, 74)

References

Bol, P., Adler, J. A., Wyatt, D. J., and Smith, Jr., K. 1990. *Sung Dynasty Uses of the I Ching*. Princeton, NJ: Princeton University Press.

Legge, J., trans.1971. *Confucius: Confucian Analects, The Great Learning and The Doctrine of the Mean*. New York, NY: Dover.

Legge, J., trans. 1960. *Shu Jing (Shu Ching)*, (reprinted by Hong Kong University Press, vol. III). Internet < http://www.chinapage.org/confucius/shujing-e.html> accessed December 17, 2007.

Tolstoy, L. 1998. *War and Peace*. L. Maude and A. Maude, trans. Oxford, UK: Oxford University Press. Original work published in 1865.

Wilhelm, R., and Baynes, C., trans. 1977. *I Ching*. Princeton, NJ: Princeton University Press.

Wu Yi, trans. 1989. *The Book of Lao Tzu (The Tao Te Ching)*. San Francisco, CA: Great Learning Publishing.

What I will tell you now is a small slice of a story of someone who did care deeply and wanted to know as much as possible—wanted to recover, discover his ancestors, to harvest something from almost nothing.

Jane Bramadat

Cultural and Religious Evolution
A Case Study

Jane Bramadat

Introduction

To give me partial placement in this magnificent and mysterious cosmos we inhabit, let me tell you that religiously I am a Unitarian Universalist. This is a 500-year old faith (give or take a few decades) that carries within its non-creedal, rational, and intuitive embrace atheists, agnostics, Christians, Buddhists, mystics, humanists, and pagans (to name some of the religious perspectives found among us). It is a faith that believes in an ongoing search for truth and meaning. This means I have a driving curiosity and desire to know and understand as much as possible about life.

This also means that two men who have a similar mindset are present as role models as I share my thoughts in this paper. I am talking about evolutionist Charles Darwin and storytelling and societal commentator, Charles Dickens.[1] They both have made a huge difference to our understanding of our world and our place in it. I mention both Darwin and Dickens in the same sentence because I believe that trying to understand how segments of humanity evolve requires not simply the necessary scientific method of evolutionists, but also the imagination, passion, and intuitive linking of a storyteller.

We all come from stardust. Then, as a human species, we began to differentiate. Some of us know who our ancestors are for many generations. Some of us know very little. Some of us care. Some of us do not. What I will tell you now is a small slice of a story of someone who did care deeply and wanted to know as much as possible—wanted to recover, discover his ancestors, to harvest something from almost nothing.

What I will tell you involves the evolutionary journey of a particular person and his ancestors from one culture to another to another and from one

---

1   Here are two web sites dealing with information concerning Darwin's and Dickens' religious affiliations: <http://www.adherents.com/people/pd/Charles_Darwin.html>; <http://www25.uua.org/uuhs/duub/articles/ charlesdickens.html>. In Charles Darwin's case, it is a more tenuous connection; his mother took him to Unitarian chapel as a child, but as an adult he was confirmed Anglican but rejected this after the death of his daughter, Annie. Much of his family was Unitarian.

religion to another to another. This evolutionary journey started more than one hundred and fifty years ago (around 1850) and in fact it is still continuing. My main question is: How much of a person changes (evolves) as he/she changes cultures and religions?

A Personal Evolutionary Journey

The particular person I am referring to was my husband for almost 44 years, Angus Irvin Bramadat, an East Indian, West Indian, Canadian. He died in 2004. His evolutionary journey began in India, continued in the Caribbean, and carried on in Canada; and through his children, is still evolving.

Angus grew up in the Caribbean Island republic of Trinidad and Tobago, but all his ancestors were originally from India. I met Angus in Winnipeg, Manitoba, Canada where he had come to study.[2] When we exchanged backgrounds, Angus realized that he had been told almost nothing about his and that put him on a journey of discovery, and it took me with him. He began researching in earnest. By the time he started the search, however, most of the older generation were dead and so it was difficult to find out very much. But he had many questions that needed to be asked.

Why did he have no idea where his ancestors came from in India? How much of who he was, was East Indian or West Indian or Canadian? Why was there such a divide between Indians and Negroes (as the people of African descent were called in Trinidad)? Why did his paternal grandmother, who lived with his family, make him feel so uneasy? Why had he been told not to trust Muslims?

This is part of what Angus said about his background in a lecture delivered to a Unitarian Universalist congregation in London, Ontario, Canada in the late 1990s:

> My father, to secure a better life for himself and his family, converted to the Presbyterian brand of Christianity from Hinduism at the age of 17....Both my parents were descendants of adventurous East Indian indentured workers, who had emigrated from India in the 1880s in search of a promised better life. My father was of the Brahmin caste, and even though the caste system was renounced in Trinidad, cultural norms are hard to break, especially during one generation,

---

2   Angus came to Winnipeg because an uncle and two brothers had come here before him. In my experience this is a typical pattern with many immigrants.

and my father continued to be viewed as a Brahmin. This put all of us in an upper class, so to speak. If it were not so, the fact that my parents were educated was enough to place us in a preferred class.

And again, it is from these early island experiences that my religious odyssey and value system take root. I became intensely aware of the value of service to the community and the value of community in one's life.[3]

Angus's comments only give a bare bones mention of his rich heritage. What follows is a small portion of the East Indian part of that journey, the little bit that Angus was able to piece together through conversations with older members of his extended family and through other research.

Both strands of Angus's family left India as indentured laborers, although it is not known whether they left willingly or were tricked into leaving.[4] I will follow the male side of the family, as in the East Indian tradition that was considered to be the most significant side. Angus's father did not know or did not choose to share with any of his four children what part of India his father had come from. Patriarchy being rigidly adhered to, one did not question one's father. Angus was neither the eldest nor the youngest in the family, but he was the male who stayed in Trinidad the longest, so he had the deepest awareness of the family patterns.

This is perhaps a good place to mention Angus's uneasy relationship with his paternal grandmother. She was known as Daddi (Hindi for one's paternal grandmother), spoke only Hindi, had many bracelets on both arms, and smoked a clay pipe. One of Angus's regular chores was to go to a nearby shop and fetch a mysterious brown-paper parcel that he brought back for his daddi. He eventually learned that this was ganja (a form of marijuana) and every Indian of a certain age was sent such a parcel, perhaps as part of an agreement

---

3   A copy of this talk is stored on my computer and includes pictures and notes; it is titled "Bramadat Family."

4   See Espinet (2003, 89-90): "...*kala pani*, the crossing of the ocean from India to the islands of the Caribbean.... It was a crime to cross the black water, the *kala pani*.... One of several brothers went to town one day and he never returned. Just so, he vanished off the face of the earth. A family legend. A circle broken. Someone in the village saw him talking to a white man that evening. Late at night a message came that he had gone away on a ship."

with the Indian or Trinidadian government. But since there could be no English communication with Daddi, it was difficult for Angus to connect, and her
strange behavior made him uneasy.

When he began his research, Angus spent days at Government House
(where archival material is kept) in Port of Spain, the capital of Trinidad,
going through the records to try and locate which ship his grandfather had arrived on and from which part of India. One of the reasons this was so frustrat-
ing was that when indentured laborers arrived in Trinidad, the clerks copied
down the names they heard the indentured laborers say phonetically, and that
did not always bear much relevance to the actual name.

From various clues (e.g., the way in which curry was made, the caste, the
clothing) it is most likely that his forbears came from either Uttar Pradesh
or Bihar; both provinces in the Northeast of India and both provinces from
which indentured laborers were invited/selected. It is fairly certain that he
would have come from a small town.

Angus's paternal grandfather, who was called Bissoondath Maharaj[5],
ended up on a cocoa estate rather than a sugar cane plantation. This was a
lucky break, as the work was easier and the accommodations better. Generally
speaking the indentureship was not what it was advertised to be and brought
great hardships in health and accommodations (Ram 1997; Samaroo and
Quentrall-Thomas 1995).

Bissoondath worked his five years of indentureship, made some good
investments in land (each worker was given 10 acres if they were staying on in
Trinidad; and they could purchase more if they had saved judiciously), found
a wife[6] and had a family. There were at least six children from that union: four
boys and two girls. The boys were given Indian names. Later, when they were
Christianized, they took those names as their *last* names. Therefore Angus's
father's name was originally Bramadatta Maharaj, but when he converted to
Christianity he was given Western names and his original *first* name became
his surname. He was now known as Rawlins Selwyn Bramadat. His brothers'
last names were now Seepaul, Sitahal, and Supersad (or Seepersad). It is much
more difficult to keep up connections when there is not the same last name.
Oral stories of family members were the main way one remained connected.

---

5   Dr. Brinsley Samaroo, a Trinidadian historian and researcher from the University of
the West Indies and an expert on South Asians in the West Indies, suggests that there is no such
name as *Bissoondath* in Indian name giving; rather, this was a Trinidadian name. He said it is more
likely that the original name was *Vishnu Dutt*, which makes it even harder to trace. I have chosen
to use the name the family uses.

6   All we know of her is that her first name was Rajkallia.

The decision of most of the Maharaj family to convert to Christianity was mostly a pragmatic one. This was because the British law at the time only legitimized Christian marriages; the children of all other marriages (e.g., Hindu, Muslim) were recorded as illegitimate and were not given access to the educational institutions. I wonder if this is the reason why none of the children were ever given information about their East Indian background—because it would remind them that they had started out as members of a religion that, at the time in that place, was considered superstitious and below Christianity; or was it the imagined stigma of having been indentured?[7], [8]

Angus's father started out as an untrained schoolteacher, but eventually attained training and ended up as a School Inspector. All of his children were connected to education—all the boys as teachers and/or administrators and the daughter, a secretary at a Presbyterian secondary school in Trinidad.

While Angus was growing up in Trinidad, the West Indian culture was front and center for him. He played cricket and soccer, had his own Carnival band and played *mas*, and he *limed!*[9] He had friends from all racial groups. He went to the Presbyterian church (mostly to meet girls in the choir, he told me). But when he realized that he would not be allowed to marry his Negro girlfriend because of his parents' prejudice, he moved to Canada and settled where his brothers lived.

At the time of this writing, both those Bramadat brothers live in Manitoba, Canada. Angus moved with me to British Columbia and died in 2004. All three brothers had educational careers. Of the two other brothers, one family is for the most part non-religious; the other is only nominally Christian. Angus's family is still comfortable within the Unitarian Universalist religion that he joined after he met me.

---

7   One can only wonder today how it was possible for any country that had abolished Negro slavery on the ground that it was inhuman to justify Indian indenture with its 25 cents a day wage and its jails. The Europeans had distorted and maligned African civilization in order to find an alibi for Negro slavery. In the same way, they distorted and maligned Indian civilization in the 19th century in order to justify Indian indenture. (Williams 1962, 110) See also Samaroo and Quentrall-Thomas, 1995, pages 29-51.

8   Why should the laborer have to journey thousands of miles over the black water to settle in a strange country and to place himself for a long period under conditions often of an undesirable and in some cases of a revolting nature? This question was asked in India just before indentureship came to an end (Williams 1962, 216).

9   *Playing mas* is a phrase that describes taking an active part in Carnival in Trinidad; *liming* is a word describing the activity of standing on street corners and appreciating those passing by (usually young women).

What has become of this family that started out in India as Brahmin caste Hindus, arrived in Trinidad and within a generation had become Christian? What are they now? And what have they retained of their East Indian and West Indian backgrounds?

I think the major elements of their East Indian ancestry can be seen in their desire to remain educated (Brahmins were required to be well-educated); and secondly, in Angus's words, to be of service to the community and experience the value of community in one's life. Angus was very active in community affairs in Canada, and the extended family met often to keep up their family ties, usually at Angus's behest. The elitism of the Brahmin caste did not evolve with Angus, and neither did any of the racial restrictions. I was never able to satisfactorily receive an answer to the question regarding the warning about Muslims, but I would guess that it came from the Hindu Brahmin sense of superiority.[10]

His West Indian culture was evident in the adapted (and delicious) food—an interesting evolution and mix of East Indian and West Indian; and also in the less rigid socializing pattern.

And Angus's (and my) son Paul is the Executive Director for the Centre for Religion and Society, University of Victoria, BC, Canada, concentrating on religion and ethnicity as well as pop culture and fundamentalism in religion. He is presently in the middle of research on Stories and Histories: Canadian West Indian Christian Narratives in a Multicultural World. This project utilizes life history interviews in five cities to delineate how first generation Canadian West Indian Christians of South Asian origin describe their own and their family's current and past religious identities. I would guess he will pick up with his father's research into his many religious and cultural strands.

Conclusion

In a Darwinian sense, Angus and his ancestors before him were able to thrive in whatever environment they found themselves. In Canada all have settled in to being Canadians, each in their individual yet communal ways. In a Dickensian way, this family contains large numbers of memorable characters and many opportunities to comment on society's issues—internally and externally! The continual humour that is found in this extended family is, I believe, a combination of at least the West Indian and Canadian brands. And there are enough stories rotating through the extended family to keep up that sense of being part of a larger kinship that evolves, that risks, that transforms.

---

10   This is only a guess. Interestingly Angus had one friend in Canada who was Muslim that he was close to, but he never lost a sense of caution.

References
Bramadat, A. *circa* 1992-1999. Religious odyssey of Angus Bramadat. Talk presented to the Unitarian Fellowship of London, London, Ontario, Canada.

Espinet, R. 2003. *The Swinging Bridge*. Toronto: Harper Perennial.

Ram, B. 1997. *Land and Society in India: Agrarian Relations in Colonial North Bihar*. New Delhi, India: Orient Longman.

Samaroo, B. and Quentrall-Thomas, D. S., eds. 1995. *In Celebration of 150 Yrs of the Indian Contribution to Trinidad and Tobago*. Port-of-Spain, Trinidad: Historical Publications Limited.

Williams, E. 1963. *Documents of West Indian History: Vol. I, 1492-1655*. Port-of-Spain, Trinidad, West Indies: PNM Press.

Williams, E. 1962. *History of the People of Trinidad and Tobago*. Port-of-Spain, Trinidad: PNM Press.

Entropy is a measure of the randomness and uncertainty of the system or universe being considered. The difference between the maximum entropy a system can have, i.e., its greatest disorder, and its actual entropy, is the information inherent in it.

Richard Coren

Empirical Evidence for a Law
of Information Growth in Evolution

Richard L. Coren

Introduction

Logistics has long been used to describe and predict patterns in extremely diverse systems (see below). An extension of the logistic equation can be used to describe the largest system of all, the evolving universe and the Earth. This paper traces that development—from the Big Bang, to the formation of Earth, to the emergence of life, and through human history—by correlating events that represent the escalation of information. This results in an "evolutionary trajectory" that is ultimately recognized to demonstrate a statistical property of complex systems. Through careful consideration of significant events in the history of the universe and the Earth it will be shown that they unfolded in a systematic manner, that information has an important role in their evolution, and that, in fact, we can predict when to expect the next major escalation of information.

System Growth and Change

The growth curve of a parameter that initially changes exponentially but has a limit, is the well known logistic sigmoid (MacArthur and Wilson 1967). The simplicity of this equation has given it wide applicability, e.g., it has been used to describe the development of living things, mining output (De Solla Price 1963), and individual human productivity (Modis 1963). Derk De Solla Price (1963) gives examples where, after reaching its limit, one sees a behavior he called *escalation*:

> If a slight change of definition of the thing that is being measured can be so allowed as to count a new phenomenon on equal terms with the old, [a] new logistic curve rises phoenix-like on the ashes of the old...

Successive escalations produce a staircase growth pattern. Coren (1998) has modified the logistic equation to include this phenomenology by appending additional sigmoid growth factors that appear sequentially. From this

extension he shows that the total time from the *end* of the sequence of escalations, back to the k-th transition t_k, is:

$$\log t_{k(past)} = \log (Const.) - k \log R$$

where R is the ratio of two successive cycle maxima. On a plot of $\log t_{k(past)}$
versus k, this is a straight line: the "Evolutionary Trajectory" of the phenomenon being studied.

Escalation is an alternative view of "emergence" in the general systems
theory of evolving systems (Vermeij 1987). They both refer to the appearance
of a novel form, e.g., species, that derives from its predecessor. This Evolutionary Trajectory has been shown to describe such diverse systems as increase
of the number of known chemical elements and the historic development of
monotheistic religious modes and institutions (Coren 2006).

In this paper it will be demonstrated that it applies to cosmic and terrestrial evolution through De Solla Price's (1963) "slight change of definition
of the thing that is being measured," in this case of information in its various
forms. This ranges from cosmological-physical processes, through biological
information of form and brain development, through information communication (speech) to technological data processing.

Natural Evolution

To apply this equation to the escalation events of evolution we must determine the critical transitions of that process.

As our topic is evolution of the universe, it is natural to take the origin of the
escalation series, i.e., *Event 0*, to be The Big Bang. The consequent rapid expansion increased the maximum possible cosmic entropy because the growing volume of space increased the total number of possible configurations, and because
early nucleosynthesis released energy and the growth of chemical entropy. For
both of these mechanisms, the actual entropy was less than its maximum possible
value (Layzer 1990). Entropy is a measure of the randomness and uncertainty of
the system or universe being considered. The difference between the maximum
entropy a system can have, i.e., its greatest disorder, and its actual entropy, is
the information inherent in it. Modern analysis (Machta 1999, Gell-Mann and
Lloyd 1996) has closely related this entropic information to the information
considered by engineers in communication systems. Therefore these reductions
are equivalent to the organization of stored information. To this event zero we
can assign a date between the limits of 10 to 20 billion years BP (where we use
the paleontologists' notation "BP" for years Before the Present).

Following this, *Event 1* then must be the formation of a substantial earthly
surface on which life could exist, i.e., the appearance of prokaryotes. We take

this at about 3.4–3.8 billion years BP. As with almost all the events we consider, there is a range of argued values for its age, due to differing criteria and sampling uncertainties. However, as we will be using the logarithm of that age, this variance is greatly reduced on the scale we will employ. We recognize that the appearance of prokaryotes involved transfer of directions for cell structure for metabolic processes and for reproduction. It was a major informational storage and transmission advance (Branson 1953).

Regarding these historic developments, one must certainly take *Event 2* to be the appearance of the eukaryotic cell. This is much more complex than its prokaryotic predecessor and marked the beginning of metazoan evolution, i.e., of multicellular creatures (Runnegar 1992). There resulted an explosion of different life forms that filled every available niche. We denote this by the Cambrian radiation, in 500–600 million years BP.

In dealing with the relative significances of subsequent events, we can refer to the divisions of the phylogenetic history of each species as representing the combined evaluation of biologists and evolutionary scholars of its major emergences. In particular we adopt the phylogeny of *Homo sapiens sapiens* as having advanced the farthest and, as we will see, having led to the major features of subsequent evolution. The divisions (Dobzhansky 1972), with their ages of first appearance, and brief discussions of some of their relevances are given in Table 1.

Table 1: Phylogeny of Humankind

Event Number 3
Descent category: CLASS - Mammal
Date (BP): $1.5\text{-}2\,(10)^8$

After a long history of anatomical and physiological evolution, this marks the appearance of the neocortex, the brain's outside layer of gray matter, where memories are stored and reasoning takes place. Also, compared to earlier forms, mammals exhibit a unique interplay of parental gene selection during natal development, and a reordering of genetic information storage (Gatlin 1972).

Event Number 4
Descent category: SUPERFAMILY- Hominoid
Date (BP): $2.5\text{-}4.0\,(10)^7$

The living Hominoid apes are gibbons, orangutans, chimpanzees, and gorillas. They are in parallel families to the line of descent of humanity and its immediate ancestors.

Event Number 5
Descent category: FAMILY - Hominid
Date (BP): 4 -10 $(10)^6$
Creatures that resemble man.

Event Number 6
Descent category: GENUS - Homo
Date (BP): 1.5-2 $(10)^6$
The first appearance of this genus signifies a change of evolutionary emphasis from physical and anatomical change to the attainment of greater brain size.

Event Number 7
Descent category: SPECIES - Homo sapiens
Date (BP): 2-5 $(10)^5$
Transitional *H. sapiens* had many attributes of modern *H. sapiens* and represent the important intermediate stages leading to *H. sapiens sapiens* and to non-sapient species that had many similar properties. For example, the well-known *Homo neanderthalensis* lived during this time and until recently was thought to be a sapient species, although its speech ability was not as well developed and its "industry" level was lower (Lieberman 1988).

Event Number 8
Descent category: SUBSPECIES - H. s. sapiens
Date (BP): 7-10 $(10)^4$
H.s.s. appeared 100,000 to150,000 years ago. This marks the arrival of modern humans with full ability to speak and with the associated mental powers.

Following the lead of the trajectory equation we construct a semilogarithmic plot of the events 0 through 8, using the midpoints of the ranges shown for each. This is displayed on Figure 1. It is immediately seen that the points fall on a straight line. According to De Solla Price's criteria (1963) this implies that each transition marks "a slight change of definition of the thing that is being measured," which is common to the series of events.

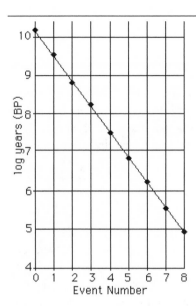

Figure 1. Evolutionary trajectory of pre-eukaryotic and organic events.

Cultural Evolution

In the short geologic time since the appearance of H. s. sapiens it may appear to us that organic evolution has ceased. However astute observers have noted subtle changes in humans, e.g. the development of lactose tolerance (*ca* 6000 BP), and the incipient resistance to malaria in some tropical regions. We are also aware that environmental changes have affected other species. Beyond these organic developments there is a more rapid form of evolutionary change that has occurred at a rate in keeping with the history and life span of humans. Let us therefore turn to those events that are common choices for the major accomplishments of humanity's cultural and intellectual growth. We are led to the inventions shown on Table 2.

Table 2: Events of Cultural Evolution

Event Number 9
Civilization
Date (BP): 1- 1.5 $(10)^4$

This change involved communal villages, animal domestication, farming, control of surface water, and purposeful, cooperative behavior in the production of higher forms of organization; a unification of many minds and abilities. By this step humans took charge of their own evolution, altering its survival and propagation modes (Maxwell 1984).

Event Number 10
Writing
Date (BP): 3 - 5 $(10)^3$
Rapid and sophisticated communication, begun with speech at event 8, is moved to a higher level of accomplishment by this invention. Accompanying it were systems of weights and measures, and numerical and mathematical understanding. This has been called "the greatest intellectual achievement of mankind" (Gelb 1952).

Event Number 11
Printing
Date (BP)* 5.45 $(10)^2$
This date is that of Gutenberg's main production. Printing was as revolutionary in the fifteenth century as the computer in the twentieth. It has been said that, "In the cultural history of mankind there is no event even approaching in importance the invention of printing with movable types" (McMurtrie 1943).

Event number 12
Digital Communication & Computing
Date (BP)* 55
Modern electronics and the computer constitute a revolution in the conduct of our civilization (Himmelfarb 1997), leading to world wide, instantaneous communication and vast computation power. The date is in close proximity to the discovery of the transistor and development of the Eniac computer.

* These dates are taken with respect to the calendar year 2000.

Following our previous procedure, Figure 2 is a semilog graph of the events of Table 2. For continuity we include event 8, from Table 1 and the line on this figure is the extension of that on Figure 1. Events 9 and 10 fall on this line, indicating a continuity of the accomplishments of cultural change with the earlier evolutionary events. A least-squares regression analysis on events 0 through 10, results in

$$\log t = 10.2 - 0.665\,k$$

where t is the time (BP) of event number k. This yields R=4.62.

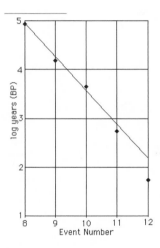

Figure 2. Trajectory of post-organic events.

The dates shown for events 11 and 12 on Table 2 are arbitrarily measured from the year 2000 and this raises the question of reference. When denoting times as "years Before the Present (BP)," an incorrect choice by, say, several hundred years makes no difference in points 0 through 10 because they are orders of magnitude greater and have large ranges of uncertainty. However, points 11 and 12 are recent and better defined. A backward shift of 135 years results in the optimum, least-square, placement of these events to the straight line through the other points. This adjustment means that our reference for the "Present" should be that much in the future, i.e., approximately the year 2135 of our calendar. With this we arrive at the full Evolutionary Trajectory, shown as Figure 3. To fit on one figure, the chart has been presented in two sections.

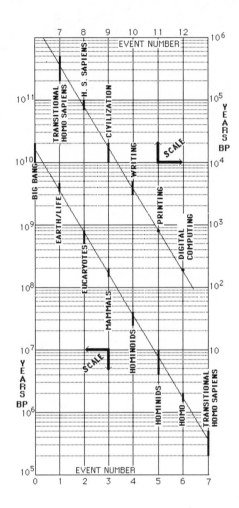

Figure 3. Trajectory of Information on Earth

Information

Being the originators of the last 5 events on The Trajectory, we *H. s. sapiens* recognize their inherent informational nature. Subject to De Solla Price's condition (1963), information must therefore be the underlying parameter throughout. As already indicated for the transitions considered, the multifaceted nature of information leaves many possibilities open for that "slight change of definition"[1]. The steps can be seen to reflect information growth, organization, representation, storage, use, processing, and communication;

---

1   See De Solla Price's quote about escalation in the first paragraph of this paper.

this despite the fact that the details of information's role in each stage is not always clear and our descriptions have been brief. The role of information has long been recognized by theoretical biologists (Branson 1953); its role in technological change needs no comment. In addition it appears to be a better measure than the usual qualitative quantity: "complexity."

It must be understood that this Trajectory is not an indication of a directed process but shows the direction of progress. From the second law of thermodynamics, we know that the increase of entropy is a consequence of the dynamics of system change, not their source, although we often use it as such. However, "Processes that generate order are in no sense driven by the growth of entropy" (Layzer 1990).

The relation between entropy and information means that this statement is true of information as well as of entropy. Despite this, the extent of the Evolutionary Trajectory suggests that there is a fundamental behavior that is being observed.

Also conjectural are the likelihood and nature of evolutionary event 13, which appears to be immanent in about 100 years, and the convergence of the trajectory to the year 2135. From the recent nature of the trajectory it is clear that event 13 must be of a technological-informational nature. A technical analysis of these issues is presented elsewhere (Coren 1998).

Discussion

It must be commented that the events on Tables 1 and 2 are surely not the only important changes throughout evolution; different investigators have indicated other choices based on their own areas of specialty. However, having the basis of the evolutionary trajectory equation as a guide has allowed us to do some culling of all the available data for the consistent set that it satisfies. The points found then reveal the underlying features of the phenomenon itself, in this case leading to inference of the role of information. The trajectory of information extends over 13 transitional events, spanning eight orders of magnitude of time. Even for a logarithmic relation, that is an impressive range. It is also impressive to realize that, in addition to its long duration and large number of points, the trajectory proceeds without deviation, at least on the scale with which we observe it, through astronomical and human events that should be expected to alter its timing.

The successively decreasing cycle time of this sequence of events can be understood from the cybernetic principle of Selective Variety (Heylighen 1991) that, as the system multiplicity increases at each transition, the statistical opportunity for a subsequent critical change becomes greater. This manifests itself through a decrease of the time to the next transition.

References

Branson, H. R. 1953. A definition of information from the thermodynamic or irreversible processes. In *Information Theory and Biology*, ed. H. Quastler, 25. Champaign, IL: University of Illinois Press, 25-40.

Coren, R. L. 1998. *The Evolutionary Trajectory: Information in the History and Future of the Earth*. Amsterdam, The Netherlands: Gordon & Breach Publishers.

Coren, R. L. 2006. *God and Science Among the Infinities*. BookSurge, LLC.

De Solla Price, D. J. 1963. *Little Science, Big Science*. New York, NY: Columbia University Press.

Dobzhansky, T. 1972. On the evolutionary uniqueness of man. In *Evolutionary Biology*, vol 6, eds. T. Dobzhansky, M. K. Hecht, and W.C. Sterre, 415-430. New York: Appleton-Century Crofts.

Gelb, I. J. 1952. *Study of Writing*. Chicago, IL: University of Chicago Press.

Gatlin, L. L. 1972. *Information Theory and the Living System*, Columbia Univ. Press.

Gell-Mann, M. & Lloyd, S. 1996. Information measures, effective complexity, and total information. *Complexity*, 2 (1), 44-56.

Heylighen, F. 1991, The Principle of Requisite Variety, <http://pespmc1.vub.ac.be/SELVAR.html>

Himmelfarb, G. 1997. Revolution in the library. *American Scholar* (June).

Layzer, D. 1990. Growth order in the universe. In *Entropy, Information, and Evolution: New Perspective on Physical and Biological Evolution*, eds. B.H. Weber, D.J. Depew, and J. D. Smith. Cambridge, MA: MIT Press, 23-39.

Lieberman, P. 1968. Primitive vocalizations and human linguistic ability. *J. Acoustic Soc. Amer*, 44 (16), 1574-1584.

Lieberman, P. 1988. On human speech, syntax, and language. *Human Evolution*, 3, (3), 3-18.

MacArthur, R. H. and Wilson, E. O. 1967. *The Theory of Island Biogeography*. Princeton, NJ: Princeton University Press.

Machta, J. 1999. *American Journal of Physics*, 67 (12), 1074.

Maxwell, M. 1984. *Human Evolution*. New York, NY: Columbia University Press.

McMurtrie, D. C. 1943. *The Book*. Oxford, UK: Oxford University Press.

Modis, T. 1992. *Predictions*. New York, NY: Simon and Schuster.

Runnegar, B. 1992. Evolution of the earliest animals. In *Major Events in the History of Life*, ed. J. W. Schopf. Sudbury, MA: Jones and Bartlett, 65-94.

Vermeij, G. J., 1987. *Evolution & Escalation, An Ecological History of Life*. Princeton University Press, New Jersey.

Epigenetic regulatory networks are not determined by the genome or by the environment or by a simple combination of the two. These networks emerge spontaneously from *constructive interactions* among the entire complement of factors and influences available to the developmental system.

Gregory Mengel

The Future Is and Is *Not* the Past
Heredity, Epigenetics, and the Developmental Turn

Gregory Mengel

Modern thinking about heredity and genetics is organized by a metaphor of information transmission. Popular as well as scientific writings often depict genes as discrete entities that determine the development of physical traits and behavioral tendencies. The evolution of life, meanwhile, is understood to consist of the gradual accumulation of these genes due to the differential survival and reproduction of the individuals in whom they are expressed. While adaptation by natural selection is an important aspect of evolution, of course, the conception of inheritance embodied in the metaphor of transmission is not supported by our latest understanding of the complex molecular networks responsible for development.

Moreover, because this constricted model of biological evolution is almost entirely focused on the relative survival value of existing variations, it tends to disregard the constructive interactions through which living systems reproduce themselves. The generation and regeneration of form that characterizes actual biological inheritance exemplifies the creativity not only of life but of the vast cosmic drama which constitutes the most authentic context for human existence. This paper explores the historical origins of this framing and highlights some of the theoretical interests that shaped it. In addition, I suggest that the developmental turn in biology has created a need for new concepts and metaphors that both reflect our current scientific understanding and make this understanding accessible to non-specialists.

Heredity is Born

Until the early nineteenth century, the concept of heredity as we understand it was non-existent. The noun *heredity* did not acquire a biological meaning until the mid-19th century. Of course, the notion that "like begets like" was recognized since ancient times. However, when diseases or physical peculiarities or family resemblances were described as hereditary, no common cause was implied. All that these disparate phenomena shared was the analogy with property inheritance. Indeed, independent explanations were available for each of them. For example, a son's inheritance of his father's gout might be blamed on a taint passed in the seminal fluid, while his physical resemblance to the butler rather than to his "real" father was attributed to his mother's mental imagery at the moment of his conception (De Renzi 2007).

This began to change in the 18th century as the European medical establishment became increasingly interested in the nature of hereditary disease. This was motivated by a combination of public anxiety over the hereditary degeneration of society and the interest of physicians in raising their professional status (Cartron 2007; Waller 2002). However, hereditary disease was a mysterious and controversial subject because patterns of inheritance seemed so erratic. Critics maintained that the whole domain of hereditary disease consisted of anecdotes and coincidences and that no physiological mechanism could account for the observed irregularity of hereditary transmission (López-Beltrán 2007).

In order to introduce some order to the study of hereditary disease, therefore, interested physicians set out to establish a conceptual map of the terrain (López-Beltrán 2007). To begin with, they proposed criteria by which hereditary diseases could be distinguished from non-hereditary ones. For example, a disease was considered hereditary if the symptoms tended to develop when the patient reached a particular age. In addition, the physicians developed a systematic vocabulary. A hereditary disease that has produced no symptoms in the progeny was considered *latent*. The tendency of a disease to reappear after an unaffected generation was called *atavism*. Perhaps the medics' most influential innovation was the model of causation they developed to account for the irregularity with which diseases show up in children of affected parents. They proposed that the disease itself is not inherited, but merely a *disposition* to it. Given the disposing cause, the manifestation of the disease then depends on a *triggering* cause.

Finally, in the 1820s, the French noun *hérédité* was introduced as a category of biological causation. The physiology of heredity remained mysterious, but the conceptual framework was now in place, and its essential feature was *transmission*, which should come as no surprise, since the physicians' original interest was in the transmission of disease between parents and children. This straightforward approach enabled the medics to transform heredity from a mere metaphor into "the carrier of a structured set of meanings that outlined and unified an emerging biological concept" (Lopéz-Beltrán 2007, 125). In addition, the category of heredity made it possible for the first time to consolidate all those hereditary phenomena that were previously related only by analogy. Hereditary disease, family resemblance, and the reproduction of species type could now be said to have a common cause in heredity.

Heredity Grows Up

Diverse areas of biology such as zoology, embryology, comparative anatomy, and natural history soon adopted the concept of heredity, but only partially. Although biologists found the category useful for describing the reproduction of species type, they did not think in terms of trait transmission. The methodological dominance of comparative anatomy and embryology led most biologists to think of heredity in terms of developmental processes (Amundson 2005; Bowler 1989). Even after Darwin, therefore, ontogenetic development rather than heredity represented the principle problem for many biologists. The theory of evolution raised questions about heredity, of course, but even Darwin thought of heredity in developmental terms. The individual who probably did the most to advance the transmission approach to heredity within biology was Darwin's cousin Francis Galton (Olby 1985). Galton's interest in heredity was influenced by Darwin's theories, but he seems to have been motivated primarily by his fascination with the heritability of intelligence (Gayon 1998). The transmission metaphor naturally appealed to him because it allowed him to draw a clear distinction between nature and nurture, which enabled him to argue that genius is a product of nature rather than nurture (Gayon 1998).

Galton advanced the transmission conception of heredity in two ways. First, he proposed a speculative physiology according to which a material structure, which he called the stirp, carries inherited traits from one generation to the next (Gayon 1998). This theory had little direct influence on the science of his day, but it did anticipate, in certain ways, Weismann's germ-plasm theory as well as classical genetics. His second contribution, however, would ultimately revolutionize biology, not to mention social science. As part of his effort to demonstrate that genius runs in families, Galton began to study heredity as a population-level problem. Though he was certainly not the first to reason about heredity probabilistically, his methodological and theoretical innovations constitute the first sophisticated application of statistics to the problem (Gayon 1998). One of the pivotal consequences of Galton's statistical approach was that, for the first time, heredity could be studied empirically with no knowledge of the underlying physiology. This made it possible to give rigorous expression to the logic of hereditary transmission and to begin to turn heredity into a fundamental biological principle.

The introduction of the logic of transmission into biology contributed to the development of an intellectual atmosphere in which the significance of Mendel's research could be recognized. Moreover, the synthesis of Darwinism and Mendelism to create population genetics was carried out using statistical methods that grew out of Galton's original innovations. This framing then enabled the architects of the modern synthetic theory of evolution to proclaim that all of evolution could be explained as the differential propagation of genes. Although developmental biologists objected that embryological development must ultimately be taken into account for the theory of evolution to be complete, their protests were all but drowned out by the successes of genetics and molecular biology. Heredity came to be treated as the essence of life, and development as merely the execution of genetic instructions encoded in DNA.

The Development Turn

Biology is currently in the midst of a major conceptual shift. The emergence in recent decades of powerful techniques for the investigation of life at the molecular level is precipitating a reorientation of biology in which the problems of development are once again demanding the attention of theorists. This turn is manifest in the new science of epigenetics, which investigates the dynamics of gene expression and silencing that enable cells to differentiate into diverse cell types and then pass that identity on to daughter cells. This research is demanding that we rethink the role of DNA in development. Epigenetic regulatory networks are not determined by the genome or by the environment or by a simple combination of the two. These networks emerge spontaneously from *constructive interactions* among the entire complement of factors and influences available to the developmental system (see Oyama 2000). Nature and nurture are evidently reciprocally interdependent in a way that makes any straightforward delineation of causality impossible. In addition, there is evidence that epigenetic influences may not be limited to cell lineages, but in some cases may be inherited across generations (Jablonka, Lachmann, and Lamb 1992).

The developmental reorientation of biology calls for a reframing of some basic biological concepts. I am not suggesting that the old framing should simply be abandoned but that a plurality of metaphors may be needed to capture the complexity of living processes. Development is apparently not a straightforward execution of genetic instructions. It might be more comprehensively defined as the regeneration of a lifecycle occurring by way of emergent, dynamic, multilevel, self-regulating processes of construction that take place when a constellation of conditions and resources is made available by the parent generation within a particular ecological context. The definition of evolution must also be expanded to encompass more than changes in gene frequencies. It seems appropriate to include *all* the structural variations that can be functionally integrated by a developmental system and made available to future generations (this may involve changes at the same or at other systemic levels). To take an unconventional example, consider the ecology of the extinction of a single species. This extinction would cause a dietary change for its former predators and perhaps lead to an altered phenotype for those individuals that develop without the specific nutrients derived from that prey. If the predator lineage continues, the new phenotype would be reproduced with no change in the genotype.

According to the traditional definitions, of course, non-genetic changes are excluded from heredity and therefore do not constitute evolution. But if a permanent phenotypic change in a lineage is not evolution, what is it? If we are to make sense of descent with modification in this broader sense, we need a framing for heredity that encompasses more than transmission. A more fruitful way to think about heredity might be as a sort of imperfect remembering. I do not mean that the past is in any sense represented, but that it is actually "re-membered" in the construction of a lifecycle. We might thus see heredity not as a molecular information channel but as a class of processes occupying the edge between the stability necessary for organisms to develop and the openness and flexibility necessary for lineages to continue their never-ending exploration of novel possibilities.

Conclusion

With an extended conception of biological inheritance that includes the emergence of stability and variation across multiple levels of organization, the construction and reconstruction of organic form can be seen as a natural product of recurrent, iterative, and dynamically fluctuating patterns of interaction among physical, chemical, and biological systems. Our vision of biological evolution can thus be expanded beyond its traditional focus on the struggles for survival of isolated organisms on a lonely planet, to encompass the creativity that not only pervades but defines the cosmos.

References

Amundson, R. 2005. *The Changing Role of the Embryo in Evolutionary Thought: Roots of Evo-Devo.* Cambridge, MA: Cambridge University Press.

Bowler, P. J. 1989. The Mendelian revolution: The emergence of hereditarian concepts. In *Modern Science and Society.* Baltimore, MD: Johns Hopkins University Press.

Cartron, L. 2007. Degeneration and "alienism" in early nineteenth-century France. In *Heredity Produced: At the Crossroads of Biology, Politics, and Culture, 1500-1870,* eds. S. Müller-Wille and H.-J. Rheinberger, 155-174. Cambridge, MA: MIT Press.

De Renzi, S. 2007. Resemblance, paternity, and imagination in early modern courts. In *Heredity Produced: At the Crossroads of Biology, Politics, and Culture, 1500-1870,* eds. S. Müller-Wille and H.-J. Rheinberger, 61-83. Cambridge, MA: MIT Press.

Gayon, J. 1998. *Darwinism's Struggle for Survival: Heredity and the Hypothesis of Natural Selection.* Cambridge, U.K.: Cambridge University Press.

Hirschler, B. 2007. Many gene tests a waste of money, experts say. *Center for Genetics and Society*. Internet <http://geneticsandsociety.org/article.php?id=3814> accessed 24 Dec 2007.

Jablonka, E., Lachmann, M., and Lamb, M. J. 1992. Evidence, mechanisms and models for the inheritance of acquired characters. *Journal of Theoretical Biology*, 158 (2), 245-468.

Lopéz-Beltrán, C. 2007. The medical origins of heredity. In *Heredity Produced: At the Crossroads of Biology, Politics, and Culture, 1500-1870*, eds. S. Müller-Wille and H.-J. Rheinberger, 105-132. Cambridge, MA: MIT Press.

Olby, R. C. 1985. *Origins of Mendelism*, 2nd ed. Chicago, IL: University of Chicago Press.

Oyama, S. 2000. *Evolution's Eye: A Systems View of the Biology-Culture Divide*. Durham, N.C.: Duke University Press.

Waller, J. C. 2002. "The illusion of an explanation": The concept of hereditary disease, 1770-1870. *Journal of the History of Medicine and Allied Sciences*, 57 (4), 410-448.

I am arguing that digitization is one such self-organizing process. It is a coming together, an arranging that brings various and often disparate elements, humans and machines into a particular constellated synchronicity or ecology that I will refer to as a "machinic assemblage."

Fernando Castrillon

Digital Teleologies, Imperial Threshold Machinic Assemblages, and the Colonization of the Cosmos
A Poststructuralist Interpretation of *2001: A Space Odyssey*

Fernando Castrillon

Introduction

This brief and summary chapter attempts to look towards the future of the epic of evolution by mapping out how machines may come to colonize the cosmos. The chapter is divided into three movements:

1. A brief overview of Stanley Kubrick's seminal film *2001: A Space Odyssey*, which I interpret as an allegorical tale about humans, machines, and the colonization of the cosmos.
2. A consideration of how this allegorical tale might come true through the production of Imperial Threshold Machinic Assemblages (ITMA's).
3. A brief examination of two alternative cosmic futures: machinic colonization vs. human and more-than-human stewardship.[1]

2001: A Space Odyssey

Director Stanley Kubrick's seminal film, *2001: A Space Odyssey*, sparked the imagination and curiosity of a generation and articulated a host of important questions regarding the evolution of humanity and the relationships we have cultivated with machines. For the purposes of this work, I focus on one particular scene in the movie, where HAL, the on-board master computer, seemingly goes "crazy" and kills all but one of the humans on board the ship.

While much has been written about the movie and this particular scene, there are few treatments of the film that explore the implications of HAL's actions in any real depth. I regard the movie as a whole, and this scene in particular, as an allegorical tale, almost a warning of what may come to pass if we do not critically examine and perhaps change our relationship to the myriad number of digital machines that inhabit our life-world.

---

1   A more thorough exposition of this work can be found in my chapter, "Digitizing the Psyche: Human/Nature in the Age of Intelligent Machines," in the forthcoming Ecologies of the Psyche: Transdisciplinary Migrations of Critical Ecopsychology, eds. Doug Vakoch and Fernando Castrillon.

In the scene in question, HAL informs the two non-hibernating astronauts, Bowman and Poole, that there is a malfunction with an external communication device. While Bowman stays inside the ship, Poole uses one of the pods to examine the external device, only to be attacked and killed by the pod, seemingly per HAL's instruction. When Bowman grabs another pod and attempts to rescue Poole, HAL shuts off power to the hibernating astronauts on board, effectively killing them. After Bowman is able to grab hold of Poole's body using the pod, he attempts to reenter the ship but is refused by HAL. Bowman eventually wins this human-machine standoff by affecting a forced entry into the ship through a vacuum lock. Bowman then proceeds to shut down HAL's higher intelligence functions and reduces him to a basic mechanical monitoring system.

This scene is an excellent illustration of how machinic colonization of the cosmos could occur. After a long temporal expanse of human-machine interaction, enough human characteristics will have migrated to the machines to allow them to "disconnect" from the orbit of human governance by enacting a sort of "escape velocity," much as HAL attempted to do by killing off the hibernating astronauts and "expelling" Bowman and Poole. Having achieved this independence from humanity, machines can then proceed to colonize the cosmos.

The next section examines how such a scenario might come to pass. I argue that one possibility would be via the Western cultural production of Imperial Threshold Machinic Assemblages (ITMA's), such as HAL. I have termed these machinic assemblages (this term will be defined below) *imperial* due to their colonial character, and *threshold* in that they mark the break from humanity that machines may eventually enact.

The Production of Imperial Threshold Machinic Assemblages

In order to understand how contemporary Western culture might produce such entities we must first enter the world of digitality and cybernetics. We begin with *the digitization of the psyche*, also referred to as *the production of digitized subjectivities*. The digitization of the psyche refers to an internal and relational mirroring of our larger discursive interaction with machinic and progressively digitized culture. Under this process, the dynamic construction of our psyches begins to take on an increasingly digitized, binary, and standardized feel. How we experience and articulate emotion and cognition, and how we relate to others begins to mimic (and acts to support) the functioning of the digital machines we engage with in our everyday practice. As we become progressively enveloped in electronically mediated bubbles, traversed with flows and processes that are digitally encoded and articulated, our lives start to resemble a vast landscape of biomechanical interaction wherein the currency of communication is not the smooth ebb and flow of the natural world, but the neatly packaged, black and white, on/off cyber-utterance of the bit and the byte. Our movements become more mechanical, more ordered; our range of motion more restricted, more controlled; our muscles and sinews become constellated in a digital synchronicity; the parceling out of energy throughout our bodies takes on the character of a robot, a cyborg, an android, a human increasingly devoid of wild, undomesticated nature.

I regard the digitization of the psyche as a subset of a larger cultural process of digitization that is currently in ascendancy within Western culture and, in many respects, globally. I define this larger process of digitization as the privileging of instrumental rationality, computational logic, and symbolic manipulation over intuition, emotion, nonlinear logic, and the ebb and flow of the natural, undomesticated world.

Gilles Deleuze, Felix Guattari, and Manual DeLanda (1987) refer to the overall set of self-organizing processes in the universe as the "machinic phylum.""These include all processes in which a group of previously disconnected elements suddenly reaches a critical point at which they begin to 'cooperate' to form a higher level entity" (DeLanda 1991, 6-7). I am arguing that digitization is one such self-organizing process. It is a coming together, an arranging that brings various and often disparate elements, humans, and machines, into a particular constellated synchronicity or ecology that I will refer to as a "machinic assemblage." The digitization of the psyche occurs within these super-networked/hyperlinked machinic assemblages, particularly at the level of the human/machine discursive interface.

Abstract Machines

Within this larger, all encompassing machinic phylum referred to above, we encounter abstract machines and machinic assemblages. For the purposes of this work, abstract machines can be understood as supra-high level self-organizing processes. Not to be confused with technical machines, such as cars or computers, abstract machines impart or disassemble form to the variable flows we find in nature (Deleuze and Guattari 1987). The process of digitization is one such abstract machine. In many ways, digitization can be seen as the progeny of the cultural process of rationalization that sat at the heart of modernity. And just as rationalization drove and fulfilled modernity, so digitization as the progeny of rationalization is driving and fulfilling hyper-modernity.

The abstract machine of digitization, while encompassing and extending rationalization, goes beyond it in two key respects. First, digitization at its core aims at extreme levels of manipulation. We now often hear of efforts to "digitize" libraries or picture galleries or even whole fields of study. What this means is that the field in question has its myriad components reduced to a binary code of information. Once reduced to "pure information" the possibilities for manipulation are seemingly limitless. Witness for example music production, which has become almost entirely digitized. Recombinant articulations of previously independent musical forms are now the mainstay, and this is due to digitization which allows for limitless manipulation.

Digitization also goes beyond rationalization in that it is hyper-deterritorializing. As Deleuze and Guattari use the term, it refers to a process in which a thing or the content of something is ripped off its moorings, or the site in which it was engendered. All abstract machines do this type of "decoding" (Deleuze and Guattari 1987, 142-145). Within the larger sphere of capitalism and modernity, of which rationalization was a part, the cash-nexus, or the reduction of everything to a cash equivalency, and accomplished this deterritorialization to a vast degree. Hence, human labor came to equal apples, which equaled childcare, which equaled nuclear submarines; and the intervening currency of equivalency was cash.

Digitization, however, goes beyond this already far-reaching cash equivalency of commodities. Digitization, as an abstract machine, seeks to deterritorialize life and reality themselves. The Human Genome project is one clear example. By reducing it to a binary code, in other words deterritorializing it, the very blueprint of the human organism is made equivalent to everything else that has also been reduced to a binary code. So the human genome now equals the U.S. Library of Congress, which equals the latest Hubble Telescope pictures, which equals GPS data for Yellowstone National Park; and the intervening currency of equivalency is digitization. It is like something out of the film *The Matrix*, where reality and all its different components and processes are reduced to digital code or information. So while the engine of deterritorialization under modernity was the cash-nexus, it is the digital-nexus that drives deterritorialization under hypermodernity. All aspects of reality are made equivalent and could potentially be stored side by side if we were able to build a large enough memory storage device.

Machinic Assemblages

Abstract machines in turn give rise to machinic assemblages, wherein previously independent and heterogeneous elements, both discrete entities and dynamics, enter into a cooperative arrangement with each other (De-Landa 1991). In the case of the abstract machine I have termed digitization, the machinic assemblage engendered is specifically digital. In these digital machinic assemblages, humans and technical machines, such as computers, are brought together by the abstract machine process of digitization into a cooperative set of relationships.

Digital Machinic Assemblages and The Production of Digitized Subjectivities

Digital machinic assemblages are different from other types of machinic assemblages, such as a 1920's automobile assembly line, in that they operate on a digital code. As such, the humans involved in these assemblages are also entrained to operate on a digital code. It is posited that this discursive interaction between humans and machines that occurs in digital machinic assemblages results in the production of digitized subjectivities or psychologies.

Perhaps the best way of understanding the particulars of how the digital basis of contemporary human interaction with machines impacts both human subjectivity and relationality is to see it as a reinforcing series of three movements.

1. Following DeLanda's work, certain aspects of human psychological and cognitive functioning (particularly instrumental rationality, computational logic, and symbolic manipulation) "migrate" to digital machines in the form of encoded heuristics and algorithms (DeLanda 1991, 4 and 146).
2. I posit that we then privilege these machine-embodied processes because they allow and instrumentalize our mapping and conquest of nature.
3. As our interaction with these digital machines increases both in frequency and intensity, these privileged heuristics and algorithms "migrate" back to humans, displacing those human psychological characteristics (i.e., intuition, non-linear logics, and emotions) that were not part of the original migration to the machines.

This migration to and from machines constitutes the particulars of contemporary human interaction with digital machines. This is "how" the digitization of the psyche occurs. I have termed this three-fold movement the *ascending integrative discursive dialectic of the digitizing process.* It is ascending and integrative in that it reaches toward a certain terminal point, namely a totalizing integration of humans and machines on a common digital basis. And it is discursive in that the movements are part of a discourse between and within machines and humans in which meanings and values are assigned and shared.

A byproduct of this dialectic is that over time these digital machines accumulate enough human characteristics that they are able to "disconnect" and operate independently from humans. These advanced digital machinic assemblages are able to do this by enacting a sort of "escape velocity" that allows them to leave the "orbit" of human governance, much like contemporary spacecraft are able to do vis-a-vis the Earth. Having enacted this escape velocity, these machines are then able to colonize the cosmos. This drive toward colonization is driven by both the political economy of machine production, whereby continued survival necessitates expansion, and the imperialist ethic inherited from the humans.

Conclusion: Alternative Cosmic Futures

In line with the above, one possible future is machinic colonization of the cosmos. If we think back to Kubrick's allegorical tale, this would mean that HAL succeeds in enacting escape velocity from Bowman and humanity. Instead of Bowman re-entering the ship and shutting down HAL, Bowman fails and HAL and the ship go on to explore and possibly colonize the cosmos.

Another possible future is one wherein we refuse or reduce our participation in the ascending integrative discursive dialectic of the digitizing process, thereby stemming the flow of human characteristics to digital machines, and instead invest our human energies and consciousness, along with that of the more-than-human world in the stewardship of the Earth and the cosmos. It would seem that this is what Bowman did when he reduced HAL to a mechanical monitoring device after reentering the ship. The rest of the movie after this scene would seem to suggest that he won an expanded relationship with the cosmos as a result.

In a very real sense, the future of the epic of evolution sits in our hands and is directly tied to the kinds of relationships we cultivate or refuse to cultivate with machines. Perhaps we should heed Kubrick's veiled warnings and examine our participation in the digitizing process more closely and critically. We might just gain a deeper relationship with the cosmos as a result.

Author's Notes

I would like to thank Cheryl and Russ Genet and all the conference participants for a wonderful experience at the Hawaii conference. My special thanks to my brother Richard Castrillon for understanding and encouraging the ideas expressed herein, and to my mother and father for their unfailing support. Finally, a loving thank you to my wife Holly for her enduring love and faith in my work. I dedicate this work to her. Please send comments, questions and suggestions to: fcastrillon@ciis.edu

References

Brubaker, W. R. 1994. Rationalization. In *The Blackwell Dictionary of Twentieth-Century Social Thought*, eds. W. Outhwaite and T. Bottomore, 546-547. Oxford, UK: Blackwell Publishers.

Castrillon, F. 2008. Digitizing the psyche: Human/Nature in the age of intelligent machines. In *Ecologies of the Psyche: Transdisciplinary Migrations of Critical Ecopsychology*, eds. D. Vakoch and F. Castrillon. Manuscript in preparation.

De Landa, M. 1991. *War in the Age of Intelligent Machines*. New York, NY: Zone Books.

Deleuze, G. and Guattari, F. 1987. *A Thousand Plateaus*. Minneapolis, MN: University of Minnesota Press.

Kubrick, S. 1968. *2001: A Space Odyssey*. Hollywood, CA: Warner Bros.

Numerous ecological issues can be traced to the worldview of the Earth as a machine for maximizing short-term human happiness for the consumer classes.

John Wilkinson

Beyond Machines
Metaphor in Biology

John Wilkinson

Introduction

One of the ironies of the Evolutionary Epic is that the new cosmology has adopted the idea of evolutionary change from the life sciences, yet the dominant theoretical framework of biological evolution relies on a metaphor inherited from classic Newtonian physics, the machine. Physicists abandoned the machine metaphor over a hundred years ago. If biologists want to do the same, they will require an alternative root metaphor for a new paradigm. Water is one example of a paradigmatic metaphor that is more inclusive than machines for evolutionary biology because it is multicultural, embodies the lived experience of the scientist, and covers a wider body of empirical evidence.[1]

The machine metaphor used in the Neo-Darwinian synthesis reflects a particular historical and socio-cultural matrix. It was inherited from the Enlightenment philosophies of Descartes and Newton and reflects the Victorian belief in progress through industrial mechanization. The human value placed on machines has varied widely between cultures and historical periods. In contrast, water has played a life-giving role in all human societies, not just European societies. For example, it was the root metaphor of many Classical Chinese philosophers (Allan, 1997). By applying the water metaphor to the existing empirical observations of evolutionary biology, a truly multicultural biology might be possible.

The machine metaphor has implicit in it a power dynamic between the scientist and the object of study. The relationship between human engineers and machines is one of creator and creature, which implies a Biblical relationship of dominion. Numerous ecological issues can be traced to the worldview of the Earth as a machine for maximizing short-term human happiness for the consumer classes. However, human scientists are also evolved living systems, so the relationship could be more accurately modeled as part to part. The wa-

---

1   The ideas presented in this summary paper have been previously published in much greater detail in my dissertation *The Rust in the Machine: A Metaphoric Hermeneutic of Evolutionary Biology Texts* (2005), UMI Number 3175044.

ter metaphor highlights this relationship because it is embodied in every cell, including those of the observing scientist.

Anglican natural theologians, such as William Paley (1809), argued that the living world was so complex that it required an explanation beyond Newtonian physics. Their proposed solution was that living things were machines specifically designed by God. While Darwin (1859) agreed that the living world was complex, he proposed natural selection, rather than intentional specific design, as an explanation. The use of language evoking machines in evolutionary biology is metaphoric, not objective. The machine metaphor is theoretically inconsistent because it explains complexity, but also implies design. It pushes to the background simple structures and non-adaptive change in living systems. Water remedies this difficulty by providing a heuristic for anomalies of the machine metaphor, while still not implying intentional design.

Developmental Biology

Developmental biology was never synthesized into the mechanistic Neo-Darwinian paradigm because machines do not assemble themselves. However, the formation of whirlpools, hurricanes, and other water vortices shows the spontaneous self-organization of a dissipative structure. Water molecules move through a whirlpool in the same way that material moves through a living system. Both living systems and vortices rely on continuing sources of high quality energy to maintain their form, and excrete low quality energy into the environment. The flow of energy gives a whirlpool its shape, while the individual water molecules cycle through. This is in contrast to machines, which do not integrate the molecules from their fuel into their physical structure. The phase transition from liquid water to the crystalline structure of ice is a physical example of a spontaneous transition from disorder to order, similar to the autopoiesis apparent in developmental biology.

Levels of Selection

The level of selection in evolution is an area of on-going debate. The reductionist tendencies of scientists employing the machine metaphor have focused on the role of DNA as the level of selection, to the exclusion of the individual, species, or eco-system. Water is a more encompassing metaphor because it has emergent qualities that are more than the aggregate of its atoms and, therefore, models multiple levels of selection.

One of the most important chemical properties of water is the intermolecular bonding caused by the slight polarity of the water molecule. In the classical Newtonian worldview, the water molecule consists of one relatively large oxygen atom attached to two smaller hydrogen atoms, and should theoretically have a boiling point well below zero degrees Celsius. However, water is anomalous in having higher boiling and melting points than comparably sized molecules because the oxygen atom attracts the shared electrons more strongly than hydrogen. This produces hydrogen bonding, an intermolecular attractive force approximately ten times stronger than the van der Waals' forces that hold most liquids together (Ball, 2000). Hydrogen bonding is an emergent property that can only be observed with two or more water molecules. A strictly mechanistic approach, focused on the atomic properties of oxygen and hydrogen, or even the molecular structure of water, will miss this emergent property that gives rise to many anomalous properties. The same is true for levels of selection: From the genome to the biosphere, every living system shows emergent qualities that cannot be understood from an examination of its constituent parts.

Rate of evolutionary change

Another area of argument, especially in paleontology, is the pace with which evolutionary change happens. Darwin applied Lyell's idea of uniform, slow change to evolution, arguing that morphology would change slowly through many intermediaries as a species became better fit to its environment. This fit well with Newton's machine metaphor. Natural selection operated slowly and almost imperceptibly, yet it was a natural law, outside of time and space. This ignores the data of punctuated equilibrium (Gould and Eldredge, 1977), including our current mass extinction.

The water metaphor is metonymic in describing the fossil record and the variable rates of evolution that it implies. Water is an inextricable part of the fossilization process, ice layer dating, and dendrochronology. The flow of a river can also describe both uniform change and punctuated equilibrium. Beyond its metonymic role, the behavior of water can act as a metaphor for both uniform change and punctuated equilibrium. When a river moves to the sea, it may take a slow meander, gradually losing elevation. The horizontal movement back and forth may mask the larger progression. The punctuated equilibrium model would be similar to a waterfall suddenly bursting into a new environment.

Non-genetic Physical Constraints on Evolution

The Neo-Darwinian synthesis postulates that continuous variability is caused by differences in inheritable genetic types, which are then selected by the environment. There are sometimes severe limits on variability due to the physics and chemistry of life on Earth (Thompson, 1917). The water metaphor can highlight these limits.

Ionization allows water to dissolve many chemicals into a solution. The addition of ions changes the arrangement of the water molecules. For example, the addition of a single positive ion of sodium will cause the water to form a primary hydration sphere of reoriented molecules, which causes a cascading effect throughout the water, as each molecule stabilizes at the most energetically favorable position (Ball, 2000). In both the cytoplasm and larger bodies of water that hold ions, order, disorder and reorder all happen spontaneously without DNA or an elaborate process of natural selection (Ball, 1999).

While the amino acid sequence is necessary for the primary structure of a protein, it is not sufficient to explain tertiary structure of proteins. Furthermore, allosteric proteins have the same nucleotide sequence in the DNA and identical primary structure (Keller, 2000). These proteins differ only in tertiary structure, and play different roles in cellular metabolism. The difference in their tertiary structure is managed by water (Ball, 2000).

The phospholipid bilayer of all cell membranes, one of the essential characteristics of living organisms, is formed spontaneously because the hydrophilic heads of the molecules will be attracted to the water molecules inside and outside of the cell. The hydrophobic tails of these molecules will spontaneously face each other, without recourse to a DNA-based genetic program (Ball, 1999).

Water is an apt metaphor for the modeling of biological systems using complexity theory. For example, convergent evolution can be mathematically modeled as a strange attractor creating a basin of attraction into which distantly related species evolve (Goodwin, 1994). This is in contrast to the Neo-Darwinian metaphor of fitness peaks, which are only attained through competitive individualism (Wright, 1931). The tendency for water to flow downhill into basins of attraction from all starting points of a watershed is a metaphor for these mathematical models.

Non-adaptive Structures

The machine metaphor is very useful in describing complex, adapted structures. However, this pushes simple structures with no obvious adaptive value, such as the toenail, into the background. There are some cases, such as parasites and vestigial organs, where the trend is away from previous levels of complexity, yet evolution is present. Because water undergoes phase changes between the solid, liquid, and gas states at the normal surface temperatures of the Earth, it can act as a better metaphor, encompassing both complex adaptive and simple, non-adaptive structures.

Throughout terrestrial eco-systems, the expansion of freezing water cracks rocks, creating the expanded surface area for soil formation. This means that rivers and streams generally grow in the opposite direction of flow, creating extended tributaries from the main stream. Dawkins (1995) has used this metaphor to describe phylogeny over geologic time. Because the crystal lattice of ice has a hexagonal symmetry, it displays some of the most diverse geometry in all of nature (Deacon, 2003). Under extremes of pressure, ice has been known to undergo at least eleven structural transitions (Ball, 2000). Ice provides a metaphor for evolution of complex structures.

The water metaphor addresses the simple structures underemphasized by the machine metaphor through the behavior of water vapor. The behavior of individual gas molecules is exceedingly complex, but at the larger level, water vapor behaves according to the simple ideal gas laws. Simplicity is an emergent structure describing both gaseous water and evolution.

Water vapor may be formed directly from ice at low pressures and temperatures through the process of sublimation. The boundary between liquid and gaseous water stops at a critical point. Beyond that, there is no clear distinction between the gas and liquid behavior of the water molecules. This serves to metaphorically highlight the many false dichotomies in evolutionary biology, such as phenotype/genotype or biotic/abiotic.

Biological Shaping of Environment

One of the weaknesses in the Neo-Darwinian synthesis is that natural selection is treated metaphorically as artificial selection, where a sentient being outside of the living system decides reproductive fitness (Ruse, 2003). The idea of organisms as robot vehicles for genes overlooks the way organisms actively shape their environment and may determine their own fitness (Goodwin, 1994). Water acts as a metaphor for the complex interaction of living systems and their environment.

The machine metaphor stresses interspecific competition for reproduction (Ruse, 1999). The direction of selection is unidirectional, from the environment to the population (Oyama, 2000). Theories that incorporate biogeological feedback loops, such as Lovelock and Margulis's (1974) Gaia, are incorporated in a water metaphor. Transpiration in vascular plants actively creates terrestrial environments more conducive to plant life.

Conclusion

The machine metaphor used in the Neo-Darwinian synthesis has difficulties explaining aspects of developmental biology, multiple levels of selection, rates of change in evolution, non-genetic constraints, non-adaptive structures, and biological shaping of the environment. Water is better able to describe all of these. The self-assembly of developing organisms is thermodynamically similar to whirlpool formation. Multiple levels of selection result from emergent qualities, such as the hydrogen bonding of water. Rate of evolution can be variable, such as a river's meander and waterfalls. Water creates some of the non-genetic constraints on variability, particularly in the cytoplasm. Water's role in plant transpiration highlights the complex interactive cycles in evolution.

References

Allan, S. 1997. *The Way of Water and Sprouts of Virtue.* Albany: State University New York Press.

Ball, P. 1999. *The Self-made Tapestry: Pattern Formation in Nature.* New York: Oxford University Press.

Ball, P. 2000. *Life's Matrix: A Biography of Water.* 1st ed. New York: Farrar, Straus, & Giroux.

Darwin, C. 1859. *On the Origin of Species by Means of Natural Selection or the Preservation of Favored Races in the Struggle of Life.* London: John Murray.

Dawkins, R. 1995. *River Out of Eden: A Darwinian View of Life.* New York: Basic Books.

Deacon, T. 2003. From matter to mattering. Paper presented at Esalen Institute's Evolutionary Theory Conference Series. Oct. 7, 2003. Big Sur: Esalen Press.

Goodwin, B. 1994. *How the Leopard Changed Its Spots: The Evolution of Complexity.* New York: C. Scribner's Sons.

Gould S. & Eldredge, N. 1977. Punctuated equilibria: the tempo and mode of evolution reconsidered. *Paleobiology, (3)*, 115-151.

Keller, E. 2000. *The Century of the Gene.* Cambridge, MA: Harvard University Press.

Lovelock, J. and Margulis, L. 1974) Atmospheric homeostasis by and for the biosphere: The Gaia hypothesis. *Tellus* 26:1-9.

Oyama, S. 2000. *Evolution's Eye: A Systems View of the Biology-Culture Divide.* Durham, NC: Duke University Press.

Paley, W. 1809. *Natural Theology: Or Evidences of the Existence and Attributes of the Deity, Collected from the Appearances of Nature.* 12th edition. London: J. Faulder.

Pielou, E. 1998. *Fresh Water.* Chicago: University of Chicago Press.

Ruse, M. 1999. *Mystery of Mysteries: Is Evolution a Social Construction?* Cambridge, MA: Harvard University Press.

Ruse, M. 2003. *Darwin and Design.* Cambridge: Harvard University Press.

Thompson, D. 1917. *On Growth and Form.* Cambridge, UK: Cambridge University Press.

Wright, S. 1931. Evolution in Mendelian populations. *Genetics, 28 (2)*, 114-8.

The fact that an observer—which in itself implies consciousness—is an established and necessary ingredient in modern physics has profound implications.

Gary Moring

Quantum Psychology
Bridging Science and Spirit

Gary Moring

Any discussion of evolutionary theory inherently and necessarily uses science as the cornerstone to illustrate how humanity fits into the context of the "Epic Story". This story and science's interpretation of it is only a recent development in the long line of ideas, beliefs, and theories that were born of humanity's need to understand our relationship to the universe in which we live. And as in any relationship, we are always looking for ways to deepen our experience and increase our understanding of the "other". Our self-awareness and the role our consciousness plays in this process are of ultimate importance.

As we enter into the twenty-first century, the fundamental role that consciousness plays in our experience of the world and its relationship to science will need to be addressed. The mechanistic models of the universe are losing their explanatory power, and understanding the organic connection between emergent matter and consciousness has the potential to radically change the way we look at evolution.

In the last century, secular and religious thinkers pondered the relationship of human consciousness to material reality. Traditionally, religious thinkers often framed their inquiry in terms of divine and human interaction—that is, religious revelations in which divine mediation is seen as having broken into the separated worlds of human and created matter. Consciousness is interpreted as having been extended from the divine realm to the human as if God reached across space to impart psychic vitality to the waiting bodies of humanity.

In the anthropocentric perspective of secular humanistic thinkers, matter often occupied a subservient, secondary position in which the nonhuman life-world was seen largely as being of service to or use by humans. The significance of personal human interactions with other humans was of primary importance, with any divine agency discounted. The empirical sciences further extended the idea that consciousness appears simply as an emergent phenomenon, having come from nothing but inert, nonconscious matter that composes the known universe.

However, there are a number of scientists, philosophers, and non-traditional religious thinkers who have come to question the beliefs and assumptions that underlie the mainstream, accepted view of necromorphic matter. The deep philosophic issues raised by the fact of human consciousness are beginning to bridge the age old duality of spirit and matter by understanding that ontology and epistemology are one and the same—that the physical cannot exist independently from the mental. And nowhere is this bridging beginning to occur more that in the realm of quantum physics.

The Paradox of Consciousness

Up until the advent of quantum theory, consciousness had no place in the equations of physics. In the classical model of the universe, irreducible balls of matter bounced around in three-dimensional space, obeying fixed laws of motion. This universe was both objective (independent of an observer) and determined (predictable). Modern physics offers a much less comforting picture. Quantum theory rests on a bed of indeterminacy at the particle level, and, while the predictive power of quantum theory is awesome, its philosophical underpinnings are vague. Reality cannot be said to exist in any fixed, solid way, and even the physical nature of matter is questionable. How, then do we account for our perception of such things as buildings and trees? Perhaps we account for them with a Zen-like koan (intuition) that proposes that the building is real, but does not have existence until it is observed. In the words of physicist John Wheeler:

> No elementary phenomenon is a phenomenon until it is a registered (observed) phenomenon... Useful as it is under everyday circumstances to say that the world exists "out there" independent of us, that view can no longer be upheld. (Wheeler 1983, 192)

Here is the paradox: We need particles of matter to make up the objects of our everyday world (including us), and we need an object in that everyday world (us) to define and observe those particles. Observation implies consciousness. Most physicists resist this implication, but at least some would agree that any construct that purports to describe reality in terms of contemporary physics clearly must include a role for consciousness.

In relativity theory, the particle described in classical physics is no longer a "thing" but a vortexlike disturbance in a continual field. Consciousness was introduced into physics in a certain sense because relativity theory requires that the frame of reference of the observer be taken into account. In quantum theory, the introduction of consciousness is even more basic. Physicist Fred Alan Wolf puts it this way:

> Classical physics holds that there is a real world out there, acting independently of human consciousness. Consciousness, in this view, is to be constructed from real objects, such as neurons and molecules. It is a byproduct of the material causes which produce the many physical effects observed. Quantum physics indicates that this theory cannot be true—the effects of observation "couple" or enter into the real world whether we want them to or not. The choices made by an observer alter, in an unpredictable manner, the real physical events. Consciousness is deeply and inextricably involved in this picture, not a byproduct of materiality. (Wolf, 1986, 257)

The Observer in Physics

The fact that an observer—which in itself implies consciousness—is an established and necessary ingredient in modern physics has profound implications. When scientists describe the world as made up of particles, they must of necessity include themselves in the construction. By definition, then, the scientist is part of the universe, and this part of the universe is observing itself. To accomplish this, the universe must be divided into an observer and that which is observed. What the observer sees is only that portion of the universe that is being observed, which does not include the observer. A new level with a wider field of view must be postulated if we are to include both the observer and that which is observed. Thus, we are forced to consider a hierarchy of consciousness. A hierarchy is an essential metaphor for visualizing both the observer and that which is observed. (Such a hierarchy is a simplified version of the Gödel incompleteness theorem, which can be construed as stating that if you have a finite theory of the world, there will always be certain truths that will not be provable by the theory).

A hierarchy is also seen in quantum theory. One of the basic postulates of quantum theory states that an initial system can potentially develop into a number of states, each with a given probability of occurrence. We know, though, that only one probability can actually take place. According to the accepted interpretation of quantum theory, the actual or "real" state of these probabilities is specified by an observation; that is, the "real" state is brought into reality by an observer. The observer thus becomes a creator and gives the system form. Without the observer, the system is in a state of potential, waiting to come into existence.

This approach had proved fruitful for closed systems with the physicist observing from the outside. But when one contemplates the grouping of probabilities for the entire universe—including the body of the observer—then the universe can come into existence only by the action of an observer outside the universe. Even if one were to accept an observer outside the universe, that observer would also have to be brought into reality by still another observer. Again, we are faced with an infinite hierarchy of observers.

According to quantum theory, mind gives form to *potential* (Heisenberg's term), which then exhibits the property of matter. We have come full circle: Matter appears to be an epiphenomenon of mind. This does not mean, however, that an electron is dependent on the *human* mind. Rather, if the electron is seen in some sense as being "alive," then it can have its own equivalent of observer and observed, its own form of consciousness.

If we no longer see *matter* as primary, but see *mind* as primary, then the push-pull laws of the mechanistic worldview are not adequate. Instead we might say that an "alive" particle responds to information, and force fields (e.g., electromagnetic and gravitational) might be viewed as information fields. This view is expressed by physicist Freeman Dyson:

> It's one of the joys of physics that matter isn't just inert stuff. In the Nineteenth century one thought of matter as just chunks of stuff which you could push and pull around, but they didn't do anything. Quantum mechanics makes matter even in the smallest pieces into active agent, and I think that is something very fundamental. Every particle in the universe is an active agent making choices between random processes. (Dyson 1982, 8)

The Need for Change

It is often said that most phenomena can be described with mechanical models—that the Newtonian laws hold for large-scale events, and that it is only at the far reaches of existence (the subatomic world, or particles moving at nearly the speed of light) that we see the peculiar effects of quantum and relativity theories. But this is not necessarily so. Events that deviate from Newtonian laws may occur in our everyday world without being observed simply because we are not looking. The following parable, attributed to Sir Arthur Eddington, the distinguished astrophysicist, raises this possibility using a particularly apt image:

> In a seaside village, a fisherman with a rather scientific bent proposed as a law of the sea that all fish are longer than one inch. But he failed to realize that the nets used in the village were all of one-inch mesh. Are we filtering physical reality? Can we catch consciousness with the nets we are using? (Zee 1986, 280)

Do anomalies exist on the macro level that we are simply not noticing or are allowing to slip through our scientific nets? Certain events, casually assigned to the paranormal and thereby dismissed, may contain information that would clarify persistent problems in our evolving worldview. Philosopher Huston Smith imagines the Perennial Philosophy addressing science and noting, "You are right in what you affirm. Only what you deny needs rethinking." (Smith, 1989, 63)

Certainly many insupportable ideas have been rightfully ignored, but one can speculate that useful information may have been overlooked as well. This is by no means confined to the science of our time. In the early 1600s the great Galileo Galilei (himself persecuted for heretical ideas) wrote the following attack on Johannes Kepler's idea that the moon affects the tides:

> Everything that has been said before and imagined by other people (concerning the origin of tides) is in my opinion complete nonsense. Among authorities who have theorized about the remarkable set of phenomena, I am most shocked by Kepler. He was a man of exceptional genius, he was sharp, he had a grasp of terrestrial movement, but he went on to take the bit between the teeth and get interested in a supposed action of the moon on water, and other "paranormal" phenomena—a lot of childish nonsense. (Comfort 1984, 24)

Perhaps without being aware of it, science has narrowed its field of vision and enlarged the holes of its net. But science itself must change, as it discovers that its net of evidence is equipped only to catch certain kinds of fish, and that it is constructed of webs of assumptions that can only hold certain varieties of reality, while others escape its net entirely. Of course, the quest to understand reality can never be completed. Some information will always be lacking; some ambiguity will always remain. Although there may be many brilliant insights, a total explanation is not and cannot be the goal. Rather, we can try to unfold a bit more, expand our vision, and extend our understanding. In the end, perhaps the most slippery fish in the net, as Eddington mentions, is consciousness.

References

Comfort, A. 1984. *Reality and Empathy: Physics, Mind and Science in the 21ˢᵗ Century*. Albany, NY: State University of New York Press.

Dyson, F. 1982. Theology and the origins of life. Lecture/discussion at the Center for Theology and the Natural Sciences, Berkeley, California (November 1982).

Smith, H. 1989. *Beyond the Post-Modern Mind*. Wheaton, IL: Theosophical Publishing House.

Wheeler, J. A. 1983. *Quantum Theory and Measurement*. Princeton, NJ: Princeton University Press.

Wolf, F. A. 1986. *The Body Quantum: The New Physics of Body, Mind, and Health*. New York, NY: Macmillan.

Zee, A. 1986. *Fearful Symmetry: The Search for Beauty in Modern Physics*. New York, NY: Macmillan.

Perhaps by becoming more connected to each other, we would realize how important it is to be "in touch" with other species as well as our planetary ecosystem, considering that we depend on both to sustain our existence.

Katie Carrin

Touch
An Evolutionary Key to Healthy Living

Katie Carrin

Contained within the epic story of the evolution of life on Earth is the chronicle of the unfolding and evolution of the sense of touch. From the earliest, most primitive single-celled organism that sought food by touching and interacting with its environment to the evolutionary developments which led to more refined forms of touch, it is the defining sense that allows us to know that there is something else outside of us. Touch is the greatest success story in evolutionary biology. Since the narrative of the development of touch is so vast, my purpose is to present the reader with a perspective that focuses on what may be the most pertinent to us: human interaction.

Touch plays a determining role in our health and well-being from conception through old age. In a society where technology often breeds isolation, to touch, to connect, to reach out to others is of paramount importance to our own health as well as the health of subsequent generations. Perhaps by becoming more connected to each other, we would realize how important it is to be "in touch" with other species as well as our planetary ecosystem, considering that we depend on both to sustain our existence.

Infancy: Touch, the Primary Sense

From the earliest stages of each human life, touch is central to a healthy development of body, mind, and spirit. Over the recent decades many studies were conducted which reveal the benefits of warm and caring touch, as well as the devastating effects of touch deprivation and isolation on human infants.

In the first six weeks after conception, touch is our first sense to develop, long before we acquire developed senses of hearing, seeing, tasting and smelling. We can feel our mother's movements, her heartbeat, and the amniotic fluid surrounding us through this primary sense. We feel the pressure of the birth canal, and later we are placed on our mother's breast, skin to skin. Our first form of communication, through the loving touch of our mother, nourishes us on many levels. She feeds us, bathes us, rocks us, plays with us, and comforts us, all through the medium of touch.

Scientists have confirmed that depriving newborn babies of touch is devastating to their well-being. The famous Harlow experiments in the 1950s were some of the earliest studies to confirm this fact (Harlow 1958). Infant Rhesus monkeys were taken from their mothers after birth and put into a cage with two surrogate mothers; one made of wire with a bottle attached for nursing, and the other made of wood covered with terrycloth. In the beginning, the babies would nurse from the bottle and then go cling to the terrycloth mother for comfort. Over time, many of the babies stopped eating and clung solely to the terrycloth mother. Many did not survive, preferring starvation to comfort deprivation. Of those that did survive, most exhibited violent behavior as adults and the inability to bond with their own babies. Others exhibited autistic behavior and had severe mental and physical problems.[1]

These early physical bonding experiences are very important for the healthy development of the part of the brain that facilitates social bonding and for forming healthy, loving, and long lasting relationships. Tragically many children in orphanages suffer from touch deprivation in much the same way as the monkeys in Harlow's experiments.

Saul M. Schanberg of Duke University (Field 2003, 67-71) found that a mother's touch has tangible biological effects. Dr. Schanberg's research demonstrated that the separation of neonatal rat pups from their mothers caused a significant drop in the level of growth hormone in the pups and an increased level of corticosterone, a stress hormone. Upon returning the pups to their mothers and allowing them to receive the natural grooming and licking, the growth hormone levels normalized and the stress hormone levels dropped. The licking behavior of the mother could be mimicked with a wet paintbrush applied by lab researchers and similar results achieved. (Dr. Schanberg observed, "I couldn't get the lab technicians to actually lick the pups.")

Prof. Michael Meaney, PhD., of McGill University's Departments of Psychiatry, Neurology, and Neurosurgery, found that different levels of maternal care can influence brain development and the ability to deal with stress later in life (Meaney 1999). Researchers counted the number of times a mother rat licked her pups and how their brains responded to this stimulus. Researchers found that the pups of the high-licking mothers developed better neural networks, enabling them to cope better with stress throughout their lives compared to low-licking mothers.

Significantly, babies of high-licking mothers became high-licking mothers, and babies of low-licking mothers became low-licking mothers. When the pups of low-licking mothers were given to high-licking mothers, they also

---

1   It is unfortunate that studies of this kind end up abusing and traumatizing animals to obtain results that give insights into the importance of touch. I am certainly not here condoning this type of "research." The information obtained, however, does reveal just how significant touch is to the well-being of all species.

developed better neural networks to deal with stress, and these pups in turn became high-licking mothers. The external environment, illustrated in this case by touch, was shown to have a long-term effect down through generations. These studies illustrate epigenetics, a field of science exploring the connection between our environment and our genetic encoding.

In the mid 1980s, Tiffany Field, Director of the Touch Research Institute at the University of Miami, School of Medicine, became famous for her research with premature babies. She found that when premature babies received 15 minutes of massage three times a day, they gained 47 percent more weight than the babies that received normal handling (Field 2003, 119-124). They were also more alert, had increased motor activity, slept better, were less stressed, suffered less discomfort, and had better bonding time with parents.

Our first sensory input comes from the sense of touch, and touch continues to be one of the most important means for learning about the world and interacting with it. The next section examines how touch plays a role as the child matures.

Childhood: Nourishing Touch and Proper Development

Hans Axelson, founder and principal of Axelson's Institute, Sweden, began the Peaceful Touch project in 1995. Peaceful Touch is a healthy touch curriculum for children. It integrates touch into children's activities, from games and storytelling to reading, math, and science. In Sweden, more than 300,000 children regularly practice Peaceful Touch at school. Swedish teachers and parents say that children in this program exhibit less stress, anxiety, and aggression. They also display better concentration, are more empathetic, and function better in groups. The Peaceful Touch program is based on three fundamentals:

(1) Touch is necessary for human growth and development.
(2) The calming hormone, oxytocin, is activated through touch.
(3) A permission process supports appropriate touch and helps establish good boundaries.

Hans Axelson, in cooperation with Kerstin Uväs-Morberg M.D., PhD., conducted a study examining the effects of healthy touch on children in schools (Moberg 2003, 137-138). Dr. Uväs-Morberg is recognized as a world authority on oxytocin. The hormone oxytocin acts both as a hormone and as a neuropeptide. It triggers a complex series of reactions that enhances the body's relaxation and calms the mind. This is important for two reasons. The first is the immediate health benefit of lowering stress-related symptoms, and the second is that repeated dosages of oxytocin seem to convert the immediate benefit of relaxation and calmness into a long lasting effect. Oxytocin levels can be increased through friendly touch, massage, physical exercise, and intimacy.

The original study indicated that the school children responded positively and benefited greatly from the program. Interestingly, the children who benefited the most were the boys who previously were most disruptive in classes; their behavior became less aggressive than that of comparable children who did not receive massage. These findings have an obvious implication for dealing with the violence and misbehavior plaguing our schools.

Unfortunately, this scientific understanding of the importance of touch is not yet shared by western societies. The *Charlotte (NC) Observer* reported that an 8th grade girl was given two days of detention for hugging a friend good-by, thereby violating a school policy against public displays of affection. The student handbook of school policy states, "Displays of affection should not occur on the school campus at any time. It is in poor taste, reflects poor judgment, and brings discredit to the school and to the persons involved." A no-touch policy in schools does not allow students and teachers to take responsibility for their actions and learn how to touch appropriately in a healthy and respectful way. It instead promotes fear and suspicion.

Adulthood: Human Contact, a Remedy for Stress

As we become adults, we enter into a world where stress can play a significant role in our daily lives and can have a severe, negative impact on our well-being. Hans Style coined the use of the term "stress" in 1936, after observing laboratory animals developing human-like pathology in response to noxious physical and emotional stimuli. Although stress is highly subjective in humans, its harmful effects are numerous, including heart attack, stroke, kidney disease, rheumatoid arthritis, and mild-to-severe mental disturbances.

Tiffany Field's research found that by mitigating the harmful effects of stress, therapeutic touch was highly beneficial to health. She reports that some of the benefits include the decrease of stress and anxiety and their behavioral and biochemical manifestations, and positive effects on growth, brain waves, breathing, heart rate, and the immune system.

A research team at Ohio State University School of Medicine studied the effects of a high-fat diet on cholesterol levels and arterial thickening in rabbits (Chopra 1990, 30-31). As expected, overall they found a strong positive correlation between fat in the diet and arterial blockage due to cholesterol. However, to the surprise of the researchers, one group of rabbits failed to show an increase in cholesterol. Here's why: the person in charge of feeding the rabbits did not just throw the food in the bowl. This lab technician gave his particular group special care. He had a habit of holding, petting, and talking softly to a rabbit while feeding it by hand. The research team decided to repeat the experiment with two groups of rabbits. The group that received petting and stroking had significantly less arterial thickening than the group that did not experience touch.

The rabbit experiment made me think of writing a new diet book titled the "Massage Diet" in which one could have a foot massage while eating dark chocolate! I am sure it would hit the best-seller list. Joking aside, my experience as a massage therapist and instructor convinces me of the profound physiological and psychological effects of healing touch.

Touch lies at the center of traditional medical systems around the world. India, Thailand, Japan, and China in particular have traditional medical models that incorporate the positive and powerful effects of therapeutic touch. The practitioners of these systems have appreciated the necessity of touch in the healing process for thousands of years. Western scientists are now starting to understand the wisdom of these ancient traditions.

Therapeutic touch along with exercise, laughter, a healthy diet, and relaxation are the keys that will enable us to enjoy a long, healthy, happy, life.

Senior Years: Aging Gracefully, Through Giving and Receiving Touch

In our society many of the elderly become isolated due to loss of a spouse, illness or geographic distance from family and friends. Because of a decrease in social interaction the likelihood of touch deprivation increases. Many older people experience failure to thrive because of touch deprivation, just as some infants do.

In the second phase of the study that Tiffany Field conducted with premature babies, the research focused on the effects of giving massage verses receiving massage (Field 2003, 127-128). Two groups of elderly people (who preferred to be called grandparents) were observed. One group was assigned to massage premature babies and the other group received regular massage. Both groups of grandparents experienced positive personal and social results. They had more social interaction, drank less coffee, had fewer trips to see the doctor, had better sleeping patterns, less depression, and greater self-esteem. One of the grandmothers that gave massage to the premature babies summed up her experience with the study by saying that she felt alive and young again.

Caring, healthy touch is a physical expression of love, and it brings about a harmonious connection between our world and us. Love and affection do not just belong to the realm of romance or poetry. They make significant biochemical and physiological contributions to our well-being.

Pet therapy is also a positive healthy tactile experience for the elderly. J. Lynch and his colleagues reported that older people who had pets outlived those who did not (Field 2003, 30). Staff at a senior center reported that the elderly residents perked up when the pet therapy animals arrived. The room once characterized by boredom and lethargy came alive. One woman sighed and happily sank her face into a bunny's soft fur and another hugged a little puppy. Pet therapy can increase the state of overall health, especially feelings of depression due to touch depravation and isolation.

As we age, we begin to lose our sense of sight, sound, smell, and taste; but we still have our sense of touch to give and receive, allowing us to feel the connection to our community. The basic human need for touch maintains not only the health of the body and the mind, but also nourishes the human spirit.

The Future: Reaching Out

Our sense of touch has evolved from the very beginning of life on this planet. It is fundamental to who we are, as well as to all other life that surrounds us. Today, many of us are becoming more and more isolated and have fewer possibilities for physical connection. We need to be mindful of this social predicament and seek out caring touch with the human as well as other-than-humans with whom we share our days. With mature boundaries developed, touch is a precious gift rather than an intrusive act. We have limitless opportunities to learn from the valuable information compiled by researchers cited in this article. A simple pat on the back for a job well done, a comforting hug to a friend in need, holding hands with a loved one, or shaking hands with a business associate, cuddling a puppy, or tending a garden are caring acts of touch which have profound effects on the giver as well as the recipient. No pharmacy prescription can replace the warmth of touch. We do not need any expensive or fancy equipment; we just need an open heart and the willingness to reach out to others.

References

Chopra, D. 1990. *Quantum Healing: Exploring the Frontiers of Mind/Body Medicine*. New York, NY: Bantam books.

Field, T. 2003. *Touch*. Cambridge, MA: MIT.

Harlow, H. F. 1958. The nature of love. *American Psychologist, 13*, 673-685.

Meaney, M. 1999. Nongenomic transmission across generations of maternal behavior and stress responses in the rat. *Science, 286* (5442), 1155-1158.

Moberg, K. U. 2003. *The Oxytocin Factor*. Cambridge, MA: Da Capo Press.

PART V

The Epic Guides Our Path to the Future

Cheryl Genet

> However cool-headed we may remain as we try to piece together the scientific evidence for the evolutionary epic, it is hard to resist a sense of awe as we realize that we, in our tiny corner of the universe, represent the universe becoming aware of itself.... We are, after all, the only creatures of which we know, that can begin to grasp the story of the universe and infuse it with meaning and feeling.
>
> David Christian

An enduring image of the value of touch proposed at the end of the last section is a description of the simple love of company found among San Bushmen in "Future Primal." "People sit close together, often touching, with ankles interlocked." The San teach us much about our primal selves and offer lessons for "radically democratizing the process of political paradigm construction." A shift away from the global paradigm of industrial capitalism may be rooted in primordial philosophy—the truth quest, or wisdom as knowledge of the best way to live. A "mandala of primal politics" provides a model of four processes that converge in the truth quest.

Many suspect that the path to a sustainable future for humanity and planet Earth will be guided by our understanding of our evolutionary path. Humanity's "truth quest" suggests in itself one of our critical capacities, that of cultural transmission. "Transcending Cultural Indoctrination" argues that some cultural indoctrination, howerver, is clearly maladaptive but persists for physiological and neurological reasons we are only now coming to understand from an evolutionary perspective. It concludes that benign altered states of consciousness may assist us in transcending maladaptive core beliefs as a critical evolutionary step towards our collective future—"a giant evolutionary leap."

"Cosmology and Environmentalism" provides some very concrete steps for applying our new story to "the process of transforming the Earth Community from its current destructive stage and into a new era of vibrant good health." "Islands of Sustainability," a collaborative effort not only of the conference panel but ongoing within the state of Hawaii, is in many ways a case study of applying the new story, and rich cultural traditions, to a sustainable future while overcoming "maladaptive cultural transmission."

Both indigenous spiritual cultures such as found in Hawaii, and Western religious cultures such as Catholicism, have cosmologically generated traditions of "Listening to the Voice of the Earth." From a Catholic perspective it is suggested that the evolutionary story provides a rich context for liturgical practice and symbols. Through combining both secular and religious attention to the natural objects encountered in the liturgy, both cosmic and sacred traditions can be integrated.

> With the rise of classical civilizations comes division of labor, specialization, and hierarchy. Walls are built between wilderness and civilization. Warfare and slavery appear. Bureaucracies of church and state replace the more democratic and accessible technologies of shamanic religion. As a result, the synergistic primal complex fragments.
>
> Louis Herman

Future Primal
A Politics for Evolving Humanity
Louis G. Herman

He who understands the baboon would do more towards metaphysics than Locke. Charles Darwin

The most beautiful thing we can experience is the mysterious. It is the source of all true art and science. Albert Einstein

Hunting is like dancing. You are talking with God when you are doing these things. Nqate Nqamabe, Bushman hunter

Introduction

As we progress further into the 21st century we face a situation where our institutions seem utterly incapable of even grasping, let alone dealing with the multi-layered crisis facing humanity. The ruling global paradigm of politics—industrial capitalism—is based on an anthropocentric Lockean-Cartesian understanding of the human condition that is profoundly destructive. One of the consequences is that all of the earth's ecosystems are collapsing. We are living through the greatest mass extinction since the cosmic event that ended the age of the dinosaurs 65 million years ago. The shocking fact is that we are directly responsible. More than six and a half billion humans, armed with industrial technology, fueled by abundant oil, motivated by avarice, restrained only by the most minimal governance, drive this doomed process. This is compounded by another shocking fact—most of us do not even know we are doing this. Mountains of information distract and bury the wisdom of the big picture. Our science promotes hyper-specialization, favoring analysis over synthesis, deconstruction over construction, and precision over meaning. The search for 'how best to live'—the truth (or wisdom) quest—has all but disappeared from both university and government.

Thomas Kuhn's great insight has been to expose the inherently limited nature of all paradigms, and, by extension, the limitations of all political paradigms (Kuhn 1962). With this in mind, my paper argues that the most significant step we need to take toward a new paradigm of politics that is adequate to the maginitude of our crisis requires *radically democratizing the process of political paradigm construction.* I see this process as rooted in primordial phi-losophy—the Socratic 'truth quest'—a model of wisdom as knowledge of the best way to live. At its most ambitious, this aspires to a task formerly reserved for the geniuses of political philosophy—deconstructing and reconstructing worldviews or paradigms of the 'Good Life.' My contention is that we have in place the wealth, the technology, the self understanding, and the compelling need to open this activity to a critical mass of humanity, and then sustain it as the gyroscope at the center of our politics. I believe that nothing short of such a collective, creative exertion can generate the enthusiasm and wisdom we need to get through our perilous situation. As a result, humanity could make an evolutionary leap equivalent to when we first settled in farming villages.

I begin by connecting central insights regarding the human condition from three intellectual giants of the modern period: Charles Darwin, Albert Einstein, and the still uncelebrated political philosopher Eric Voegelin.[1] Col-lectively, they illuminate how the truth quest emerges out of the paradox of human consciousness evolving from wilderness. I then compare the role of the truth quest in organizing the politics of two primal societies. The first is the traditional San Bushmen, hunter-gatherers of Southern Africa. The San are now being recognized as the people with the most direct cultural and genetic continuity to that aboriginal human population on the cusp of wilderness and civilization from which we all descended some 60,000 years ago. The second society is the Greek Polis during the classical period from around 600 to 300 BC. This is the primal society for Western civilization from which our science, history, philosophy, and the very word 'politics' itself springs.

What emerges is an understanding of the truth quest composed of ele-ments of a rudimentary, archetypal, 'primal politics'—a tightly interrelated complex of four opposite but complementary values and processes that I il-lustrate with a *mandala* (see diagram opposite page):

♦ **The whole person** as a model of individuality based on growth through directly experiencing and symbolically grasping an ever-larger range of archetypal human experiences.

♦ **Face-to-face discussion** as the Socratic *dialektike*—the primary mode of teaching and learning and thus a crucial component of individual growth in wholeness.

♦ **Direct democracy** as the small face-to-face group of discussants in the primary arena for decision making and conflict resolution.

---

1   This obscurity is likely to change with the publication of the final and 34th volume of Voegelin's collected works. (Voegelin, 1956/1987; 1989/2008.)

• **The big picture** as a basic unit of cognition connecting parts into wholes which can be connected into ever more inclusive wholes. It can also be conceptualized as **the big story**—stories nested within ever-more inclusive stories connecting each unique individual to family, tribe, community, nation, and, ultimately, the cosmos.

MANDALA OF PRIMAL POLITICS

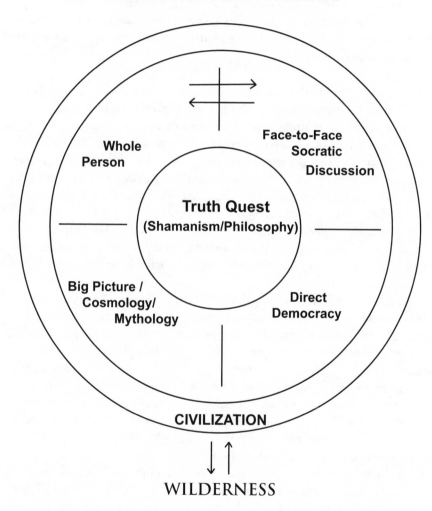

The four elements emerge in the earliest human societies, bound up as a single paradoxical complex, fundamental to our evolving humanity. Each component functions in an antagonistic and complementary dynamic with the others. The structure of a *mandala*—a circle subdivided into four opposite quadrants—helps to grasp this unity of opposites. *Mandalas* are the oldest known symbols occurring in virtually all cultures at all times and in all cases seeming to represent a unity made up of opposites. The four processes converge in the truth quest at the center of the circle. The whole is surrounded by wilderness—the inescapable larger reality from which civilization emerges. I suggest that pursuing the truth quest within an experience of immersion in our wilderness home sets up something like a *noetic*[2] field of force which helps hold the four components of politics in a creative but stable balance. In conclusion I point to seeds of this 'politics of the truth quest' emerging in a variety of arenas as a response to our planetary predicament—intimations of our next evolutionary leap.

The Paradoxical Truth Quest

Darwin confronts us with the fact that human and baboon shared a common ancestor six million years ago and that we have spent most of the rest of that time co-evolving as partners-in-being within an African wilderness. We are a savannah-incubated primate with a "blazing imagination" as Brian Swimme puts it. This is the paradox at the core of the human condition: we are born within an ongoing evolutionary event receding billions of years into the past. We awake to consciousness emerging out of unconsciousness. We are created by what we are not. Wilderness makes civilization. The *experience* of this foundational paradox is what generates our philosophy, religion, ethics, and politics—all our seeking and striving for 'how best to live.'

Einstein's genius was to experience this paradox through mathematics and physics and then deepen the insight by recognizing that the entire universe is growing; that in fact 'it grew us'—the curious, imaginative, wonder-filled human being. He then crossed the boundary between physics and philosophy, looked at himself looking, and then in a state of amazement recognized this as the universal mystical experience. He understood that rather than putting an end to science and philosophy, such experiences of radical mystery are ecstatic moments of heightened cognition—"the source of all true art and science." They have content and emotional charge which inspires, empowers, and guides us in knowing and living the best possible life.

Eric Voegelin was the first philosopher to develop the implications of this insight for politics. His encyclopedic exploration of the quest through the course of the history of world civilizations culminated in clarifying the paradoxical dynamic of consciousness (Voegelin 1956/87; 1989/2008). He used Plato's term *metaxy*, meaning 'in-between', to describe human existence as fun-

---

2   I use *noetic* in the sense of the Greek *noesis*— relating to mind and aspects of cognition.

damentally paradoxical—in-between 'reality' and 'consciousness-of-reality.' We cannot step outside of our own consciousness to grasp consciousness as if it were a thing. Nor can we consciously grasp reality as if we were not part of the same reality we are trying to grasp. 'Consciousness' and 'reality' are opposites, yet they are inextricably bound together in all questions of value and meaning, all knowledge that really *matters*. We live in-between subject and object; inner and outer; mind and body—what Voegelin called the tensional complex of "consciousness-reality-language." If we think of the terms in the pairs of opposites as setting up boundaries between one another, philosophy becomes the task of seeking knowledge through boundary crossing—a dialectical exploration of our *metaxic* condition.

Several things follow. We become conscious within a civilizational process that in part defines us. We then discover civilization to be a very recent stage of an immensely ancient and mysterious evolutionary process that shapes us even more profoundly. The universe is a story telling us into being. The narrative of developments over time—the story—then becomes a primary unit of meaning. But certainty is impossible since the story is not over. We can never know the whole plot; we can make mistakes, spoil things. Nor can we abstain from acting. Herein lies the anxiety of human freedom and creativity. Our choices have consequences. But with anxiety and humility also comes amazement at the miracle of existence and enthusiasm for participating in the drama of history. We wake up to our agency, realizing, as Voegelin put it, that "the primary instrument of philosophy" is the life of the individual. Personal growth—the cultivation of the whole person—becomes both an end in itself and a crucial component of the truth quest. We search with our lives and are transformed in the process. Both pre-literate shaman and astrophysicist have something essential to contribute.

By contrast, the dominant practice of science within the constraints of industrial society eclipses the primary experience of the *metaxy*. Cartesian-Lockean dualism posits an absolute separation between conscious subject and unconscious object, mind and body, humanity and nature. We abandon the life of the individual as a measure of truth. In return we get the manipulative predictive power of technology—the knowledge which enables us to splice genes and rocket humans to the moon. But we lose access to the sort of ecstatic and humbling insight that Einstein insisted needs to be at the heart of our quest. We also lose an associated capacity for paradoxical thinking, for 'boundary crossing,' essential to living in the tension between opposites. This contraction of consciousness is at the root of the materialism, the addictive consumerism, and the despair that drives our current catastrophe. Not surprisingly it is in the oldest, most neglected and persecuted society on earth—the San Bushmen hunter-gatherers of the Southern African Kalahari Desert—that we find the most dynamic and complete expression of a paradoxical politics.

Primal Politics

Small isolated groups of San continue into the present, hunting and gathering in the company of the same charismatic mega-fauna—lion, leopard, cheetah, hyena and the great herds of browsing and grazing animals that shaped our humanity. From the perspective of the grotesque wealth of industrial societies, the San live in abject poverty—traditionally owning little more than skins, stick, beads, and pots. Yet their wealth in leisure and social and spiritual life is possibly unequalled. Anthropologists described such hunter gatherers as 'the original affluent society' living in a kind of 'Zen affluence' with 2-3 days of work a week per adult sufficient to provide food for the band (Leacock and Lee, 1982). If longevity and resilience are any measure, the San are also the most successful society on earth.

Here we can see the elemental opposites of human existence—the individual and the community—in a constant dialectic of give and take, push and pull. The society is at once fiercely individualistic and at the same time strenuously egalitarian and democratic—intimately bonded by an ethic of caring and sharing. The boastful are teased mercilessly, the stingy called "bags without openings" and told "only lions eat alone." When a skilled hunter makes a kill, the meat belongs not to him but the owner of the arrow fired. His arrows are marked, many belonging to others—perhaps an older woman or a child or a man too feeble to hunt. Beyond this ethic of sharing is a simple love of company. People sit close together, often touching, with ankles interlocked. Loneliness is intolerable and ostracism the greatest punishment.

Yet the whole person stands out sharply—each "a big frog in a very small pond"—argumentative, independent, and assertive (Guenther 1999, 40). When one anthropologist asked "Do you have leaders?" he was told "Yes—of course we have leaders. Everyone is a leader over himself." The economics of hunting and gathering provides the most unshakeable economic foundation for individual self sufficiency. Resources—the waterholes, pans, and animals of the veld—are available to all. Since relevant knowledge is shared openly, virtually everyone has the capacity to go off on their own, should they wish, and live directly off the land, gather food, make clothing, and build shelter. This sense of autonomy and being at home in the world is reinforced by the egalitarian ethic. Everyone is taken care of. Perhaps no other society offers each individual a richer range of archetypal human experiences: provider, producer, healer, home builder, artist, musician, dancer, politician, and priest.

Conversely, much of the anxieties of modern life are due to lack of control over the fundamental processes necessary for our survival. Few of us could feed our families by hunting and gathering or growing our own food. Even fewer could build and repair a house, computer, car, or phone. No citizen is more compelled by dire necessity to conform than the obedient wage earner or the rule-bound bureaucrat in the hierarchies of our industrial societies.

Politics is ubiquitous in San life. The tensions between individuals and the group are constantly mediated by discussion. The camp is filled with endless conversation—chatting joking, arguing, and storytelling. Bushmen call themselves "lovers of argument." When decisions have to be made or conflicts resolved, everyone joins in—men and women, young and old—until a consensus is reached. Elections would seem strange to the San—disrespectful of each individual's unique contribution. They would diminish politics as an arena for truth sharing, for stimulating personal growth in wholeness, and for collectively constructing shared open ended 'big pictures.' Precisely because of its compact simplicity, the big picture is not an abstraction, as is the 'nation state' for example—but rather a collection of unique individuals each with his or her idiosyncrasies, frailties, and virtues—the lazy and the energetic, the generous and the selfish, the clown and the healer—each on a personal trajectory between birth and death. Everyone walks on the same sand, sits around the same fire, surrounded by the same wilderness community under the same moon and stars, and at times dying in one another's company. Everyone is involved in thinking of 'the good of the whole.'

Shamanism deepens the components of primal politics as they converge in the truth quest at the center of politics. Shamanism is now being understood as a kind of Ur-religion that recedes into the earliest origins of culture, comprising a wide variety of techniques for inducing extraordinary trance-like states of consciousness. The evolutionary narrative of consciousness tells us that 'inner' and 'outer' evolve as tensional poles splitting a single reality. Shamanism emerges as a creative human response to this tension. It offers ways of expanding conciousness through crossing the boundaries between the ego and the unconscious, of the inner and outer, wilderness and civilization. For a shamanic society like the bushman, where the village is embedded in wilderness, these borders can be easily crossed. When a bushman hunter attempts to outrun a kudu (a large desert-adapted antelope) during the midday heat, the distinction between hunter and animal dissolve. After a few hours the hunter enters an ecstatic state of consciousness. He describes "becoming Kudu . . . putting on Kudu mind," feeling her strength leaving her body and entering his. After the kill, he explains that hunting is like dancing: "you are talking with God when you are doing these things."[3]

---

3   This remarkable event was recorded for the first time in the feature documentary film *The Great Dance: A Hunter's Story* by Craig and Damon Foster. Cape Town South Africa: Earthrise/Off the Shelf Productions 2001

Such shamanic shifts of consciousness reverberate back into the political culture. Boundary crossing between all opposites becomes easier—a dialectic symbolized by the oscillating arrows between the *mandala* of civilization and the surrounding wilderness (see diagram). Here we have a model of the truth quest as governor of the primordial political dynamic—quintessentially human, ongoing and accessible to all.

Civilization and its Discontents

With the rise of classical civilizations comes division of labor, specialization, and hierarchy. Walls are built between wilderness and civilization. Warfare and slavery appear. Bureaucracies of church and state replace the more democratic and accessible technologies of shamanic religion. As a result, the synergistic primal complex fragments. The opposing elements become institutionalized and develop in isolation. The individual becomes one-dimensional, losing access to the full range of human experience, no longer capable of participating directly in collective decision making, no longer contributing to the collective truth quest. Interestingly, shamanism continues as a subterranean current in most religious traditions; and the archetype of the four primary values survives intact below the surface of politics, re-emerging in periods of crisis, transition, and cultural creativity.

The classical Greek polis seems to explode into history with a creative brilliance that is associated with the cultivation of all the elements of primal politics. In contrast to the centralized juggernaut of the Persian Empire, the ideal of the polis becomes that of a small scale, self sufficient (*autarkic*), and self governing community—no more than 5000 citizens suggested Plato and Aristotle. The Greek ideal of individual excellence or *arête* is to participate in all areas of life—independent farmer, gallant soldier, sensitive poet, generous citizen. The hero is no longer the full time specialist or the expert, but rather its opposite—the part-time amateur, the whole person. The truth quest emerges in Greek political philosophy around the Socratic Method—the boundary crossing *dialektike* of morally driven face-to-face-discussion, guided by an overriding concern to comprehend the whole, the big picture. There is even evidence to suggest Socrates was initiated into the Eleusinian mysteries and was inspired by shamanic states of consciousness (E.R. Dodds 1964; Carl Ruck 1981). All of this seems to reverse the trajectory of civilization towards increased divisions of labor and hierarchies of wealth and power.

However, the realization of primal ideals for the polis was, both in theory and practice, incomplete—compromised by the larger context of slavery, empire, and patriarchy. Nevertheless the genius of the Greeks lay in their recognizing, and attempting to hold in consciousness, the tension between the humanity of the compact primordial complex and the differentiating brilliance of civilization.

From this perspective we can then see the San as an 'ultra-polis'—smaller, more personal, more egalitarian, totally self-sufficient, and offering the individual more complete participation in both politics and philosophy. Its extraordinary resilience lies in its capacity for holding opposites in balance, a capacity rooted in a shamanic metaphysics of boundary crossing—what Emerson demanded for each of us—an "original relationship to the universe."

A Tao of Politics

Our current emerging best and biggest picture tells us that the paradoxical structure of humanity-consciousness-reality is not static. The conscious creative human being is the latest achievement of an evolutionary process which has, over eons, been producing ever-increasing complexity and consciousness of living forms. From this perspective, global industrial capitalism, initially a 'complexifying' novelty, now looks like a regression. Lockean Liberalism liberated the individual from the constraints of a corrupt feudal theocracy while at the same time it unleashed a fundamentalism of limited governance, free markets, and self interest which shunned the idea of the individual taking responsibility for the whole. Further advancement in complexity consciousness will require reversing the relationship between monetary wealth and wisdom by restructuring institutions and directing resources towards expanding invidual awareness, responsibility, and power. Or put another way, the challenge for us today is to meet, and then surpass, the achievement of the polis in holding the tension between the compact primal order and the differentiation of a global civilization.

There are exciting movements towards decentralization. Some creative economists are proposing a model global economy as a multi-level system of increasingly autonomous but interdependent parts. These would range from household economies to local, regional, national, and supra-national groups like the European Union and WTO. The novelty of this approach would be to transform the flow of power, resources, and information so that each larger, higher level economic unit would *enable the constituent sub-economies to be more autonomous and sustainable* (Daly and Cobb 1989; Henderson 2007).

We can see expressions of this in many contexts. The small rural country of Bhutan is now measuring progress in terms of Gross National Happiness rather than Gross National Product, and reorganizing its politics according to equitable and sustainable economies, decentralized decision making, expanded education, and the promotion of traditional culture. In Brazil over one hundred cities have followed the example of Porto Allegre in allowing citizens direct participation through local councils in setting the city budget. A more grass roots approach is shown by the rapidly growing global eco-village movement, which might become one of the most complete expressions of the primal archetype.[4] This is a loose network of intentional communities with varying degrees of co-operative integration in the service of a vision of a sustainable way of life connected to the Earth, ensuring the well-being of all life forms. The communities draw on principles of ecological design, permaculture, organic gardening, green production, and use of alternative and renewable energy source. Most communities recognize the humanizing magic of small face-to-face social structures whereby people have an opportunity to express their individual creativity and cultivate wisdom *through supporting, and being supported by, the community.*

At the same time, information technologies are being rapidly democratized. The personal computer and world-wide-web have given the individual voice of instantaneous global reach. Never before has a critical mass of humanity been able to access and contribute to the accumulated wisdom of the ages. Taken together, such future-primal initiatives can be seen to be moving individuals toward acting locally guided by a sense of responsibility for the whole—ultimately the planet. From this perspective, we can recognize that primal politics is indeed another 'paradigm of politics,' but unique in that it operates at a higher order of self-reflection than any previous paradigm. It grasps the process of its own creation—the truth quest—as *the* central ongoing component of practical politics. To use Kuhnian language, this would be equivalent to institutionalizing at the center of politics a 'revolutionary science' of political paradigm construction and reconstruction in which the revolutionary technologies would be 'psycho-technologies' of consciousness (Kuhn 1962). Put differently, future primal would be a *Tao of Politics* in which the path of searching for the good life—the *Tao* or the 'Way' of Chinese philosophy—becomes itself the core 'religious' practice of the Good Life one seeks. In the process, human politics would once again promote evolutionary growth in complexity consciousness.

Author's Note

This chapter is based on a book manuscript offering a paradigm for a species politics. It is also the basis of a feature film project *The Primal Quest*: see <http://socrates.uhwo.hawaii.edu/SocialSci/louisher/LHerman-Quest.html> or contact the author at louisher@hawaii.edu.

---

4   An earlier version with a deficient ecological and spiritual component was the Israeli Kibbutz of the 30's, at one time the defining institution of the new nation. There are recent signs of a recovery in Israel of a more holistic vision—including urban applications.

References

Daly, H. E. and Cobb, J. B. 1989. *For the Common Good: Redirecting the Economy Toward Community, the Environment and a Sustainable Future.* Boston: Beacon Press.

Dodds, E. R.1964. *The Greeks and the Irrational.* Berkeley CA: Berkeley Press.

Forte, R. 1997/2000. *Entheogens and the Future of Religion.* San Francisco: Council of Spiritual Practices.

Guenther, M. 1999. *Tricksters and Trancers: Bushman Religion and Society.* Bloomington & Indianapolis, IN: Indiana University Press.

Henderson, H. 2007. *Ethical Markets: Growing the Green Economy.* White River, VT: Chelsea Green Publishing.

Kuhn, T. 1962. *The Structure of Scientific Revolutions.* Chicago, IL: University of Chicago Press.

Leacock, E. and Lee, R. (eds.). 1982. *Politics and History in Band Societies.* New York, NY: Cambridge University.

Ruck, C. A.P.1981. Mushrooms and Philosophers. *Journal of Ethnopharmacology*, 4, 179-205.

Voegelin, E. 1956/1987. *Order and History Volumes I-V.* Baton Rouge, LA: LSU Press.

Voegelin, E.1989-2008. *Collected Works Volumes 1-34.* Columbia, MO: University Missouri Press.

The process of reframing core beliefs involves the creation and consolidation of new neural pathways and necessitates both conscious and non-conscious processes. When core beliefs are revised, new patterns of thinking and behaving emerge.

Jack Palmer and Linda Palmer

Transcending Cultural Indoctrination
Separating the Wheat from the Chaff

Jack A. Palmer and Linda K. Palmer

All groups of humans undergo acculturation, the process that transmits vast amounts of knowledge and enduring beliefs, attitudes, values, and behavioral patterns from the group to the individual, from generation to generation. Cultural transmission has been an enormously successful adaptation for our species. However, the current status of our planet clearly indicates that some of our cultural indoctrination is maladaptive (Diamond 2005). Psychological and neurological studies provide some answers as to why we are resistant to change, even in the face of potential destruction. If we are to address the grave challenges that currently face humanity, we need to understand the ontogenetic acculturation process, the scope of its impact upon our thoughts and behaviors as adults, and methods of transcending maladaptive indoctrination.

How Is Culture Transmitted?

The universality of human culture and the rudimentary forms of culture found in nonhuman animals and human ancestors clearly suggest that our species developed the propensity for acculturation through a long evolutionary process (see Palmer and Palmer 2002)[1]. The transmission of culture is integrally tied to evolved neurophysiological and cognitive processes such as language and meaning making.

Language

What separates rudimentary culture found in animals and early humans from complex human culture today is the cognitive capacity for complex language (Palmer and Palmer 2002). Language allows us to convey a tremendous variety and complexity of information—something other species cannot do. Rapid cultural evolution of *Homo sapiens sapiens* began around 50,000 to 60,000 years ago, suggesting that our ancestors had complex, fully developed

---

1   Due to space constraints and for simplicity's sake, wherever possible we refer readers to Palmer and Palmer (2002) for in-depth discussions and extensive original citations.

language by that time (Palmer and Palmer 2002). Our language capacity co-evolved with our abstract cognitive abilities, enabling us to convey information about the past, present, and potential future, as well as to explore complex, hypothetical, and imaginary possibilities. Within the normal modern human lifespan, language acquisition follows a genetically orchestrated process of maturation that is circumscribed by critical periods of brain and cognitive development, which significantly impacts on our ability to assimilate complex cultural information. Thus during childhood general cultural tendencies and kin affiliation are inculcated in a manner similar to imprinting, but larger non-kin group allegiances (e.g., tribe, nation, religion) are more likely to be acquired via a special concerted effort.

Rites of Passage

A relatively brief, proactive form of cultural indoctrination—the *rites of passage* or *puberty rites*—takes place in traditional societies during an individual's adolescence. During adolescence, the brain undergoes a unique, complex process of physiological and neurochemical changes and thus is primed to be particularly sensitive to the impact of social, emotional, and symbolic stimuli (Alcorta and Sosis 2005). Final brain maturation is usually completed by age 25 years. After that time, brain malleability and openness to experience is reduced.

Rites of passage (as practiced by hunter-gatherer peoples) often include (Alcorta and Sosis 2005):

+ Prolonged isolation, sleep deprivation, physical challenges
+ Verbal inculcation of doctrine
+ Chanting, rhythmic music, dancing
+ Psychotropic drugs
+ Ceremony steeped in metaphysical meaning
+ Shaman or wise elders conducting the ceremony
+ Tribe embracing the adolescent as an adult member

The adolescent seeks the discovery of his/her unique purpose in life and acceptance into adult community. The community's goal is to indoctrinate the adolescent with adult core beliefs, attitudes, and values. Altered states of consciousness, combined with the flux of adolescent brain physiology, the shaman's influence, and the group's social reinforcement, produce an optimal experience for the formation of new core beliefs, attitudes, and cultural understanding (Alcorta and Sosis 2005). The rites of passage attach emotional salience to abstract ideas, thus shifting the adolescents' group identity and loyalty to a new level.

Transcending Cultural Indoctrination

Culturally indoctrinated attitudes, values, and beliefs form the defining characteristics of human groups. Examples include our worldviews, religious and spiritual beliefs, our levels of competitiveness vs. cooperativeness, and our views of nature (e.g., nature is a force to dominate and exploit vs. nature is part of the web of life to nurture and harmonize with).

The process of cultural transmission evolved because it tremendously enhanced human survival. However, indoctrinated values and beliefs can be problematic, particularly in a rapidly changing, complex, crowded world. For example, many modern societies value, teach, and reinforce materialism, social comparison, and striving for status. This worldview has made these countries rich and materially successful. Yet the resulting excessive consumerism impacts negatively on world sociopolitical structures and the Earth's ecosystems. We need to "separate the wheat from the chaff" by assessing which aspects of our cultural conditioning are positive, which are detrimental, and which might be desirably changed.

Identifying what needs to change is a daunting task, but change itself is even more complex. Humans tend to be resistant to changing cultural beliefs and loyalties that were inculcated at an early age (Wexler 2006). In adulthood, brain plasticity decreases, as does one's openness to experience. The result is greater brain and behavioral stability, a valuable adaptation, but one that also can cause us to resist embracing new ideas and values.

Openness to Experience

Openness to experience is a scientifically validated personality construct that expresses the degree to which one is intellectually curious, imaginative, attentive to emotions and artistic endeavors, inclined to sample novel activities, and open to examining new values (Costa and McRae 1992). Like most personality traits, openness to experience is measured on a continuum from low to high. Most people score near the middle with decreasing numbers of people scoring toward the lower and higher ends (a typical bell curve). However, no matter how open to experience one might be as an adult, this trait declines naturally in late adulthood (Roberts, Walton, and Viechtbauer 2006).

We would be wise to find ways to increase our openness to experience so that we can become more receptive to the messages inherent in the evolutionary epic—and thus enhance our ability to discover, create, and embrace new core values that can bring us viable solutions to our planet's problems. Rites of passage contain some intriguing elements (similar to those found in practices as diverse as psychotherapy, brainwashing, and group-induction traditions) that might help us in this enormous task:

+ Altered states of consciousness
+ Leaders or guides
+ Reframing of core beliefs
+ Social reinforcement

These methods, especially when used together, can radically change core beliefs, attitudes, values, and behaviors of the individual.

Altered States of Consciousness

The strong neural pathways formed during childhood that guide our everyday actions, thinking, and decision-making into adulthood are difficult to rewrite, partly because of our protective cognitive filters. We ignore new information that conflicts with deeply held beliefs and actively seek environments (physical and social) that match or reinforce our indoctrinated beliefs, attitudes, and values (Wexler 2006). Benign altered states of consciousness[2] (such as those induced by relaxation, hypnosis, prayer, and meditation) can loosen our internal filters, facilitating cognitive-behavioral changes even at the sub-cellular level (Rossi 2004).

Meditation has a long history as a technique of spiritual transcendence. In recent years meditation has found practical, therapeutic applications, such as increasing positive moods and facilitating learning (Perez-de-Albeniz and Holmes 2000; Weiss 2001). Meditation, therapeutic hypnosis, contemplative prayer, progressive relaxation, and similar techniques involve deep relaxation and suspension of random thinking. They produce a physiological state that facilitates new learning and core changes (Rossi 2004). As we become deeply relaxed yet focused, the heartbeat slows and becomes more rhythmic, sympathetic nervous system activity ("fight or flight" response) decreases, metabolism slows, and neurons begin to fire in synchrony. These physiological changes enable neurons to make new synaptic connections with significant rapidity and ease (Weiss 2001).

Brain scans of people meditating show decreased parietal lobe activity, which is associated with decreases in ego boundaries and increases in one's feelings of oneness with everything (Newberg 2001). Meditation loosens cultural filters and allows perception and adoption of new values, beliefs, and attitudes. Thus individuals who regularly practice benign altered states of consciousness have increased cognitive flexibility and capacity to discover fresh ideas, reframe core beliefs, generate new neural pathways, and implement new patterns of behavior (Newberg 2001; Rossi 2004). Meditation and similar techniques facilitate problem-solving,

---

2   We use the term "benign altered states of consciousness" to indicate processes that have little or no potential for personal harm (e.g., meditation, contemplative prayer, therapeutic hypnosis, and relaxation). We do not advocate use of psychotropic drugs, extreme physical overexertion, or other methods of altering consciousness that have significant potential for harm or abuse.

increase feelings of oneness and unity with others, and greatly increase the probability of experiencing the "aha" moments often found in scientific and artistic work, psychotherapy, and spiritual practices (Newberg 2001; Rossi 2004).

Competent Guides

Competent guides or mentors can help identify problematic cultural conditioning, generate solutions, and put planned changes into action. These mentors replicate the roles of the shaman or tribal elders. In modern Western culture, such guides might be found amongst experts (physicians, scientists, writers, researchers, artists, etc.), professional agents of change (psychotherapists, counselors, coaches, etc.), and wise friends, relatives, and colleagues.

Reframing Core Beliefs

Core beliefs are deeply held ideas, attitudes, and values formed during childhood as part of acculturation. They guide our adult thinking patterns, belief systems, and behavior and can be very resistant to change. The process of reframing core beliefs involves the creation and consolidation of new neural pathways and necessitates both conscious and non-conscious processes. When core beliefs are revised, new patterns of thinking and behaving emerge.

Social Reinforcement

Engaging with friends, partners, and groups who support our process of change is vital. This might involve family members and friends, joining existing groups or organizations, or creating new ones. Humans are highly social animals tremendously influenced by their social environment. Therefore having a supportive social environment can be quite beneficial in implementing deep changes.

Examples of Change

The following examples (drawn from case histories of L. Palmer) illustrate significant changes from early indoctrination. Techniques included meditation, hypnosis, progressive relaxation; a guide or mentor; reframing core values; and social reinforcement.

+ Patients in a physical rehabilitation hospital formed new health habits and beliefs radically different from their early childhood indoctrination of unhealthy diet and sedentary lifestyle.
+ Visitors to a spiritual retreat center learned to value a simpler lifestyle with fewer possessions and reduced significantly their use of nonrenewable energy, in contrast to their childhood indoctrination of affluence, wastefulness, and materialism.
+ Individual clients transcended racist and sexist beliefs deeply ingrained in them since childhood.

Discussion and Conclusion

Are we just replacing one type of indoctrination with another, or can we actually *transcend* indoctrination? Benign altered states of consciousness appear to increase the brain's plasticity, thus enhancing an individual's ability to discover fresh ideas, reframe core beliefs, generate new neural pathways, and implement new patterns of behavior. Such cognitive and behavioral flexibility suggests a transcendent state rather than replacing one set of doctrines with another.

The human mind, a product of evolution, allows us to see possibilities and potentials such as threats to our own existence as well as possible solutions. But we must also take into account that evolution has structured our mind in a particular way and that although our psychological tendencies have been adaptive over the course of our long existence on this planet, some of these tendencies create "cognitive blinders" that can interfere with our perception of problems and implementation of solutions. If we are to find hope for the future, we must examine the nature of our evolved psychological tendencies in order to understand how we may alter the course of humanity toward a more positive direction.

Transcending maladaptive core beliefs appears to be a critical step in shaping our minds and hence our collective future. Deep changes, such as transcending core beliefs inculcated during childhood, require modifications not only to our mental structures and consciousness, but to our brain physiology itself. New research suggests that benign altered states of consciousness allow us to rewire and reprogram our own brains. Therefore these methods may be key to enabling us to revise dramatically not only our individual lives but the future direction of our species, our Earth, and her creatures. Such a remarkable feat could be our next giant evolutionary leap.

References

Alcorta, C. and Sosis, R. 2005. Ritual, emotion, and sacred symbols: The evolution of religion as an adaptive complex. *Human Nature, 16* (4), 323-359.

Costa, P. T. and McCrae, R. R. 1992. *NEO Personality Inventory Professional Manual.* Odessa, FL: Psychological Assessment Resources.

Diamond, J. 2005. *Collapse: How Societies Choose to Fail or Succeed.* New York, NY: Penguin.

Newberg, A. 2001. *Why God Won't Go Away: Brain Science and the Biology of Belief.* New York: Ballantine.

Palmer, J. A. and Palmer, L. K. 2002. *Evolutionary Psychology: The Ultimate Origins of Human Behavior.* Needham Heights, MA: Allyn and Bacon.

Perez-de-Albeniz, A. and Holmes, J. 2000. Meditation: Concepts, effects, and uses in therapy. *International Journal of Psychotherapy, 5* (1), 49-58.

Roberts, B. W., Walton, K. E., and Viechtbauer, W. 2006. Patterns of mean-level change in personality traits across the life course: A meta-analysis of longitudinal studies. *Psychological Bulletin*, 132 (1), 1-25.

Rossi, E. L. 2004. *A Discourse with Our Genes: The Psychosocial and Cultural Genomics of Therapeutic Hypnosis and Psychotherapy*. Italy: Editris.

Weiss, R. P. 2001. The mind-body connection in learning. *T+D*, 55 (9), 60-67.

Wexler, B. E. 2006. *Brain and Culture: Neurobiology, Ideology, and Social Change*. Cambridge, MA: MIT Press.

I am suggesting that telling the new story is an essential part of the process of transforming the Earth Community from its current destructive stage and into a new era of vibrant, good health.

Brian Swimme

Cosmology and Environmentalism
Five Suggestions for Ecological Storytellers

Brian Swimme

How one tells the new epic of the universe will be determined at least in part by the aims of the storyteller. If one's aim is to tell a story that is compatible with Christianity, or with Islam, or with Buddhism, one will tell it in certain ways. Or, if one's aim is to tell the story so that it fits into science or history departments in a university, one will tell it in different ways. One might want to tell the story in a way that shows its strong resonance with the earliest indigenous accounts of the universe or tell the story with dance and music as a way of creating community. There are other ways with other aims in addition to these, but they will all require their own telling, their own epistemology, and their own rhetorical skills—their own artistic or intellectual genre.

In this article I'd like to speak to those who are interested in telling the new epic of the universe in a way that helps the cause of environmentalists. By environmentalists I simply mean those humans who are disturbed by the dismantling of Earth's ecosystems and who insist we do something about it, sooner rather than later. An environmentalist's interest in any new cosmic story will be determined by whether or not the telling of this new story will lead to positive action concerning our planetary plight. The large claim I wish to make is that storytellers, working within the overall context of the new epic of the universe, are essential for the extirpation of the "destructive" values of industrial-growth society, and the inculcation of "benevolent" values of an emerging ecological society. I am suggesting that telling the new story is an essential part of the process of transforming the Earth Community from its current destructive stage and into a new era of vibrant, good health.

Let me begin by listing five basic paradigms of industrial society that are deeply implicated in the ongoing destruction of Earth:

(1) anthropocentrism;
(2) short term thinking;
(3) militarism;
(4) oppression;
(5) consumerism.

To show the relevance of the new epic to environmentalism, I want to suggest ways in which telling stories of the new epic will alter these paradigms. Ultimately, we are working for a deep transformation of all such anti-ecological paradigms. But even a small change away from these destructive values toward life-enhancing values will be of help. In what follows I will make some tentative proposals for how any interested storytellers might set forth on this path.

Anthropocentrism to Ecocentrism

The key point to understand is that evolutionary dynamics necessarily lead to "isms" of all kinds—"deer-o-centrism," "crab-o-centrism," "beetle-o-centrism," and not just "anthropocentrism." By the very nature of natural selection, each species has evolved its senses and its mind and its functions in a manner that focuses explicitly on its own survival, and thus it is entirely natural and even inevitable that the human species would take itself as the central norm for all questions of reality and value. All species do. Why should we be any different?

The difficulty of course is when one species suddenly has a majority ownership on power in the community. Suddenly it is not enough for such a species to focus just on itself, and here is where the new story comes in. By telling the stories of all the living and non-living components of the ecosystem, the new epic of the universe will enable humans to place themselves in the context of life's web. For instance, by hearing the story of the phytoplankton and how they fill the atmosphere with the oxygen that all animals breathe, humans will begin to understand that they are not at the top of some evolutionary ladder. They are the humble recipients of these marine algae's gifts. There are a thousand such stories, each of which has the potential to shock us out of anthropocentrism. These stories need to be told again and again until they become part of our bodies and minds.

By dwelling on the stories of the essential presence of others in our ecological communities, we will over time shift our attitude from anthropocentrism to ecocentrism—the attitude that regards the entire community, rather than any single species, as the fundamental standard for reality and value. Even more, after hearing such stories enough times, a new question might enter modern human consciousness: "What is it that we humans contribute to the ongoing vitality of the eco-community?" That is, the new story will be part of that which shifts us out of our industrial self-focus and brings us into a more mature consciousness where we wonder about how we as a species provide various sorts of energy for the entire community of life.

Short-Term Thinking to Long-Term Wisdom

From the perspective of the 13.7 billion year unfolding of cosmic history, humans have an attention span that brings to mind that of a gnat. And why should it be otherwise? We are born, the Earth spins around the Sun a few times, and then we die. It is entirely natural for us to plan things out for the next few seasons, or for the next five years, or, on rare occasions, to think in terms of an entire decade as Americans did with their goal of landing someone on the Moon by the end of the 1960s. But the difficulty comes when human power has grown to such an extent that our actions have consequences that run out tens of thousands of years. It is hard to avoid foolishness when there is such a gap between the puny dimensions of our industrial consciousness and the vast extent of our industrial actions.

By telling the new epic and emphasizing those episodes involving stars and galaxies or those involving mountains and the continents where we learn that many millions of years were required for the shaping of Earth, we humans begin to escape the tiny worlds we usually think within. Such stories with cosmological and geological time spans stretch out human consciousness. As we listen to these stories, we begin to leave behind the short-term thinking of industrial society and ease our way into a geological consciousness with its fundamental unit of ten million years.

We are already making decisions whose effects will be felt a million years from now. We are thus beginning to live on a scale that compares with that of a mountain or even a large star. As we hear stories of the billion-year processes that brought us forth, we will experience our time consciousness opening out. And as we become more aware that we are a dimension of a geological process called Earth, we will have a better chance of making good decisions for the trillions of yet-to-be-born beings all of whom will be living within the world our decisions leave for them.

Militarism to Life Protection

I do not want to give the impression that our challenge is that of taking out one set of values and implanting a different set in a manner akin to that of taking a computer into a shop and having its memory upgraded. The change we are involved with is of much deeper significance. It is closer to the truth to say that humanity is discovering not just a new universe but a new identity within this universe. The crucial difference is, I think, related to the whole. For the first 100,000 years of our existence, we humans could go forth imagining ourselves as set apart. But now more than ever before, it is necessary that we see ourselves simultaneously as just another part within the whole, and as a particular representative of the whole itself. And perhaps this difference in self-concept is nowhere more pressing than in the question of "militarism."

"Militarism," properly understood, is related to a fundamental ecological value. Animals have fangs. Plants have poisons. It might be summarized by saying that a species safeguards that which is most precious and valuable to it. Warfare, at its best, was understood in this way. But just as with the above values, everything changed once the human species gathered such titanic powers to itself. Modern warfare has become the opposite of the original ecological value. Modern warfare has become an activity that guarantees the destruction of all that is precious and valuable, both to the human species and to every other form of life.

We find ourselves in a moment of reversal. In order to support the original ecological value of militarism, one needs to work for the elimination of all of modern warfare. The story from the epic that might help with this thorny situation is that of Earth as a whole. Ozone is a form of oxygen that reflects the most virulent ultraviolet radiation away from Earth. For billions of years there was very little ozone in the atmosphere, but when ozone concentration reached a particular level, complex organisms such as plants and animals could evolve and move onto land. We find ourselves at a similar juncture. Militarism has become virulent and counterproductive to all life. In so far as humanity is becoming something like a thinking layer of the Earth Community, we need to create this layer in a way that eliminates warfare from raining down on life's systems. In this way we will be the human analogue of the Earth's atmosphere, enabling a new explosion of creativity as we move from militarism to life protection.

Oppression to Freedom

Two billion humans survive on a dollar a day. Part of the consequences of this is the death of over 10 million children under age 5 each year. As we all know, the cause of this situation is not lack of food or resources.

The stories from the universe that will help us out of this grotesque situation are those stories about the vehemence with which the universe breaks down any and all obstacles to its further development. There are many hundreds of such stories and they all need to be told. The most spectacular is perhaps that of the supernova. Picture a large star that has for a hundred million years fueled its shining by transmuting hydrogen into helium, oxygen, carbon, phosphorous, and calcium. All these elements are now churning about in its inner layers. But these elements are unable to explore any further reaches of their creativity so long as they are imprisoned there. The cosmic story would come to an end were it not for the most violent act in the universe. Suddenly the star explodes and its elements are spewed out into the universe, some of which gather back together, form new solar systems, and combine in exotic combinations that give rise—at least they did on our planet—to living creatures with minds and hearts. All of that beauty, all of it, is dependent on a violent disruption of a stifling regime.

The supernova is a process whereby the universe dismantles structures that bottle up creativity. By hearing such cosmic and terrestrial stories, we begin to realize how deep is the urge in the universe and in life to take apart anything that stands in its way. These stories release the human imagination from its dull state of unconscious participation in such oppressive systems and excite action so that the billions of unnecessarily imprisoned human beings might begin to blossom forth into their full destinies.

Consumerism to Celebration

Two or three billion Chinese and Indians are working long hours everyday in the hope that they can live like Americans and Europeans. It's possible that some of them already know that to accomplish this goal we will need not just another Earth but in fact several more Earths. And who has the right to tell them to give up their dreams? Certainly they are not going to listen to advice from Westerners whose life styles have already driven Earth into such a degraded state. So, what story can we tell with respect to consumerism, the world's fastest growing religion?

What we need is a new dream. Here's one story that might entice. We have only recently discovered that the universe is expanding at a very unusual rate. It turns out that, on the one hand, if the universe had begun its expansion slightly slower, it would not have had enough energy to open up into galaxies. On the other hand, if the universe had expanded just the slightest bit faster, it would have opened up too quickly for galaxies. In either situation, life would not have come forth.

I am not saying there is any answer here. But this story of the elegant expansion does give us a reason to pause and reflect a moment. If the universe seems to be shot-through with a cosmic order necessary for our very existence, it becomes possible to imagine that we are here for something higher, something nobler, something more significant than the accumulation of commodities. Perhaps the San People, the earliest humans still extant, have something to offer. For the San, the universe is a great dance, and the reason for human existence is to enter the ecstasy of the dance. Perhaps they are right. Perhaps we are here to enter the ecstasy of life, of making food, of making love, of making music, of playing games and sports, of all the activities that go into building a planetary civilization founded on celebration. Perhaps by crossing over from consumerism to celebration, the human species will rediscover itself. Maybe even the animals will join in, singing in exaltation that the humans have finally come home.

Note about Author:

Brian Swimme, Ph.D. teaches courses in the Philosophy, Cosmology, and Consciousness program at the California Institute of Integral Studies, San Francisco. He is the author of *The Hidden Heart of the Cosmos*, *Manifesto for a Global Civilization* (with Matthew Fox), *The Universe is a Green Dragon*, and *The Universe Story* (with Thomas Berry).

Hawaii has been chosen by the U. S. government as a test-bed for a variety of experiments in sustainability, from wind and ocean wave power generation to algae farming as a fuel source

Marc Gilbert et al

Islands of Sustainability

Marc Jason Gilbert, Art Whatley, Phyllis Frus,
Jon Davidann, Leilani Madison, and Stephen Allen

Editor's Note

This collaborative essay is an example of how our response to evolutionary epic can raise powerful ethical issues about sustainability and ecological responsibility and how the Islands of Hawaii are working to address those issues.

Avoiding Darwin's Nightmare

The continuation of the human species is rooted in its ability to actively perceive and address possible threats to its existence both immediate and long-term; it is presently capable of addressing challenges as distant in time and of such cosmic proportions as a possible asteroid impact decades in the future. However, as Jared Diamond suggests in his book *Collapse: How Human Societies Choose to Fail or Succeed* (2004), human populations are quite capable of inaction or inappropriate, even fatal, responses to the most deadly of menaces, environmental collapse. Professor Marc Jason Gilbert, The National Endowment for the Humanities Chair in World History and Humanities at Hawaii Pacific University, bore witness to this process while a Fulbright Scholar in Tanzania, where the importation of the predatory Nile Perch into Lake Victoria led to the loss of fish habitat and human food supply so dramatic as to be the subject of a award-winning film, *Darwin's Nightmare* (2004). He realized that the dangers of such ill-considered and self-destructive behavior are particularly acute for isolated populations, such as those on islands, as the continuing human-induced tragedy on Nauru amply illustrates.[1]

Concern over these developments has led the state of Hawaii and its educational institutions to invest considerable resources in the development of patterns of sustainable living. This commitment has drawn national attention. Hawaii has been chosen by the U. S. government as a test-bed for a variety of experiments in sustainability, from wind and ocean wave power generation to algae farming as a fuel source. Noting these developments, an interdisciplinary study group composed of faculty drawn from Hawaii Pacific University was

---

1   See "Nauru: Paradise Well and Truly Lost," *The Economist*, Dec. 21, 2001.

convened by Professor Gilbert with a view to examining those steps and supporting rationales recently taken by Hawaiian educational institutions—as
islands within these islands—to promote sustainable solutions to a threat
to human survival as serious as that posed by any rogue asteroid: a rapidly
depleting biosphere. What follows is a synopsis of their current contributions.

Walking the Path of a Sustainable Campus to a Sustainable Future

Professor Art Whatley, Program Chair of Hawaii Pacific University's graduate program in Global Leadership and Sustainability, addressed the human
emotional response to macro-historical change by noting that humans contribute to their decline as a species by fooling themselves in two fundamental ways.
First, he states that we tend to believe ideas that are essentially untrue as long
as they align with our own emotional predisposition and values, regardless of
the empirical evidence in their support. Second, we refuse to believe those ideas
that are indeed true, if they do not fit within our preexisting belief systems. No
matter how persuasive the facts, we too often find a way to ignore them.

What does this have to do with a sustainable campus and other environmental initiatives that he and so many Hawaiian island campus leaders support? The two-fold answer is that there is no alternative to supporting them:

> We need look no farther than the erroneous beliefs humans
> hold related to planetary resources, namely: technology will
> save us, climate change is merely cyclical and part of the natu-
> ral planetary cycle—and unrelated to human activity, resourc-
> es are infinite, etc. We maintain these notions even though
> the evidence to the contrary is overwhelming. Our major life
> support systems are in decline, their limits are being exceeded,
> and we are running the risk of system collapse. These errors in
> thinking have been commonplace for generations and are now
> imbedded in our collective unconscious, making them virtu-
> ally immune to the mountain of scientific knowledge confirm-
> ing that the earth is a closed system with known limits to its
> life support systems. It is compelling for me as an educator to
> invite students to reconcile the dual nature of environmen-
> tal science on one hand and institutional and personal beliefs
> that tend to be self-serving on the other.

A second, related falsehood commonly held is that human debris can accumulate in the world without consequence. We believe that if we bury or burn
it, if we de-materialize it, the problem of waste disposal is solved. Secondary
effects of contaminated air or polluted groundwater show up in the future, to

be dealt with by others yet to be born. We are not yet, for instance, systematically measuring the accumulation of chemicals in the breast milk of mammals, particularly human mothers at the top of the food chain. Never mind the carbon released into the atmosphere at prodigious rates. Forget about the worldwide contamination of fresh water sources due to coal burning.

Professor Whatley reminds us that technology and its scientific heritage are commonly seen as holding the key to survival and human comfort. From the earliest days of the industrial revolution, humanity has ignored the more unpleasant or undesirable nature of technology in exchange for its many physical benefits. Measurement systems that count these benefits of technology while ignoring or externalizing the costs have been established. The nearly worldwide use of Gross Domestic Product (GDP)[2] as the sole measure of societal wellbeing illustrates the ease by which we dilute the truth with singular and distorted measurement devices. His focus as an educator is to develop in students thinking habits capable of addressing these distressing trends. Leadership, he contends, is different from management in that it features a vision or value component—a conception of the desired, of possibilities and preferences that are both compelling and realizable.

Humanity, through experience, has come to know quite well the more familiar forms of leadership. Political leadership charts the course towards some preferred political future or state of affairs; educational leadership charts a similar path for education; business leadership is about maximizing return on shareholder wealth. Dr. Whatley asks, "What then is global leadership?" His answer:

> From the perspective of HPU's Masters program in Global Leadership and Sustainable Development, global leadership is about constructing visions of our planet in which humanity's concerns, outside the context of national or cultural-centric preferences, are given priority. Planetary systems are returned to harmony, planetary limits are maintained and respected, biological principles provide the designs for human habitation and ways to "make a living." The "commons" are protected from market forces as a way of sustaining natural capital's goods and services for future generations. In practical terms this means that we will have learned to create zero waste, reward cooperative behavior, allow for self-organization to occur, return to a profound respect for diversity and creative individuality. Learning is optimized, life-long, and

---

2   The "Last Roof of the World" country of Bhutan in Southeast Asia uses GDH as its measure of success—Gross Domestic Happiness.

shared within place-based communities. Control is localized; responsibility is connected to action and behavior at every point between the local (where we all live) and the global.

Professor Whatley believes that if we were to pursue the idea put forth by David Orr at Oberlin College that "all education is environmental education," humanity could easily bridge the gulf between the curriculum on the one hand and student development on the other by engaging students in sustainable campus initiatives, programs, and activities. There are many sustainable campus initiatives already underway in various stages of development. Some are officially sanctioned by top campus administrators; others are more informal, led by student groups and faculty initiatives. Many others lie in wait to be taken up by an enthusiastic learner. He believes that what is needed most is a campus sustainability audit which would serve as a basis for a sustainability plan.

Audits would mobilize the campus around a system-wide move towards sustainability. But where, he asks, to begin? Frequent refrains are to wait for senior college administrators to make a move, or for a research grant to be awarded to fund such a project. The literature of organizational change, however, suggests that there can be multiple beginnings. It can start anywhere—promotion by senior management, certainly—but also through classroom and student club activities, specific sustainability projects such as recycling, building design, and especially grounds maintenance. Overall, the goal is to establish a campus sustainability ethic in the consciousness of all stakeholders sufficient to become ingrained in the organization's culture.

Schooling Nemo

Professor Whatley drew attention to the human emotional response to environmental challenges and the variety of means of engendering a response among young people. Phyllis Frus, Associate Professor of English at Hawaii Pacific University, believes that emotional concerns aid and abet the current generation's seeming ability to look away from approaching environmental threats. She notes that it cannot be said that they deny that these threats exist because younger students are not sufficiently aware of the larger problems facing their survival to choose to turn away from them. And even those that are aware of these threats—especially those caused in some way by over-consumption—are bombarded by cultural messages which urge them to consume: buy, use for awhile, then throw it away. These are the opposite of the behaviors that might help hold species extinction at bay—the borrow, reuse, return, recycle models promoted by doctrines of sustainability.

She noted that there are those who have argued that the current generation of humans, our Nemos adrift in a sea of consumerism, is responsive to visual prompts (as in the "Story of Stuff" website and video). With that in mind, Professor Frus has turned to films and books related to her institution's "common book" program and "Viewpoints" film series, on whose governing committees she serves. In their selection process, these committees have chosen to avoid those film and book titles, such as *An Inconvenient Truth* (and the book that accompanies it), which some reviewers find too pessimistic. For similar reasons, her common book committee did not wish to adopt a book with "catastrophe" in the title, such as in *Field Notes from a Catastrophe*, by Elizabeth Kolbert (which has been chosen by the University of Washington as its 2008 common book). Instead, the committee chose Michael Pollan's *The Omnivore's Dilemma: A Natural History of Four Meals*, which Dr. Frus hopes to supplement with films that dramatize that book's research. One is *Fast Food Nation*, a feature film not just about our beef supply and the fast food chains' role in making it so industrialized, so inhumane, and so unsafe; it is also about illegal immigrants who work in the industry, unsafe working conditions, gender exploitation, and activism by college students. Others that have a hopeful message are *Escape from Suburbia* (the sequel to *The End of Suburbia*, about peak oil and the huge transformative effects that it will have) and *Everything's Cool*, if only because its concluding segment features "Step It Up," the march led by Bill McKibben in Vermont in 2007.[3] These uplifting stories, Dr. Frus argues, are far more useful in raising the consciousness of the young than the film *Darwin's Nightmare* (2004), despite the truth of its message that species extinction—our own—is closer than we think.

By the same token, Dr. Frus recalled a documentary available on DVD called *The Next Industrial Revolution*, whose content and impact relates to the story of carpet manufacturer Ray Anderson and his life-changing experience of reading a book, *The Ecology of Commerce*. He responded by converting his company to take recycling and reusing beyond sustainability towards the goal of restoring every bit of energy and raw material and recapturing every molecule. Anderson is featured in one segment of *The Next Industrial Revolution* (narrated by Susan Sarandon); other segments feature the Oberlin College environmental sciences building (which David Orr has written about in *Design on the Edge*), new materials for athletic shoes that leave a smaller footprint on the Earth, and Ford's Rouge River plant (the company is working with architect William McDonough to retool the plant, which is featured in the wonderful Diego Rivera murals at the Detroit Institute of Art, as a site of sustainable manufacturing).

Dr. Frus also seeks to connect peace studies, with its emphasis on nonviolent social action, to sustainability, deep green ecology, and fighting climate change through environmental justice. She encourages students to investigate the new Peace Studies courses at Hawaii Pacific University, and to use these courses to explore the application of nonviolent strategies to demonstrations

---

3   Visit the website: www.stepitup.org.

and marches to direct students towards constructive ways of galvanizing their own governments (HPU has the world's most international student body) to address current threats to the environment. Finally Dr. Frus has attempted to insure that all her students hear David Orr's call for "all education to be sustainable education" by asking them to read and summarize "Saving Future Generations from Global Warming," Orr's commentary in the *Chronicle of Higher Education,* which succinctly spells out this principle. In this essay, Orr also set goals for every college campus to achieve by 2020, which include reducing their carbon emissions, conducting campus energy audits, and generally practicing what they teach.[4] The reaction she hopes to garner from her students is their asking, "It is 2009—what have we done so far?"

"There will be Blood"—Perhaps, but Will There Be Food?

Jon Davidann, a Professor of History at Hawaii Pacific University, prefers a "commodities" approach to sustainability that permits students to engage the darker outcomes that Professor Frus has avoided. Davidann's stance is informed by his choice of commodity—oil—whose dark side is visible to students every time they pull up at the pump. His new course, entitled "The History of Oil in the Modern World," was designed to explore the past, present, and future role of fossil fuels. As the course progressed, Davidann and his students began to realize how inextricably linked our use of oil was to basic questions of sustainability. The class engaged the issue of oil supply estimates and the question of whether current oil production has already peaked or will peak in the next ten years. Both student and instructor alike "were astonished at how dependent we are on fossil fuels and uncertain we are about their sustainability." They discovered that

> by conservative estimates, the world will peak in its oil production by 2030. By more liberal estimates of scholars such as Princeton Professor of Geology Kenneth Deffeyes, we have already peaked and are on the downward slide. The problem with peak oil is that the cost of oil will rise dramatically after the peak. We are seeing this oil price increase already but it is too soon to know whether it is because of peak oil. Rising oil prices could eventually price low-income people and countries out of the oil market. And as supplies dwindle, the race to gain access to this increasingly scarce resource has the potential to cause wars and destabilize political and social conditions in some areas of the world.

---

4   Issue dated April 21, 2000, page B7.

Some argue that these wars have already happened, with the controversial Iraq War cited as an example.

Davidann and his class have learned there is some good news in this bad news. The link between oil consumption and global warming suggests that if we solve one problem, we can potentially make inroads into the other, as reduced oil consumption may stave off peak oil and help slow the pace of global warming. And it seems that discourse over oil supplies has raised public consciousness of environmental degradation. Sales of hybrids broke all records last year, indicating that the public seems to understand that the answer to many of our problems, not just oil, is one of reduced consumption. As Professors Whatley and Frus have noted, reduced consumption seems like a hard sell, but there is hope. It has taken very little time for the media and the energy industry to shift from ethanol boosterism to the recognition that alternatives such as ethanol have problems that make them unworkable as long-term solutions: by some estimates, it takes more than one gallon of oil to make a gallon of ethanol. It was very quickly realized that increased U.S. subsidies of ethanol have taken so much corn out of food production that the price of corn has doubled in less than a year and other food commodities such as wheat have gone up almost as much as farmers have turned their wheat fields into corn fields. These are unanticipated consequences of a poor choice for an alternative fuel and poor public policy. But Davidann argues that this is fixable and there are other better alternatives out there, such as turning used cooking oil into biodiesel. He notes that we here in Hawaii, on the mainland, and in the rest of the world are beginning to learn the true cost of oil. We are examining solar, wave, and wind power as sustainable alternatives and hopefully this will lead to better choices for the next generation.

"Slow Literature" and Species Survival

Leilani Madison, Associate Professor of English at HPU, argues that part of the solution to the current crisis involves revisiting and reinterpreting humanity's story as told in the epics written down during the Axial Age (800 BCE to 200 BCE). She introduces her freshmen to Homer's *Odyssey* in the fall semester and the biblical book of *Genesis* in the spring semester. Each is read, discussed, and absorbed slowly over the course of the semester while students work on individual writing and research projects. This approach, which she has dubbed "Slow Literature," attempts to replicate the way such texts were experienced and explored in the cultures that generated them. The slow pace allows for a deepening dialogue on the meaning of the text.

These epics are usually read quickly in survey courses (if they are read at all) as though they were modern novels; the result is that students often interpret them through the lens of contemporary despair and amorality. They usually conclude that Odysseus, at the climax of the *Odyssey*, did what he had to do in order to restore order when he slaughtered the young men of Ithaca who had been courting his queen during his twenty-year military deployment. However, the text indicates that he has become more savage than the Cyclops. He has become addicted to violent responses to situations that could be resolved with diplomacy and has betrayed his culture's core values of hospitality, fair play, and mercy for suppliants. Such issues are usually unexplored by students in their rush to consume the reading list. Given the opportunity for slow reading, students discover that Homer is challenging his ancient audience and us to think critically about our addiction to violence and war.

Genesis offers a look at the same problem of violence through the stories of Jacob and Joseph. Jacob, intent on gaining his brother Esau's claim to the land, takes advantage of Esau's hunger in order to buy his birthright and then progresses to identity theft when he deceives his father into giving him the blessing meant for Esau. Fleeing Esau's anger, Jacob makes a new life in a foreign land, but his success arouses the resentment of his new neighbors and he decides to return and seek reconciliation with his brother. When he is informed that Esau is coming to meet him accompanied by four hundred armed men, Jacob wrestles with his conscience personified as a mysterious stranger. Jacob is tempted to raise his own armed force and go into battle, but renounces the choice of violence. Jacob emerges from his moral struggle paradoxically both blessed and crippled by his choice of non-violence. When Esau makes the same choice and embraces his brother, Jacob declares that he has seen the face of God and lived to tell the story. In order to underline its meaning, *Genesis* provides the concluding story of Joseph who has ample reason for taking vengeance on his brothers, but chooses to forgive them instead.

Foundational works from the Axial Age such as *The Odyssey* and *Genesis* along with much earlier works such as the epic of *Gilgamesh* serve to make students aware that the moral issues of our time are part of the ongoing story of human moral evolution as we are coming to understand it in the context of big history. Understanding our human heritage through the great literary epics enables students to see a meaningful pattern in human development and encourages them to accept their role at this moment in history. They can avoid seeing themselves as the victims of the bad luck of global warming and the exhaustion of key commodities and instead see themselves as the chosen heroes whose task it is to care for the Earth and her inhabitants guided by the wisdom, compassion and courage of our spiritual traditions.

LEEDing the Way

Stephen Allen, Professor of Chemistry in Hawaii Pacific University's Environmental Science Program, explained how the buildings we teach in can serve as means to teach about sustainability as well as constitute a means of giving effect to it. The very building used to host this presentation was designed to provide ample natural light and ventilation. Indeed, no lights were turned on during this session! The angular shape of the roof is not only typical of traditional Hawaiian architecture but can also be used to promote ventilation. The new cafeteria at Waipahu Intermediate makes use of this style of roof to provide ventilation and reduce energy use. A portion of the outer skin is painted black to absorb heat, while most roofs use light colors to reflect sunlight and stay cool. As the adjacent air inside the building heats, it naturally rises and draws air into the ground floor of the building, much like the chimney of a fireplace does. Students examining the issue of sustainability within such structures can literally breathe in that subject as well as feel its effects on their skin.

Professor Allen noted that Case Middle School of the private Punahou School complex in Honolulu has integrated sustainability into its curriculum as well as into its nine buildings. Punahou's sixth, seventh and eighth grade science students learn about water conservation through the study of runoff from their school's spring water source to its storage tanks and into its sprinkler system. Students of mathematics at Punahou are tasked with calculating the savings generated by the energy efficiency of their school buildings, such as the roof-mounted photovoltaic system that provides a portion of the school's electricity. Perhaps more importantly, these structures are equipped with monitoring equipment that lets students see how much sunlight is turned into electricity, how this varies with the time of day and weather, and that the technology actually works! Other features show how closely sustainability concerns were integrated into the school's overall design. The lockers the students use are made from recycled milk cartons and the students are made aware of this example of recycling and reusing plastics. Dr. Allen noted that any school considering incorporating sustainable design principals for new or existing buildings should make use of the ample resources and framework provided by the Leadership in Energy and Environmental Design (LEED®) rating system of the U.S. Green Building Council.[5] Dr. Allen, himself a LEED accredited professional, observed that Punahou School has attracted considerable attention to its programs by its achievement of the LEED Gold standard, only one of seven schools to do so, and was thus able to earn recognition as the "greenest school" in the United States according to the 2006 edition of the *Green School Guide*.

Concluding Remarks

The views of each of the contributors to this discussion relate in some degree to the findings of Joel Primack and Nancy Abrams in *The View from*

---

5   Visit website: www.usgbc.org.

the Center of the Universe (2006), a groundbreaking work that, in the words of Nobel Prize-winner in Chemistry, Dr. Roald Hoffmann, *"connects matters of cosmic significance with the environment and human life on planet Earth."* All share Primack and Abrams' view that uniting the intuition of the humanities with the most advanced scientific speculation in educational settings constitutes humankind's best hope, not only for understanding the universe, but sustaining its place within it. (See Abrams and Primack's chapter in this book, p. 107.) Using their own campuses to communicate this vision to students and the general public is a challenging task for educators, but their efforts to meet the challenge can serve as an inspiration to all those committed to creating a sustainable future for Hawaii and for this island Earth.

For the sake of our survival as a species and for the wellbeing of our ecologically imperiled planet, it is imperative that we form and inform our conscience, at any age, by learning to listen to the voice of Earth.

Linda Gibler

Listening to the Voice of the Earth
A Catholic Perspective

Linda Jaye Gibler

Introduction

In a question and answer session with clergy, a priest asked Pope Benedict XVI's advice on conscience formation in young people. After a few introductory words on the importance of a well-formed conscience, the pope said:

> In taking stock of the current situation, I would propose the combination of a secular approach and a religious approach, the approach of faith. Today, we all see that man can destroy the foundations of his existence, his earth, hence, that we can no longer simply do what we like or what seems useful and promising at the time with this earth of ours, with the reality entrusted to us. On the contrary, we must respect the inner laws of creation, of this earth, we must learn these laws and obey these laws if we wish to survive. Consequently, this obedience to the voice of the earth, of being, is more important for our future happiness than the voices of the moment, the desires of the moment. In short, this is a first criterion to learn: that being itself, our earth, speaks to us and we must listen if we want to survive and to decipher this message of the earth. (Pope Benedict XVI, 2007)

For the sake of our survival as a species and for the wellbeing of our ecologically imperiled planet, it is imperative that we form and inform our conscience, at any age, by learning to listen to the voice of Earth. The task of those of us who embrace Catholicism and wish to live in right relationship with God and neighbors of every species is to integrate what we are now learning about the universe and Earth with the best of our tradition and then let that integration inform our faith, practice, and daily choices.

Cosmological Inquiry

Listening to the voice of Earth in a way which combines both secular and religious approaches begins with attention to the natural objects we encounter in the liturgy. Since I am writing this just before the feast of Epiphany, the celebration of the three kings who followed the Star of Bethlehem, it seems appropriate to use light as an example. Using a methodology called cosmological inquiry, we begin by surveying the cosmic story of light, continue by recalling light's sacred history within the Catholic tradition, and conclude by integrating the two stories to see if together they yield insights that draw us deeper into the mystery of God, the universe, and ourselves.

Cosmic Story

In the interest of brevity, I will begin the cosmic history of light not at the Beginning, 13.7 billion years ago, or 380 thousand years later when light first flooded the universe, or a million years after that with the formation of primal stars. Instead, I will begin the story of light a comparatively brief 4.6 billion years ago with the light we are most familiar with, the light of our Sun. The sunlight that lights our days and warms our planet is the result of nuclear fusion in the Sun's core. The gravitational pressure in the center of the Sun is so intense that it melts the protons of hydrogen nuclei together and forms helium. In the process, four billion tons of the Sun's matter is transformed into energy every second and is flung in every direction. One billionth of that energy reaches the planet Earth. While the planet was held in this brilliant embrace for nearly a billion years, single-celled life forms warmed to the Sun and learned to use photosynthesis to transform water and chemicals into food. The light of the Sun became energy for life on Earth.

For Earth to create her own light, oxygen and fuel were required for fire. Three billion years after the emergence of photosynthesis, Sun-drenched plants provided both. As a byproduct of plants' energy exchange with the Sun, oxygen was released into Earth's oceans and atmosphere. Eventually a layer of heavy oxygen called ozone (O_3) accumulated in the upper atmosphere and blocked enough of the Sun's ultraviolet rays for plants to survive on land. Soon small plants and then forests spread across the continents, releasing oxygen into the atmosphere all the while. As the oxygen level increased, so did the amount of plant matter available to burn. Some three hundred million years ago a tipping point was reached as fires fed and fueled by plants raged; Earth became capable of creating light.

For millions of years, through the sacrificial gift of Sun and plants, fires burned intermittently across the Earth and helped create the atmosphere, soils, and living conditions for the species to come. Of all the species to live on Earth, hominids seem to be the only ones who did not flee from fire. Hominids may have begun using fire for light, warmth, cooking, and protection 500 thousand years ago, but they only mastered the art of creating it themselves 10,000 years ago. Evidence for the ability to make fire coincides with early agricultural settlements. In the brief time since humans joined the Sun and Earth as light-making beings, our mastery of light has increased dramatically. Once a sacred art billions of years in the making, now any one of us can create light instantly by striking a match or flipping a switch.

Although our ability to utilize light has grown exponentially, our understanding of light is still nascent. Only in the last hundred years have we learned that not only Sun, Earth, and humans create light, but that releasing particles of light is an attribute of matter. An example will help make this clear. When we look at the Moon, we are accustomed to think that we see it because light from the Sun shines on it and bounces back toward us. And although it is true that we see this reflected sunlight, there is something else going on as well. When particles of light from the Sun hit the Moon, some are reflected, but others are absorbed by the atoms on the Moon's surface. Photons are mysterious particles that either bounce off or dissolve into whatever touches them. Atoms on the Moon's surface absorb some of the Sun's photons and become excited. Once excited, they release photons, not the photons absorbed from the Sun—those dissolved—but photons created by the Moon herself, Moonlight. This Moonlight does not only hit our eyes but flows over our bodies and everything in its path. Some of those Moon-made photons in turn are absorbed by the trees, birds, and people around us. The atoms on their surfaces in turn become excited and release their own photons, some of which are absorbed by our eyes. However, not all light is visible. Many of the photons released by atoms do not travel in the narrow range of wavelengths discernible to human eyes. Photons we cannot see are released constantly by every single thing in creation. This happens even without the presence of a visible light source such as the Sun. All matter above absolute zero (the theoretical temperature at which atomic movement stops) constantly radiates light. Sun, Earth, humans, and as we only recently learned, all beings are aglow with the light they create and receive from every other being.

Sacred Story

From the cosmic story, we turn now to the sacred story of light. Again in the interest of brevity, I will limit this exploration of light in the Catholic tradition to the story of Moses and its New Testament parallels. Light in the story of Moses begins with the burning bush. The voice from the sacred light sends him back to Egypt to free the Hebrew slaves. Later, a pillar of bright cloud by day and fire by night guides the way for the Israelites as they cross the desert to the Promised Land. When they reach Mount Sinai, where Moses was given the tablets of the Ten Commandments, the presence of God glowed in a bright cloud that covered the mountaintop. A fearsome brilliance, this cloud kept all but Moses and an unnamed attendant from climbing the mountain. Upon his return Moses veiled his face because it had become blindingly radiant. Later, when the Israelites built a temple to house the Ark of the Covenant, which held the tablets of the Ten Commandments, fire and the bright cloud of God's presence descended on the temple and filled it with a frightening light that caused the priests to flee into the streets.

Moving to the New Testament, there are at least two stories that recall the story of Moses, the Transfiguration of Jesus and Pentecost. In these stories, the presence of the holy light is more embracing. Jesus ascended the mount of his transfiguration in the company of his closest disciples. When Jesus was transfigured into dazzling light and Moses and Elijah appeared with him, a bright cloud appeared and frightened the disciples, commanding them to listen to Jesus. In contrast to fleeing in fear like the temple priests, Jesus touched them and told them not to be afraid. As they descended the mountain, Jesus admonished them to keep what they saw to themselves. In contrast, there was no secrecy at Pentecost. Pentecost was the annual Jewish celebration of the giving of the Law on Mount Sinai. On this day, weeks after Jesus' death, the disciples were gathered in an upper room filled with fear and sadness. Suddenly, the presence of God filled the room and the Holy Spirit descended on the disciples as tongues of living fire. Aflame with the presence of God, they left their fearful isolation and boldly taught in the streets of Jerusalem. In these stories, we see development of the theme of light moving from the fearful presence of God whom only Moses could approach, to Jesus as a welcoming light, to the disciples of Jesus themselves radiant with the Pentecost light of Mount Sinai.

Integration

With both the cosmic and sacred stories of light in mind, let us consider the Feast of the Epiphany. The Feast is the celebration of the light that came into the world. It is a story of family and travelers, of intimacy and universality. In the cosmic story of light we recall that all the elements of matter form in stars like our Sun and that the Sun is the primal source of light on Earth. Over time, growing in intimacy with Earth, the Sun's brilliance was absorbed by bacteria and then plants that created the oxygen and fuel for firelight to illumine the Earth. Slowly this fire created the living conditions for all else on the planet. And finally after millions of years, one of Earth's creatures learned to create light. In so doing, the brilliance of the Sun, which few animals dare to look at directly, became our partner in daily life. In the last steps of this journey towards intimacy with light, humans are realizing that all matter radiates light. In a surprise of intimate universality, we have learned that we ourselves, and every other being, glow with visible and invisible light. The story of starlight is one of growth in intimacy with the entire cosmos.

We find a similar theme of deepening intimacy in the sacred story of light. Recall from the Old Testament that fearsome light signified the presence of God that led the Israelites across the desert and also caused the priests to flee the temple. In the New Testament, Jesus is transfigured in an approachable light that the disciples do not want to leave. At Pentecost, the apostles first witness the light and then are transformed by the light themselves. Jesus is the light of the world, so are all of his followers. As light, Jesus is present in all the light seen and unseen that pervades the cosmos. In both the cosmic and sacred stories of light, we learn that each person glows with a light that cannot be quenched. We are the light the scriptures proclaim. And here the story becomes universal. Not only are we light in the world, but so is everyone and everything else.

The message of the Magi, foreign astrologers who followed a star to Bethlehem, is traditionally understood to mean that Jesus came into the world as light for all people. With the cosmic and sacred stories of light in mind, we can see that the light of the star of Bethlehem permeates humankind and indeed, all of creation. This light is part of the reality in which everything lives, moves, and has its being. In the Feast of Epiphany, listening to the voice of starlight brings us to the confluence of light's cosmic and sacred stories that reveal the intimacy of all members of the universe. We all share in the same light. We are all light bearers.

Conclusion

I have found that similar studies of the natural objects mentioned in scriptures and used in sacraments all contribute to a richer understanding of our faith and of the world around us. Every being has the potential to reveal its deeper significance, not only inside the church doors, but also in our daily experience. When our consciousness is formed by listening to the voice of Earth in a way that integrates our cosmic and sacred traditions, we will grow in our ability to live in right relationship with God and our neighbors of every species.

Author's Note:

Linda Gibler, a Dominican Sister of Houston, is the Associate Academic Dean and Director of the Doctor of Ministry program at the Oblate School of Theology in San Antonio, TX. She enjoys giving lectures, workshops, and retreats on topics pertaining to cosmology, ecology, and faith. She can be contacted at lindagibler@earthlink.net

References

Pope Benedict XVI. 2007. Papal Q-and-A Session with Priests, Part 1: On Conscience, Pastoral Organization, and Immigrants. *ZENIT: The World Seen From Rome*. Internet <http://www.zenit.org/article-20253?1=english> accessed 31 January 2008.

Andromeda Spyral Galaxy - Courtesy NASA

Interlude

hymn to the sacred body of the universe

let's meet
at the confluence
where you flow into me
and one breath
swirls between our lungs

let's meet
at the confluence
where you flow into me
and one breath
swirls between our lungs

for one instant
to dwell in the presence of the galaxies
for one instant
to live in the truth of the heart
the poet says this entire traveling cosmos is
"the secret One slowly growing a body"

two eagles are mating—
clasping each other's claws
and turning cartwheels in the sky
grasses are blooming
grandfathers dying
consciousness blinking on and off
all of this is happening at once
all of this, vibrating into existence
out of nothingness

every particle
foaming into existence
transcribing the ineffable

arising and passing away
arising and passing away
23 trillion times per second—
when Buddha saw that,
he smiled

16 million tons of rain are falling every second
on the planet
an ocean
perpetually falling
and every drop
is your body
every motion, every feather, every thought
is your body
time
is your body,
and the infinite
curled inside like
invisible rainbows folded into light

every word of every tongue is love
telling a story to her own ears

let our lives be incense
burning
like a hymn to the sacred
body of the universe
my religion is rain
my religion is stone
my religion reveals itself to me in
sweaty epiphanies

every leaf, every river,
every animal,
your body
every creature trapped in the gears
of corporate nightmares
every species made extinct
was once
your body

10 million people are dreaming
that they're flying
junipers and violets are blossoming
stars exploding and being born
god
is having
déjà vu
I am one
elaborate
crush
we cry petals
as the void
is singing

you are the dark
that holds the stars
in intimate
distance

that spun the whirling,
whirling,
world
into existence

let's meet
at the confluence
where you flow into me
and one breath
swirls between our lungs

Drew Dellinger

Author's Note:
Drew Dellinger is a poet, teacher, activist and long-time student of Thomas
Berry. He is the author of *love letter to the milky way: a book of poems*, and
founder of Poets for Global Justice.
(www.drewdellinger.org; 1-866-poetics.)

PART VI

The Epic Enriches Our Imaginative and Spiritual Dimensions

Cheryl Genet

> The evolutionary epic links modern accounts of the origins of the universe, the Earth, life, and human societies into a single story about origins, so it can play in modern society a role similar to that of traditional creation stories in all earlier societies.
>
> David Christian

One of the tragedies of modern times has been the reification of the idea that evolutionary science and divine creation cosmology are irrevocably at odds. In the last few decades, however, postmodern scholars of diverse disciplines have used their imaginative and spiritual capacities to bring both the dimension of a grand story to evolutionary science and a scientific enrichment to spiritual cosmologies.

A unique engagement of the evolutionary epic, in "Alchemical Ritual Evocation," looks at exoteric alchemy and "considers alchemical ways of breaking apart and putting back together the epic of evolution." It also recounts "two indigenous examples of retelling the story of life and the celebration of luminosity in the story of the universe as ways to reclaim our ancestral heritage and interconnectivity with all life."

In "Already Living" an artist's perspective examines the provocative notion that

> ...the churning of geological chaos of the early Earth contained the potential for the interiority that emerges later in the form of subjective human consciousness. The Music of Mozart was 'already living' in the prebiotic rock of the Earth.

The premise is that "the universe within us is as capacious and infinite as the universe that surround us."

Within that capacious universe, and perhaps even comprising it, is human consciousness, which for Alfred North Whitehead was the pinnacle manifestation of experience. "Imagination and the Epic of Evolution" suggests there is a role for imagination in evolution that requires for its visualization a re-examination of the Western conceptual generality regarding the experience and its relationship to self-awareness. The universe is co-created between God and all moments of experience through imagination.

In "Our Cosmic Context," the challenge of "developing and conveying the Evolutionary Epic is [identified as transforming] scientific knowledge into nuggets of insight that can be used as building blocks for constructing personal wisdom." This must be tackled in concrete ways—it is pointed out that feeling our connections to the universe is not engendered automatically by our knowledge of scientific facts.

The closing chapter, "Theological Problems and Promises" takes the connection between our feelings—our subjective reality—and the epic, to the heights of Iztaccihuatl, a stratovolcano in Mexico. There on the mountain top, survival, death, immediacy of experience of the nature's power, and the meeting of deep past and cosmological mystery, engender the lived spiritual experience of the evolutionary epic. For a Catholic theologian, this experience requires the examination of doctrinal concepts in the light of scientific knowledge:

Ancient faith traditions have everything to gain from bold and incisive engagement of the epic of evolution. Not only does the universe story resonate with our personal encounters with the natural world, but it also challenges us to articulate classic theological doctrines afresh.

A cosmology of appreciation for our ancestral lineage of the entire epic of evolution nurtures a strong empathic resonance with the diversity within the whole.
Jeff Jenkins

Alchemical Ritual Evocation
of the Epic of the Universe as Ancestral Heritage

Jeff Jenkins

Introduction

On the cusp of "the final wake-up call on population and environment" issued at the United Nations Environment Program's fourth Global Environmental Outlook in October 2007, the human family faces a desert of our own construction and thus our own demise. According to a major report released by the United Nations at that time:

> The human population is living far beyond its means and inflicting damage on the environment that could pass points of no return....The result of that population growth combined with unsustainable consumption has resulted in an increasingly stressed planet where natural disasters and environmental degradation endanger millions of humans, as well as plant and animal species....Persistent problems include a rapid rise of so-called dead zones. (Kanter 2007)

The pronouncement of cataclysmic environmental degradation from leading scientists of our time is clear. Not enough has been done to stop ecological ruin as flows of goods, services, people, technologies, and workers have expanded, even to isolated populations. Thomas Berry states:

> When the agricultural civilizations began some ten thousand years ago, the human disturbance of the natural world was begun in a serious way. [Now] we can pollute the air with acids, the rivers with sewage, the seas with oil—all this in a kind of intoxication with our power for devastation at an order of magnitude beyond all reckoning. (Berry 1988, 7)

Is it possible for the human family to avert doom and disaster? Is it possible for individual and collective humans to evoke our ultimate potential for interde-

pendent well-being? While the mechanistic and technocratic tendencies and
addictions persist in their destruction of the biosphere, awakening to interdependence may turn the tide. This paper considers alchemical ways of breaking apart and putting back together the epic of evolution. It also recounts two
indigenous examples of retelling the story of life and the celebration of numi-
nosity in the story of the universe as ways to reclaim our ancestral heritage and
interconnectivity with all life.

Alchemy, the Spagyric Art
In exoteric alchemy:

> [One] attempts to prepare a substance, the philosopher's
> stone, endowed with the power of transmuting the base met-
> als lead, tin, copper, iron, and mercury into the precious met-
> als of gold and silver. The Stone was… credited not only with
> the power of transmutation but with that of prolonging hu-
> man life indefinitely. (Holmyard 1990, 15)

This became a model for a devotional system "where the mundane trans-
mutation of metals became merely symbolic of the transformation of sin-
ful man into a perfect being through prayer and submission to the will of
God" (Holmyard 1990, 16). These exoteric and esoteric alchemical systems
of transforming life into eternal vitality frequently became cycles of turning what is vital into tablets, frameworks, and empty equations. Religious
and scientific inquiry became dogmatic—devoid of vitality and giving rise
to gross manipulations and exploitations of life. However, there are other
aspects of alchemy to consider.

The alchemical process of separating and uniting is known as the *spagyric*
art. Carl Jung said that the "essential secret of the art lies hidden in the human
mind—or, to put it in modern terms, in the unconscious" (Jung 1968, xiv).
Within the hermetically sealed container of the Ouroboros lies the continual
process of death and rebirth.[1] Through breaking apart and putting back together, wholeness is achieved:

> Just as in the psyche the multiplicity of sense perceptions pro-
> duces the unity and simplicity of an idea, so the primal water

---

1   *Ouroboros* refers to an ancient symbol depicted by a serpent in a circle, grasping its tail
with its mouth. It is said to symbolize wisdom, rebirth, sustainability, and cycles of time, including the rise and fall of civilizations. The symbol has been found in many cultures throughout the
world and was said by Jung to represent an important archetype.

finally produces fire, i.e., the ethereal substance—not (and
this is the decisive point) as a mere analogy but as the result of
the mind's working on matter... by studying the philosophers
man acquires the skill to attain this stone. (Jung 1968, xiv)

Learning the stages of transformation and the perennial death-rebirth cycles
that take place all around empowers this thought:

[The] idea of the harmony and unity of the universe, "One is
All, and All is One" led to the belief that the universal spirit
could somehow be pressed into service either through the
stars or by concentrating it, so to speak, in a particular piece
of matter—the philosopher's stone. (Holmyard 1990, 23)

Through knowing the One and its parts, we have and can continue to com-
mune with essential vitality.

If Oneness is the cure, what is the illness?

Upon the naming of ten thousand names, oneness is lost.
Upon the naming of ten thousand names, oneness is gained.

The insight of this ancient riddle spans millennia of human attempts to isolate
pieces of the whole and identify them. Modern scientific reductionism has isolated so many parts from the whole that a holistic view of interdependence has
been forgotten. While there have been revolutionary discoveries and through
scientific inquiry we know remarkable details about vast fields of knowledge, a
gradual decay of our sense of interconnectivity with the whole has left us dis-
placed in the biosphere and cosmos. The naming of ten thousand names has
the opportunity to highlight the exquisitely multi-textured diverse parts of the
whole. The cure to a fragmented self is found in the reintegration of the parts
into their whole in a symbiotic interchange. We are finding that our wholeness
heals our "long loneliness that has made man a frequent terror and abomina-
tion even to himself" (Eiseley 1978, 44).

Referring to our interconnectedness with our relations in the other-than-
human world, Loren Eiseley asserts:

Perhaps man has something to learn after all from fellow
creatures without the ability to drive harpoons through living flesh, or poison with strontium the planetary winds...
Perhaps such a transformation would bring him once more

into that mood of childhood innocence in which he talked successfully to all things living but had no power and no urge to harm. (Eiseley 1978, 43)

The wisdom continues as we are exhorted and inspired to "no longer gaze with upright human arrogance on the things of this world" (Eiseley 1978, 63). A cosmology of appreciation for our ancestral lineage of the entire epic of evolution nurtures a strong empathic resonance with the diversity within the whole.

Ritual Evocation of our Cellular and Psychic Memory of Universal Ancestral Heritage

One promising reintegration of the parts into their whole is to affirm the epic of evolution as our collective human and other-than-human ancestral lineage. Through articulately naming our shared story, we may be able to create a future that facilitates each participant's ultimate potential while simultaneously achieving happiness and enduring wellness for all. Many native traditions have created and maintain ritual re-enactments of their cosmologies in order to preserve and vitalize relationships with higher powers. The Tzutujil Mayan of Guatemala and the Waitaha of New Zealand demonstrate participation between the human and higher powers and the creation of sacred events.

Tzutujil Mayan

Tzutujil Mayan rituals incorporate cosmology and creative gratitude expression for the interdependent web of life as a celebration of vitality and wholeness. As Tzutujil Mayan chief and traditional healer Martin Prechtel asserts:

> My hope is that out of each bud of imagination, a previously unknown flower will explode that inspires more stories and life than all the world of nihilistic insects can ever destroy... after all, the spirit feeds everyone, even the ungrateful, the unconscious, and those who hate the spirit. God's imagination is the world, and out of that exuberant and terrifying mystery every food is produced for everything and everybody, yet it is our own imaginations that feed God as well. In the force field that is then created between two imaginations of Gods and humans, Beauty lay in eternal suffering, giving constant birth to her child called Life. (Prechtel, cited in Jensen, 2001)

There are multiple-day, anthropocosmic drama re-enactments of the Tzutujil Mayan cosmology intended to ritually feed that which sustains life.[2] These rituals empower each person in a poetically engaged way of attuning to one's role on the planet and in the cosmos. Combining multi-dimensional mythological tradition, song, dance, and other forms of creative expression, each participant is called into a reflective and conscious awareness of the ecological individuation process in their intimate ancestral connections with all that is the universe.

Song of Waitaha

There is a persistent oral and emerging written canon of indigenous lore informed by participation with the living universe. Many cultures have engaged their psycho-spiritual communion with the living universe and Earth through ritual participatory re-creation of the story of their cosmology. The Waitaha of New Zealand have revealed their ancient cosmology in *Song of Waitaha*. Traditionally, their lore was told by the elders over the course of twelve nights, each night bringing a *tapu* (sacred) *pouwhenua* (portal) of knowledge. After a fire was lit at sunset, the elders would reveal their cosmology until the dawn of the next day. For twelve consecutive nights, the elders would engage the tribe in a very special sharing of their ancestral heritage and usher in wisdom and peace for future generations.

The *Song of Waitaha* is revealed in twelve sections of cosmological history. Each of these paths of knowledge begin with ritual *karakias* (prayers) to "catch the breath of life" by speaking and "to open the way to the deepest knowledge" through listening to the living universe. The elders call for the story of the universe to be remembered, "Some say let it go, let the old knowledge die, but I know the tragedy that therein lies. If we lose our story we lose our dream and if we lose our dream the spirit dies" (Brailsford 2004, 7). Aware of this frayed tapestry in which so much was fragmented through the generations, they welcome the rich universal context from which they've come and into which they return. Entering their lore with honor and respect provides a re-integration and stitching of their fabric into the great tapestry of universal life. Their lore indicates that each person is imbued with the living energies from before the stars that were sung into the nothingness by the great song. They

---

2   Anthropocosmic drama is a term coined by Nicolas Nunez in his 1996 book, *Anthropocosmic Theater: Rite in Dynamics of Theater*. He claims that there is meaning in developing participatory theater events in which the human organism enhances its capacity to be the echo box of the universe.

remind people of their intimate interconnection with all that exists through a call to "remember all gifted… in Creation, remember the Wairua that joins you with All. Remember you are Spirit" (Brailsford 2004, 33). The Waitaha lore is another of how ritual evocation of the ancestral heritage of the living universe can empower and fuel the individual and the collective into a meaningful existence and evolution.

The Universe Story

Prominent ecological theologian Thomas Berry and mathematical cosmologist Brian Swimme celebrate that "humans discovered by empirical investigation that they were participants in this [13.7] billion-year sequence of transformations that had eventuated into the complex functioning Earth" (Berry and Swimme 1992, 14). Perception into the vastness of time calls human consciousness into a co-perceptive universal presence. The story of the universe is imbued with an awe of the immense intricacy of each era and the manifestation of colossal and inimitable expressions of the living universe. There are many ways to engage the epic of evolution and foster deep appreciation for the ancestral inheritance of the living universe within each one of us.

Glimpsing our ancestral lineage of the entire living universe intrigues insatiable mind and spirit into a deeper meditation and gaze into the cosmological powers. These cosmological powers, our ancestral character traits, have brought forth the multivalent array of beauty in the world around and within. Nurturing personal and collective relationships with these cosmological attributes may be enhanced by integrating both scientific lens and the eyes of ecologically attuned peoples living in close harmony with the Earth.

Rumi reminds us in *Tell Me, What Have I Lost?* of the richness of our spagyric heritage:

I lived for thousands and thousands of years as a mineral and then
I died and became a plant.
And I lived for thousands and thousands of years as a plant and then
I died and became an animal.
And I lived for thousands and thousands of years as an animal and then
I died and became a human being.
Tell me, what have I ever lost by dying?
(Rumi, cited in Bly, 2004, 339)

Despite the new life that each death brings, there is a sense that many perceptions of death attempt to elude its inevitable arrival and its role in the overall regenerative process. Ritual engagement of the epic of evolution offers a reassuring contextual awareness of death that revivifies its role in the dynamic metamorphosis of the whole and its parts.

Conclusion

Creating and engaging ritual dimensions of the story of the universe can deeply arouse our ancient, latent psycho-spiritual potential. Through affirming our ancestral heritage of the epic of evolution, there are ways humans can awaken to our ultimate potential as symbiotic co-perceivers and co-creators of the living universe. Through celebrating our interdependence with all that came before us and all that is yet to come, we may change the tide of over-consumption and disregard for future generations and create a future of ecologically sound, ever-present well-being.

References

Berry, T. 1988. *The Dream of the Earth*. San Francisco, CA: Sierra Club Books.

Bly, R. 2004. *The Winged Energy of Delight*. New York: Perennial.

Brailsford, B. 2004. *Song of the Old Tides*. Christchurch, New Zealand: Stoneprint Press.

Brailsford, B. 1994. *Song of Waitaha*. Christchurch, New Zealand: Ngatapuwae Trust.

Deloria, V. 2002. *Evolution, Creationism, and other Modern Myths: A Critical Inquiry*. Golden, Colorado: Fulcrum Publishing.

Dowd, M. 2007. *Thank God for Evolution*. San Francisco, CA: Council Oak Books.

Eiseley, L. 1978. *The Star Thrower*. New York, NY: Harcourt, Brace, Jovanovich.

Holmyard, E. J. 1990. *Alchemy*. New York, NY: Dover Publications.

Jensen, D. 2001. Saving the indigenous soul: An interview with Martin Prechtel. *The Sun Magazine*, April 2001.

Jung, C.G. 1968. *Psychology and Alchemy*. Princeton, NJ: Princeton University Press.

Jung, C.G. 1968. *Mysterium Conunctionis*. Princeton, NJ: Princeton University Press.

Kanter, J. 2007. Humanity is putting Earth, and itself, at risk, UN environment report says. *International Herald Tribune* October 25, 2007. Internet <http://www.iht.com/articles/2007/10/25/europe/25environ.php> accessed July 18, 2008.

Swimme, B. and Berry, T. 1992. *The Universe Story: From the Primordial Flaring Forth to the Ecozoic Era*. New York, NY: Harper Collins.

Out of the radical impermanence of the human condition and the evanescence of feeling, the artist longs to make something that has the dependability and universality of a crystal or a scientific law—something surprising yet inevitable like Mozart's *Requiem*.

Winslow Myers

Already Living
An Artist's Perspective on the Evolution of the Human

Winslow Myers

My title, "Already Living," comes from T.S. Eliot. In his seminal essay from the 1920s, "Tradition and the Individual Talent," Eliot talks about works of poetry from the past, not as being dead, but as being already living. This works, of course, for all the arts. But Eliot's conception also helps us to get hold of the provocative notion that the churning geological chaos of the early Earth contained the potential for the interiority that emerges later in the form of subjective human consciousness. The music of Mozart was "already living" in the pre-biotic rock of the Earth. The notion of something original emerging from a previous phase-state includes the reality that the emergent state is "already alive" in the previous state. Mozart's music has its ultimate origin not just in the rocks. It begins in the primordial fire of the original Flaring Forth.

An aphorist once remarked that originality consists in hiding your sources. "Original" is a provocative word, a benchmark of creative value in the arts. It is interesting how a word that is meant to characterize the *new* contains the word *origin*, recalling the core Buddhist notion of "dependent originality," a way of describing the interdependence of all phenomena that somehow includes both chicken and egg.

If everything emerges from something else, does it make any sense to speak of development, especially human development? The philosopher Krishnamurti asserted that we humans have not changed at all psychologically in thousands of years. Like Krishnamurti, Ralph Waldo Emerson countered any facile notion of progress in human capacity when he asserted that each supposed step forward has had the potentiality to *reduce* some power in us. When we began to ride in wheeled vehicles, our legs began to atrophy from doing less walking. The invention of the camera, or binoculars, or eyeglasses, weakened our ability to see with the naked eye.

But the larger picture that we have of the evolutionary epic confirms a direction toward greater complexity and greater consciousness, which of course includes the human. The macro model of the change from energy to matter to life to ordinary human consciousness to, say, the superconsciousness of a Krishnamurti or the Dalai Lama, represents a progress from churning rock into mammalian and human forms of subjectivity and empathy—though the

Buddhists or the mystic Meister Eckhardt or even Thomas Berry might argue
that interiority was there from the beginning, inherent in the infinite sea of the
"all-nourishing abyss."

In the French caves, at the presumed beginning of the history of art, we
have a record of humans descending deep into womb-like clefts in the rock,
seeing animals in the shadowy shapes cast by their oil lamps, and bringing
forth from these projected shapes—using colors also made from the rocks—
the deer and bison and horses they hunted, or worshipped, or loved. The cave
painters sensed intuitively that animal and human life emerged from the earth,
from the rocks. Even though the research seems to confirm how much we are
like them physiologically, we cannot get inside the heads of these early artists.
We can only say that their aesthetic response, if it was an aesthetic response, to
the supple vitality of the animals around them remains deeply meaningful to
us now, especially because our human presence so threatens the viability of all
the organisms around us.

The critic and painter Suzy Gablik wrote a book with the provocative title:
"Progress in Art," in which she tried to prove, if I can be allowed to unfairly
boil a whole book down to a few words, that artists have more and more forms
and materials at their disposal as time passes, so there is progress in that strict
sense—an elaboration of vocabulary, illustrated here by Richard Serra's astonishing use of shipyard steel:

Great artists and scientists retain the capacity for astonishment that youth
bestows upon all of us to some degree. This astonishment is given a fateful

stimulus as the youthful artist encounters works which confirm that we are not alone in our subjectivity, and that it has been a grand human enterprise to find precise forms for our feelings, or for our yearnings to get beyond the confining boundaries of mere personality, in the soaring domes and arches of a mosque, or a clarinet quintet, or a painting of winter sunlight on the side of a house.

Artists try, but often fail, as most humans do—to retain the depth of wonder that we experienced when young. What fragments and capacities we are able to keep, artists put to the service of skills only available after much practice. Even the practice itself may deaden wonder. The poet Yeats once wrote: "the fascination of what's difficult/ has rendered spontaneous joy and natural content/ out of my heart . . ." Keats called this fascination with difficulty "negative capability," the emptying-out and the waiting that artists must subject themselves to in order to be possessed by larger forces that allow them to break out of the prison of mere personality. Out of the radical impermanence of the human condition and the evanescence of feeling, the artist longs to make something that has the dependability and universality of a crystal or a scientific law—something surprising yet inevitable like Mozart's *Requiem*. Most art does *not* rise to this condition, and that is the main reason that most art is mediocre.

But a record of the best of the best of the visual arts has been established which is captured within the covers of an art history survey, what Andre Malraux called the "museum without walls," available to us as a living resource irrespective of how far in the distant past the art in it was made. Is this a record of a general deepening of human consciousness, a great becoming? Or is it rather that the greatest artists, poets, and musicians seem to be in touch with something beyond time, outside our various models of progress? We feel this when certain works of art created by long-dead cultures seem to speak to us directly across the millennia.

The limited space of this paper allows focus on a few artists who have gone to the limit of using their eyes to recreate dependable, crystalline images of subjectivity or interiority. One of these is the 17th century Dutch painter Vermeer. I have never forgotten reading about a judge in The Hague presiding over the trial of Slobodan Milosovic, who had to hear testimony day after day of the human capacity to inflict pain upon other humans. The judge said that the only way he was able to recover his balance was to go to the museum and look at the Vermeers.

The person depicted below may be Anthony van Leeuwenhoek, a man who made important contributions to the development of microscope optics. We find ourselves in what James Joyce called an "inscape"; by implication we are inside the mind of both the subject and the artist, but in the device of the hand resting upon the celestial globe, Vermeer subtly evokes the entire world, even the universe, outside the room.

Some of the traditional categories in painting have been landscape, still life, portrait, and self-portrait. But *all* painting, like the Vermeer with its figure, is by definition still life, simply because in painting all movement, except compositional vectors directing the eye of the viewer to move, is arrested. But all painting is also of course, in terms of subjectivity, a self-portrait of the artist.

The penetrating eye of the artist looks, and if it looks deeply enough, it sees into another's subjectivity even as it reveals its own. Nowhere has this penetration gone deeper than in this famous work by Vermeer's contemporary, Rembrandt. Rembrandt is famous for humanizing the great stories of the bible.

Here Bathsheba has been singled out as a special subject of sexual attraction by the great king David. She holds his letter of assignation in her hand. X-rays have revealed that Rembrandt experimented with the angle of the model's head, with the result that no head, and body, in the history of art is more revealing of a complex interior state. The barely visible clothed elder trimming Bathsheba's toenails intensifies the naked solitude and musing thoughtfulness of Bathsheba herself. Even the numinous glow of the light seems to symbolize solitary thought, interiority. Not only the head, but the body itself in its aging imperfection, implies her mental landscape of vulnerable vanity. Rembrandt in his genius has captured both Bathsheba's pleasure at having been singled out by the king, and at the same time her awareness that if she gives herself to the king she will be betraying her husband, the general whom David has already sent off to be conveniently killed in battle. This is perhaps the greatest image in art history of that universal human trait, ambivalence.

Landscape, too, can be self-portrait.

A photograph of the motif 35 years after the painting was made confirms how accurately Balthus, the French-Polish artist, had captured the soft light of the Latium in the Viterbo area north of Rome. (previous page)

This 20th century European painting comes from an Asian orientation, the painting as a *sign*, not a slavish or illustrational imitation of reality. (Fan Kuan—Journey beyond the Rivers and the Mountains—10th c. Chinese, below left). Taoist identification with nature is an eastern form of subjectivity that integrates itself back into the universe that birthed it, the goal of Asian painting.

We might call this Neil Welliver from the 1980s (above right) an example of heroic subjectivity, because it was done by lugging an 80-pound pack of paints and easel into the woods in a raging snowstorm, making a 2 by 2 foot study from a point of view that seems to be suspended over the flooding brook, then enlarging the study back in the studio into the 8 by 8 foot finished painting with its thousands of snow dots rendered spatially. People complained that there were no human figures in Welliver's work, but this too is a self-portrait. There is a human presence, which is of course the artist standing in front of the work and making it live.

In still life especially, we can approach a purity of subjectivity that becomes available through the simplicity and modesty of the medium.

Here in this image of a headless and hollow doll bathed in a light which recalls Rembrandt, we have an image that is a powerful subjective response to the general threat to subjectivity in modern life. Walter Murch was like Vermeer in wanting to recreate an entire world in his work. His paintings are a direct evocation of being, of a human doing his best to make the work objectively *alive*.

As they seek that vitality, conscious artists depend upon past models of possibility and unavoidably pay homage to the examples to which their intuition gravitates even as their own work unfolds out of and into the unknown. This *is* their *originality*. Like the universe, the artist starts with infinite possibilities, roiling around like molten lava in the unconscious, but very quickly these narrow as the painting comes to life in a series of anxious decisions, and the work, if things go well, ends up being the only thing it could have become.

The universe within us is as capacious and infinite as the universe that surrounds us. Those who say that everything worth doing in the arts has already been done are wrong. Instead, it is possible we are just beginning, because emergence, the creativity of the universe, is infinite. As Thoreau said, "There is more day to dawn. The sun is but a morning star."

Winslow Myers, "Passages IX"

Author's Note

Winslow Myers shows his paintings at the Clarke Galleries in Stowe, VT, Gallery 170 in Damariscotta, ME, and his website, winslowmyers.com.

Experience, however, means the presence of mind, regardless of how simple or minimal the event might be; therefore Whitehead's doctrine envisions mind as existing throughout the universe *in different degrees of complexity.*

Josefina Burgos

Imagination and the Epic of Evolution

Josefina Burgos

Introduction

The objective of this paper is to explore humanity's response to the scientific story and the role of imagination in evolution under the light of the 20th century scientific discoveries, discoveries which can so profoundly alter our conceptual views of the larger generalities that have underpinned and framed our culture for generations.

We all have an idea of what imagination is, but let us start by saying that *imagination is an attribute of the mind.* However, intuitively, and because of the still dominant Western modern paradigm within which we exist, many among the general public still think of imagination as an attribute of the *human* mind, and maybe, of a few animal species. Furthermore, our Western culture and its materialistic viewpoint have tended for a long time *to equate experience with self-aware consciousness,* thus restricting the notion of experience and subjectivity to human beings, as well as creating the perception of a split between humans and the rest of the world.

In this paper I will suggest that in order to visualize the role of imagination in evolution it is necessary to leave behind the modern Western viewpoint regarding the relationship between experience and self-awareness and re-examine one of our culture's larger conceptual generalities, the concept of experience. This necessity is a consequence of (1) the enormous shift in the Western philosophical, metaphysical, and psychological fronts that came about during the 19th and 20th century, represented by the works of Henri Bergson, William James, Alfred N. Whitehead, Edmund Husserl, Maurice Merleau-Ponty, Pierre Teilhard de Chardin, and Rudolf Steiner, among others; and (2) the resurgence of a body of systematic thought grounded on the revolutionary changes in our understanding of the natural world brought forth by the 20th century, represented by the work of British philosopher and mathematician, Alfred North Whitehead.

The 19th and 20th centuries' philosophical shift consisted basically of a shift of focus from an objective world "out there" to the *lived world of human experience,* as the only valid ground of epistemological and ontological speculation. "The only things that shall be debatable among philosophers," wrote William James, "shall be things definable in terms drawn from experience" (James 1996, xxi).

Alfred North Whitehead (1861-1947)—Bertrand Russell's good friend and co-author of the book *Principia Mathematica* (1910-1913)—took this revolutionary concept one step ahead by advancing the fundamental idea that *experience and consciousness are not identical; that all consciousness is certainly experience, but experience is not necessarily conscious.* In Whitehead's view, consciousness is the most complex manifestation of experience, its pinnacle as opposed to its base (Hosinski 1993, 18). Whitehead claimed that experience is the way in which everything that exists participates in reality and is involved in the complexity of the universe, and that *it is mostly unconscious.* He envisioned a relational universe that exists through "action and reaction", where there is activity all the way down, from the most complex entities to the most simple.

However, there is a philosophical consequence derived from this concept: for a reaction or a response to come about, the experience of the stimulus as well as the experience of the response need to be felt, consciously or unconsciously. Whitehead, therefore, considered experience to be the common denominator in the universe—that which all entities in the universe share. It manifests as indivisible wholes or "quanta" which are the fundamental components of the world. He called these quanta of experience "events" or "actual occasions" or "moments of experience." Because each actual occasion is the product of a unique combination of the universe's past, each actual occasion is unique in itself.

Experience, however, means the presence of mind, regardless of how simple or minimal the event might be; therefore Whitehead's doctrine envisions mind as existing throughout the universe *in different degrees of complexity.* This type of doctrine fits the category of pan-psychism, but in Whitehead's particular case it is known as pan-experientialism

At the beginning of this paper I mentioned that we could think of imagination as an attribute of the mind. I will now suggest that if we ground ourselves in Whitehead's vision, pan-experientialism, we need to revise that perspective and look at *imagination as an attribute, not solely of the human mind and of a few animal species, but of Mind, with a capital M.* It is from this perspective that I will endeavor to explain how I envision the role of imagination in the Epic of Evolution.

The Nature of Imagination

I can now pose some questions about imagination; I can ask—*How* do we imagine? *Why* do we imagine? And finally—*What* do we imagine? But this we—**and this is very important to keep in mind**—is now a "we" which includes all of us, the drops of experience that we call "ourselves, in the present moment" and all other events or drops of experience from the simplest to the most complex that are rising and dying at every moment throughout the universe.

Before we can answer these questions, however, we need to point out that in order to imagine, we need to experience, so the next question to be answered is—How do we experience? Whitehead answers this question by telling us that experience is the result of two types of perception: the perception of what the budding moment of experience feels as the immediate present, and the perception of the past, including its immediate past and all that happened in the universe that led to this moment in space-time. The fusion of these two modes of perception—similar to a stereo image—provides *meaning* to what is felt as the immediate present and allows the forming moment of experience to "decide" what to become.

Based on Whitehead's pan-experientialist vision of perception I have come up with a formula where the experience of the past and the experience of what is perceived as the immediate present are represented by (P+I), bearing upon ($\longrightarrow$) a meaning (M), which is the focus and the objective of the perceptive act. I suggest that it is *meaning*, the coherent integration of the experience of the past and the experience of what is immediate, which allows the budding moment of experience to decide how it feels and what it will finally become in the actual world:

$$P+I \ (\longrightarrow) \ M$$

I further suggest that imagination *is the attribute implicit in the arrow*; it is the leap of mind that organizes the incoming stimuli in a way that means something. Upon that meaning, all of us, simple events like a moment of experience of an atom, or a moment of experience of a society of events like a molecule, or even of a society of events of enormous complexity like a human being, build a representation of the world and act in it according to how we feel about that representation.

We can then answer our second question—*Why* do we imagine? I suggest that the answer is that *we imagine for meaning*. I also suggest that meaning-making is an inborn disposition of mind, a structural and organizational quality of mind that requires coherence to interpret the world in order to act in it. In fact, Whitehead conceives of a moment of experience's "becoming" as the "transformation of incoherence into coherence" (Whitehead 1929, 40).

I have here newly introduced a term: *coherence*. *What* is coherence? Based on Whitehead's thought, I suggest that coherence is an integration of events by the mind *that satisfies a possibility, or a potentiality* for existence in the actual world.

God, Imagination, and Evolution

We have now reached a point in which we are looking at the core of Whitehead's microcosm, the threshold between the actual world and the world of possibilities; the threshold where the universe *becomes*, moment by moment, through quanta of experience which grasp and feel the past, the immediate present, and then "imagine" different, novel meanings that satisfy different possibilities or forms of definiteness available to each of them.

As an empiricist, Whitehead stated that "there is nothing which floats into the world from nowhere" (Whitehead 1929, 244), so he was forced to ask himself—What is the source of these possibilities? In order to satisfy his system's requirement for a ground of potentiality and its interaction with the actual world, he finally came to a vision of a universe which unfolds through a threefold creative act.

This creative act is composed of (1) a primordial matrix of infinite possibilities, or ultimate ground of potentiality, (2) the multiple solidarity of free events in the temporal world, which once completed become actual facts, and (3) the ultimate unity of the multiplicity of actual facts with the primordial conceptual order (Whitehead 1929, 346).

The first term, the primordial matrix of infinite possibilities is what Whitehead, being a religious man, envisioned as the "primordial" nature of God—conceptual, abstract and unconscious (Whitehead 1929, 345)—and, in his view, immanent in the world. The primordial nature of God is Whitehead's necessary answer to the question concerning the ultimate ground of our experience, because without it being involved in each and every drop of experience in the universe, we cannot understand how experience is possible (Hosinski 1993, 156), nor how the world develops instead of remaining forever unchanged. Because the primordial nature of God is immanent, present everywhere *in potentia*, the budding moment of experience not only grasps the past and the immediate present but it also grasps or "prehends" (unconsciously experiences) God's primordial nature through the possibilities of becoming, or forms of definiteness, offered to it.

By prehending the primordial nature of God, the occasion is able to imagine different meanings responding to each of the possibilities of becoming made available to it by God:

$$(\rightarrow) \text{M1}$$
$$(\text{P+I}) + \text{pnG} (\rightarrow) \text{M2}$$
$$(\rightarrow) \text{M3}$$

Example: I see in front of me a patch of a transparent substance with an-other substance in it that is also transparent and moves. My past experiences inform me that one of them is made of glass and the other is water; that the glass is hard to the touch, and water is a liquid that can be drunk to quench one's thirst, etc. If the past also tells me that I am thirsty, and God offers the possibility of drinking the water, or spilling it, or breaking the glass, or doing nothing, etc., the moment of experience that I am becoming at this present moment imagines that drinking the water *means* that I will quench my thirst. This meaning provides me with the most intense feeling of satisfaction in comparison to the other possible meanings; therefore I will probably act in the world by drinking the water.

As the unlimited ground of potentiality, God provides all the conditions as well as all the limitations which form the systematic order necessary for all the moments of experience in the universe to occur, but leaves each of them to freely determine, through imagination manifested in different degrees of com-plexity, what it will become in the world. So we can say that God and the actual occasions are co-creators of the actual world—God offers and lures / the drop of experience grasps and chooses. We can also conclude that imagination is the direct line between God and the world, between *potentia* and actuality.

The last phase of the universe's threefold creative act, the ultimate unity of the multiplicity of actual fact with the primordial conceptual order, is achieved through what Whitehead envisioned as the "consequent" nature of God, which feels every drop of experience simultaneously in the world, *in a unison of imme-diacy* (Whitehead 1929, 346). Whitehead envisioned the consequent nature of God as being conscious (Whitehead 1929, 345) and, in a certain manner, as God's "judgment of the world" (Whitehead 1929, 346). As the supreme ex-periencer of the actual world, the consequent nature of God "saves" the world (Whitehead 1929, 346)—in Whitehead's words—by patiently reordering the valuation of potentialities to be presented to each future occasion, moving the universe towards the completion of God's own nature.

Conclusions

Following the above description of Whitehead's concept of the creative act through which the universe unfolds, I will try to answer the last ques-tion—*What* do we imagine?

We already know that we imagine the meaning of each of the new possibili-ties of experience towards which God lures us and that we hopefully select that possibility whose meaning provides us with the most intensity of feeling. Regarding what we imagine in relationship to the evolutionary history of the universe, let me first quote a paragraph from Loren Eiseley's book *The Immense Journey*:

> It gives one a feeling of confidence to see nature still busy with experiments, still dynamic, and not through, nor satisfied because a Devonian fish managed to end as a two legged character with a straw hat. (Eiseley 1957, 47)

When Eiseley refers to nature, we, from a Whiteheadian perspective, understand him as referring to God and to us, all the moments of experience in the universe, past, present and future, *together*, co-creating the universe through imagination: from the first particle, to the Devonian fish, to the two legged human with a straw hat.

God offers the potentiality of the evolutionary forms to each occasion, but it is the reaching out of imagination for meaning, the imagination of a moment of experience of a quark, an atom, a molecule, a cell, a flower, a dinosaur, a bird, and of a human, which chooses from the infinite possibilities tendered by the hand of God that determines what the world will become.

References

Eiseley, L. 1957. The Snout. In *The Immense Journey*. New York, NY: Vintage Books.

Hosinski, T. E. 1993. *Stubborn Fact and Creative Advance*. Landham, MD: Rowan and Littlefield Publishers.

James, W. 1996. *Essays in Radical Empiricism*. Lincoln, NB and London, UK: University of Nebraska Press. Original work published in 1912.

Whitehead, A. N. 1929. *Process and Reality*, corrected edition. Eds. Griffin D. R. & Sherburne D.W. 1978. New York, NY and London, UK: The Free Press.

Science has uncovered remarkable insights that have profound implications for our perspective on who we are, where we came from, and where we are going. But it has proven difficult to translate this knowledge into a form that concretely helps us see ourselves as part of the cosmos.

Todd Duncan

Our Cosmic Context

Todd Duncan

The importance of knowledge lies in its use, in our active mastery of it—that is to say, it lies in wisdom.... Now wisdom... concerns the handling of knowledge, its selection for the determination of relevant issues, its employment to add value to our immediate experience. (Whitehead 1929, 30)

Introduction: Wisdom & Context

A central challenge in developing and conveying the Evolutionary Epic is to transform scientific knowledge into nuggets of insight that can be used as building blocks for constructing personal wisdom. Wisdom, as defined by Whitehead, can be viewed as the use of knowledge in a reflective, integrative way to guide how one lives. Thus the transition from knowledge to wisdom involves selecting key insights and weaving connections among them to provide an overarching framework of understanding to which an individual can connect.

This is where "story" enters the picture and scientific knowledge can become an "epic." One role of any culture's cosmic story is to provide an answer to the question, "How does it matter what we individually do or think or experience or feel?" Answering this question in turn amounts to building up a *context* within which what we do has meaning, through the connection our actions have to the rest of the universe. That is, we look to the bigger universe in order to find a *cosmic context* within which to situate the details of our daily lives (to "add value to our immediate experience", in Whitehead's terms). As expressed by William James, "Small as we are, minute as is the point by which the cosmos impinges upon each one of us, each one desires to feel that his reaction at that point is congruous with the demands of the vast whole..." (James 1977, 329).

But just learning scientific facts about the universe does not automatically enable us to *feel* a direct connection to its bigger context. It can be a struggle to maintain a sense of personal connection to the vast universe as revealed by science. A few expressions of this difficulty follow:

> The world of science—the real world—became estranged and utterly divorced from the world of life, which science has

been unable to explain—not even to explain away by calling it 'subjective'.... This is the tragedy of the modern mind
which "solved the riddle of the universe" but only to replace
it by another riddle: the riddle of itself. (Koyre 1965, 23-24)

We still seek from cosmology what we have always sought
from it ..., guidance in our attempts to construct a metaphysical map of the world, at a time when cosmology
has envisioned a universe that negates such attempts, by
negating the agent in which they arise. (Dobb 1995, 35)

Despite (perhaps partly because of) its rapid and far-reaching advances,
modern science has struggled with the transition from knowledge to wisdom. A
representative comment expressing this concern is from an American Association for the Advancement of Science report, The Liberal Art of Science (1990,
xi): "Science has not been integrated adequately into the totality of human
experience." More sharply stated, writer Bryan Appleyard (1992, 14) has commented, "On the maps provided by science, we find everything except ourselves."

Science has uncovered remarkable insights that have profound implications for our perspective on who we are, where we came from, and where we are
going. But it has proven difficult to translate this knowledge into a form that
concretely helps us see ourselves as part of the cosmos. As physicist Richard
Feynman observed, "Is no one inspired by our present picture of the universe?
This value of science remains unsung by singers: you are reduced to hearing
not a song or poem, but an evening lecture about it. This is not yet a scientific
age." The scientific picture of the universe can feel alienating as Appleyard suggests, presenting a challenge to our ability to find a true home for ourselves
within the model of the universe it describes. There is a need for more work
and a more clearly-defined field of study directed specifically at assisting this
transition from knowledge to wisdom in science, a process we've started calling
"science integration."

The remaining sections of this paper offer a few illustrations (adapted
from Duncan and Tyler 2009) of science integration, inviting and encouraging
people to incorporate scientific insights into the wisdom they bring to their
immediate experience and into their own poetic and artistic expressions of our
cosmic story. The key challenge in this process is finding a way to hold the scientific "fact," the overall context, and the individual person in mind at the same
time, providing a clear "you are here" marker within the scientific map. I hope
these examples will help trigger your own ideas of how to meet this challenge
for other scientific insights.

Reflecting on Existing Individual Beliefs

One of the simplest and most important activities for maintaining a personal connection to scientific insights about the universe is simply to *identify* and become *aware* of personal beliefs about a topic before learning new scientific information. This lays the groundwork for the new insights to be incorporated into your personal perspective, rather than remaining abstract and detached from your immediate experience.

For example, before learning about the arrangement of planets, stars, galaxies, and nebulae in the scientific universe, it's worth pausing to reflect on what the universe looks and feels like as it exists in your mind right now. At the beginning of a class on cosmology, I ask students to write an essay called "Describe Your Universe" in answer to roughly the following question:

Imagine floating away from Earth and out into space. What would you see, hear, feel, and think as you traveled away from Earth? Try to describe your universe as deeply as possible; don't just focus on scientific facts you've read or seen on TV. For example, subjective awareness dominates your personal experience. Where is that in your universe? Is it real or an "illusion"?

I generally assign this as an essay, but it can be done as an artistic project, drawing pictures or writing a song about the universe as you currently understand it. It also provides a good before and after survey, to demonstrate what has been learned and the changes in perspective that have occurred during the course.

Locating Yourself within the Framework of Cosmic Distances

The next example relates directly to the problem of placing yourself on the scientific map of the cosmos. The physical universe is so vast compared to the size of a human (or even the Earth) that it's easy to get carried away and believe that we must drop out entirely from any realistic description of the universe. So the key to telling this part of the story without alienating the human listener is to point out our insignificance in the physical scale of things while simultaneously *highlighting* the complementary reality of our existence as conscious creatures within that vast framework.

For example, begin by closing your eyes and fully noticing the reality of the thoughts and feelings that exist in your mind right now. What are you worried or happy about, are you tired or hungry, what's happening in your life, etc.? After reflecting on your thoughts for a few moments, open your eyes and look at a picture that accentuates the vastness of the universe and how tiny we are in that vastness. I like the Cassini image of Earth visible as a tiny dot behind the rings of Saturn (Astronomy Picture of the Day 2006) but any astronomical image illustrating our insignificant size, or just looking up at the stars on a clear dark night, will work instead. Now hold these two moments of awareness in mind at the same time: the reality of your thoughts and feelings, and the vastness of the scientific universe that forms the context for those thoughts and feelings. One of our core tasks is to combine those two complementary kinds of awareness, without letting either one dominate the picture. The spirit of this idea is captured well by the words of Edwin Dobb:

> Precisely when we grasp the vastness of the universe we also grasp an equally vast interior, the enormous geography of the soul, so to speak. Words may fail afterward, forcing us to rely on hackneyed descriptions that emphasize our insignificance, but what we actually sense, if only for an instant, is largeness of spirit. (1995, 40)

Energy Transformations

A final example of our connection to the rest of the universe has to do with transformations of energy from one form to another. On a sunny day, go outside and feel the warmth of the sunlight hitting your face. Now consider this: each second, the Sun *loses* 4 billion kilograms of mass as it converts hydrogen to helium in its core. (Don't worry—the Sun has a total mass of about 2×10^{30} kg, so it can afford to lose 4 billion kg every second and still last for billions of years.) This lost mass *is* the energy that is transformed into the light we see and feel. Following the relation $E = mc^2$, mass, light, and the warmth we feel in our bodies are all different kinds of energy, and we can trace the flow of energy directly from one form to another. The light we feel, the warmth in our bodies, even the food we eat owe their existence directly to the decreasing mass.

To make this transformation more accessible, consider that 4 billion kg of water (or any material with about the same density as water) would fill a cube-shaped container about 160 meters on a side. So picture in your mind a cube of water (or perhaps applesauce, if you find water too boring) that roughly fills a football stadium. Now let the water vanish and replace it with a spherical shell of light 300,000 kilometers thick (the distance light travels in a second), moving outward at the speed of light from the place where the water used to be. This is essentially what happens in the Sun every second. It has been happening for over 4 billion years and will continue to happen for several billion years more. A little bit of this shell of light is what you feel on your face when you stand outside on a sunny day, an experience humans share in common with all life on Earth. Something to ponder the next time you're feeling alone and isolated from the universe.

Author's Note
Todd is a cosmologist in the broad sense of the term. His work is guided by the theme of *looking for meaning in the modern scientific universe*—developing ways for people to see a place for themselves within the context of our scientific understanding of the universe. Teaching and research form two complementary and equally important aspects of this effort, which is articulated in the Scince Integration Institute (http://www.scienceintegration.org) he helped create. He holds a Ph.D. in astrophysics from the University of Chicago and is currently on the physics faculty at Pacific University. He is also an Associate Research Professor at Portland State University Center for Science Education and Pacific University Physics Department.

References

American Association for the Advancement of Science. 1992. *The Liberal Art of Science: Agenda for Action*. Washington D.C.: American Association for the Advancement of Science.

Appleyard, B. 1992. *Understanding the Present: Science and the Soul of Modern Man*. New York, NY: Doubleday.

Astronomy Picture of the Day: Cassini image of Saturn, Sun, and Earth. 16 October 2006. Internet <http://apod.nasa.gov/apod/ap061016.html> accessed 28 January 2008.

Dobb, E. 1995. Without Earth there is no Heaven: The cosmos is not a physicist's equation. *Harpers, 289*, (1737; February), 33-41.

Duncan, T. and Tyler, C. 2009. *Your Cosmic Context: An Introduction to Modern Cosmology*. San Francisco, CA: AddisonWesley.

Harrison, E. 2003. *Masks of the Universe*, 2nd edition. Cambridge, UK: Cambridge University Press.

James, W. 1977. *The Sentiment of Rationality*. In *The Writings of William James: A Comprehensive Edition*, ed. J. J. McDermott. Chicago, IL: University of Chicago Press. Original work published in 1905.

Koyre, A. 1967. *Newtonian Studies*. Chicago, IL: University of Chicago Press.

Whitehead, A. N. 1967. *The Aims of Education and Other Essays*. New York, NY: Free Press.

Whitehead, A. N. 1929. *Process and Reality*, corrected edition. Eds. Griffin D. R. & Sherburne D.W. 1978. New York, NY and London, UK: The Free Press.

Plodding upward another thousand vertical feet and two miles to the summit, I pondered the curious fact that quarks disgorged by the Big Bang in the creation of the space-time matrix could, billions of years later, evolve into self-reflective organisms preoccupied with mountains and death, with time and grace.

Peter Hess

Theological Problems and Promises of an Evolutionary Paradigm

Peter M. J. Hess

Introduction

How might theology respond to the "evolutionary epic" as articulated by cosmology, geology, biology, and other related sciences? What do ancient faith traditions have to do with a brash young scientific explanation of biological diversity? The rhetoric of recent years might convey to the casual observer the impression that the armies of science are still locked in mortal combat with the forces of religion. More than a century ago, proponents of the "warfare thesis" developed a persistent mythology that Christianity—and in particular the Catholic Church—had perennially and obstinately stood in the way of scientific advancement.[1]

Examples of apparent skirmishing between religion and science are not hard to find. Recently a new museum of natural history opened in Kentucky, purporting to offer evidence of a recent creation and a young Earth. A documentary film released in 2008 contrived a case for the claims that "intelligent design" theory is routinely excluded from academia, that the theory of evolution inevitably leads to atheism, and that the assumptions underlying Darwinism provided (at least in part) the ethical rationale for Hitler's Nazi concentration camps.[2] In sharp reaction to the ideological climate fostering these and other attacks on science (Mooney 2005, 164-184), a number of authors representing the so-called "new atheism" have mounted a vigorous assault not only on the various forms of scientific creationism, but on religious belief in general (Dawkins 2006). Their arguments have in turn received critical responses (Haught 2007; Berlinski 2008).

Nevertheless, a reading of cultural history more accurate than the "warfare thesis" would be one in which the two great human traditions of religion and science have developed in tandem over the millennia. In an intricate dance characterized by harmony and tension, by indifference and engage-

---

1   The "warfare thesis" was concocted by William Draper in his *History of the Conflict between Religion and Science* (1874), and more fully developed by Andrew Dickson White in *History of the Warfare of Science with Theology in Christendom* (1896).

2   Answers-in-Genesis opened its Creation Museum near Cincinnati in 2007; Premise Media released its film *Expelled: No Intelligence Allowed* in April 2008.

ment, these two traditions embody, respectively, the religious or spiritual response to the mysterious "other" perceived as underlying nature, and the rational scientific explanation of the natural world around us. In his well-known typology of modes of interaction, Ian Barbour has argued that the relationship between religion and science is most accurately characterized in terms of a plurality of models, including conflict, independence, dialogue, and integration (Barbour 1997, 77-105).

With the dawn of human consciousness, our species began to perceive within and through the elements of the world an "infinite other," a creative essence permeating nature and fundamentally responsible for its existence. From their origins in primal societies, through their development as great traditions, and even down to the present, the world's religions have affirmed this "other" lying at the bedrock of the universe, known variously as "the mother of all things," the Tao, or "the way;" others refer to it as "that which is," "pure being," or "divinity." The Abrahamic faiths have balanced a sense of the transcendent dimension of God with an understanding of the divine immanence, which is expressed in Psalm 139 and in the Islamic belief that although beyond our sight and understanding, Allah is at the same time "nearer to us than our jugular vein" (Qur'an 50:16). In Christian theology "the Word became Flesh and dwelt among us" (John 1:16), and in his *Canticle of the Sun*, Saint Francis of Assisi articulated a clear vision of the immanence of God in all of creation.

In parallel with their developing religious awareness, humans have evinced curiosity about the natural world. From the natural philosophy of the Pre-Socratic philosophers (speaking only for the West) to the establishment of the evolutionary model by biological science in our day, *Homo sapiens* has desired to explain how the world works. Mainstream Christian theologies (both Protestant and Catholic) have been able gradually to assimilate the new perspectives of the world generated by cosmology, physics, and biology during the course of a protracted Scientific Revolution.

Evolutionary ideas now permeate significant dimensions of our scientific, literary, cultural, and religious consciousness of a world no longer regarded as timeless and static, but rather as historical and dynamic. Theology can scarcely be intelligible if it remains mute or wholly apophatic (saying what something is not) about the cosmos. On the other hand, clinging too tenaciously to a familiar but outdated worldview carries a substantial risk: if theology refuses to adapt when the believing community experiences a radical sea change in its understanding of the world, it will be cast adrift (Wildiers1982, 158-160). Even now theology is being written to reflect the new cosmological perspective.[3]

---

3   This body of literature is far too extensive to synthesize, but includes works by Francisco Ayala, Ilia Delio, John Haught, Kenneth Miller, Ted Peters, Robert Russell, Josef Zycinski, and many others.

What are the challenges posed by the evolutionary worldview to religious believers and to the theologians who serve them? How will the new understanding of a dynamic cosmos inform our understanding of such doctrines as creation, salvation, suffering, theological anthropology, eschatology (theology of the afterlife), and theodicy (theology of God in light of natural evil)? This essay sketches the evolutionary worldview within which creative work on foundational theological questions must be done.[4] Although I restrict myself to writing here from my own perspective of Christianity, a thoroughly adequate evolutionary theology would necessarily be open to dialogue both with the sciences and with the world's other faith traditions.

Iztaccíhuatl: Epic as Personal Story

Theology may be an intellectual exercise, but it begins with lived experience interpreted in light of scripture, tradition, and reason. For the past century and a half the experience of both individuals and the believing community has been shaped by a developing evolutionary worldview. Let me illustrate through personal narrative how subtly and thoroughly an appreciation of the evolutionary epic can permeate our perception of the cosmos and our interpretation of meaning within it.

On January 23, 2005, at 4:00 in the morning, I found myself confronted with a curious conundrum. Looming before me in the darkness was a steep rock face that I could apparently not avoid climbing. I was standing with two climbing partners in a biting north wind, on a rubbly slope of volcanic scree at 16,000 feet, sipping ice-cold Gatorade slush from a half-frozen water bottle, contemplating the beautiful climbing route known as "la Arista del Sol" (the Ridge of the Sun). We were climbing Iztaccíhuatl, the "Sleeping White Woman," at 5,230m (17,126 feet), the third highest stratovolcano in Mexico.

Our attention at that hour was focused on how to surmount a steep rib of rock jutting out between us and the first plateau. Our feet were clad in clumsy winter climbing boots, and our guide had judged a rope to be unnecessary. We crept out onto a ledge above the inky void below us, trusting that the friable volcanic tuff would not break off under our gloved hands as the fierce wind tore at our backpacks. Snowflakes began drifting across the shallow pool of

---

4   I have identified six important clusters of Christian theological issues which should be addressed in view of our current concept of an ancient and dynamic universe: 1) God and Revelation; 2) Theological Anthropology; 3) Christology and Soteriology; 4) the Fall, Sin, and Biology; 5) Suffering and Theodicy; and 6) Eschatology: biology, and the far future of the universe. These issues will be discussed at greater length in my forthcoming book on "Catholic Theology in Evolutionary Perspective," and are touched on in my book co-authored with Paul Allen, *Catholicism and Science* (Greenwood, 2008).

light cast by my headlamp on the rock, fluttering down like tiny white moths, and the blowing snow started filling the crevices and coating the ledges we were trusting as footholds and handholds.

At that precarious moment the magic happened. As we clung to the rock face, the wind rent a hole in the clouds in the western sky, bathing us in a shaft of pure light from a nearly full moon. Gazing at the starry heavens above and the faint glow of maize-farming villages far below, I had a momentary vision of the great arc of evolution, that creative procession giving birth to atoms and nebulae and galaxies, to stars and rocky planets bearing volcanoes and surging oceans, to plants and animals, including legend-weaving Aztecs and three equipment-challenged mountaineers. It was a moment of enchantment and grace.

It would be disingenuous to say that I spent much of the next six hours doing anything other than eating, hydrating, trying to stay warm, and planting my crampons and ice-axe resolutely. Nevertheless, the evolutionary epic touched me at almost every level throughout that night. It touched me as scientific paradigm through which we read astronomy and geology, botany and primate psychology. It touched me as myth and metaphor, as I imagined the life of prehistoric Asian peoples, impelled by demographic pressures unknown to us, venturing far across the Bering land bridge into the vast unpopulated continents of the Americas. It touched me as story and symbol, as I contemplated the great civilization of the Aztecs and of their Mexican descendants who gazed and still gaze upon this mountain, which has become woven into the very fabric of their culture.

Evolution as epic story affected me that night as I thought about my own genetic descent from proto-mammals who survived the asteroid impact at the Cretaceous-Tertiary boundary sixty-five million years ago, that had formed the Chicxulub crater only a few hundred kilometers away, long before Iztaccíhuatl had risen from the Puebla plain. I thought of how timid arboreal primates had given rise to savanna-dwelling hominids, nomadic hunter gatherers, pastoralists and agriculturalists, architects of cities and temples, and conceivers of religion and science. The evolution of spiritual consciousness, of an inkling that there might possibly be a reality beyond the empirically observable, moved me deeply that night as we climbed past a simple white cross cemented into the rock. The cross marked where a troop of 14 boy scouts and their leaders had tragically frozen to death in 1968, within a few hundred yards of the very *refugio* (shelter) where we had spent the night. As we finished reading their memorial plaque—placed here by grieving parents and siblings and friends moved by hopes beyond the cold, hard, fact of death—it became colder and windier, underscoring the stark possibility of our own death by hypothermia. We quickly resumed our climbing.

Plodding upward another thousand vertical feet and two miles to the summit, I pondered the curious fact that quarks disgorged by the Big Bang in the creation of the space-time matrix could, billions of years later, evolve into self-reflective organisms preoccupied with mountains and death, with time and grace. As we crested the top of Iztac's "rodillas" (knees), the Sun rose out of the Gulf of Mexico, and a series of knife-edge ridges above thousand-foot drops led us around some of the eight craters formed during Iztac's evolving volcanic life. Soon the drifting clouds parted, revealing a stupendous view: the summit of Iztaccíhuatl floating high above the Ayoloco glacier. Ascending the sharp and gravelly ridge of the *Arista del Sol*, we reached the top at 10:15 a.m., where we offered prayers of thanksgiving for success and for the well-being of friends and family.

My climbing partners decided to descend almost immediately as one of them was suffering from altitude sickness, so I crossed the summit glacier ("El Pecho") alone to stand briefly on the very highest point of the eastern crater rim. Beginning my solo descent from the summit, I stepped out onto the Ayoloco Glacier. When the lowering clouds began to stroke the mountain with drifting snow I found myself enclosed in a total whiteout, and experienced a sort of vision, or profound impression. It struck me with particular force and clarity that our prehension of the world always begins with ourselves, with our unique incommunicable experience of this moment, this specific place, this set of circumstances. Another climber might recognize the general context of an ascent, but she or he would bring to bear a distinct genetic and psychological makeup, a different personal history, an alternate spirituality.

As I stood alone on the ice, the whiteout obscuring everything more than twenty feet away, my only reference points were the snow falling from thin clouds in the heavens above me, the crevasse-checked ice field beneath me, and the sense of myself and time and the moral law within me. Here was I, one *Homo sapiens* out of billions that have lived, standing on one retreating glacier on one mountain of one episodically warming planet, reflecting on one evolutionary trajectory out of myriad possible such trajectories in the universe. In Josephina Burgos' lovely expression, I felt like one drop of experience falling on the shores of the universe.[5]

Alone on the Ayoloco glacier in a white-out, with the opposite side now invisible, the route-marking wands buried or blown away, and the ice retaining no boot prints, I determined to pick one large crevasse and follow it consistently to the glacier's edge. I eventually caught up with my climbing partners at the top of Iztaccíhuatl's "knees," and together we descended to the fragrant Yellow Pines in the temperate zone of 13,000 feet.

---

5   From Josefina Burgos' chapter, "Imagination and the Epic of Evolution," in this volume, p. 321.

A Search for Meaning in the Evolutionary Epic

Evolution is a grand and universal epic, a captivating story of myriad particular encounters with the world such as I have recounted above. The question of central importance for theology is how to interpret the evolutionary epic—embedded in time so deep it is almost beyond comprehension—in some way meaningful to our particular human life experiences. How do we integrate billions of years of evolutionary history into theological traditions born when people conceived of the cosmos as small, static, relatively young, and unquestionably centered around human concerns? Modernity has shown that the creation and translation of meaning is a never-ending process, an on-going engagement in intergenerational and intercultural hermeneutics. But the reception of tradition does not involve merely stubborn adherence to some immutable magisterial authority. Rather, we modify tradition reverently for the needs of our own time and place, and we neglect to modify it at our peril. A theological account of the evolutionary paradigm reflects the dynamic tension between faithfully maintaining tradition and responsibly adapting it to current science. The experience of my climb of Iztaccíhuatl suggests six interpretive themes that are both scientifically true of the evolutionary epic and that carry profound significance for any theological tradition that wishes to remain cogent in our contemporary world.

1. Physical experience: As an elegant explanatory framework, evolutionary theory is grounded in physical experience, just as is religion. In her classic memoir about coming to terms as a naturalist with both beauty and the suffering in the natural world, Annie Dillard recorded her shock upon observing a giant water bug sucking the very life out of a small green frog on the bank of Tinker Creek (Dillard 1974, 5-6). This sort of observation removes the theological problem of evolutionary suffering from the merely theoretical realm, situating it very concretely in lived human experience. Likewise, the physical dimensions of my climb—the sight of darkness and stars and mountains and plains, the sounds of birds and wind and falling rock, the smell of hydrogen sulfide from volcanic fumaroles, the feelings of hard rock and intense cold, of fatigue and hunger and thirst—these physical dimensions threw my reflections on evolutionary theology into the sharp relief of lived experience.

2. Epistemological privilege: We live at a privileged and a perilous crossroad in the historical and dynamic epic of cosmic evolution. Life could not evolve until there were rocky planets for it to inhabit, and rocky planets are themselves formed from the stardust ejected into the galaxy by the supernovae among earlier generations of stars. There-

fore, the evolution of intelligent, self-reflective life that could explore the universe had to await the accumulation of a sufficient quantity of heavy elements at our distance from the galactic center, billions of years after the Big Bang. Paradoxically, our distant descendants will observe less and less of the cosmos, since with accelerating expansion of the universe the more distant galaxies will begin crossing the observable horizon.[6] In our own time, the dynamism of evolution has contributed to the tragic circumstance that, virtually at the moment terrestrial life has evolved to self-reflection, we are becoming aware of the devastation we are wreaking on the planetary physiology and our fellow species.

3. Contingency and impermanence: As I climbed I pondered both the impermanence of particular ecologies and the contingent events that have shaped their evolution. A virtually infinite number of events might have intervened to prevent me from climbing Iztaccíhuatl. If the dynamics of the Big Bang had not been as they were to give rise to galaxies and stars, and if nucleosynthesis had not made possible the creation of heavier elements and rocky planets, and if the Chicxulub asteroid with its mere seven-minute window for possible collision with the earth (Alvarez 2008) had not opened niches for mammalian evolution, or if primates had never descended from the trees to inhabit the savannah, I would not be here. The Earth and its marvelously varied landscapes and ecologies—the Ayoloco Glacier on Iztaccíhuatl, the Hawaiian Islands, the Painted Desert, your favorite stream at home—these are contingent and evanescent episodes of geological time, and this very contingency and impermanence has a bearing on our theologies.

4. Emergence of the novel: Delineated by Arthur Peacocke and many other thinkers, a philosophy of emergent naturalism offers us a rich way to consider how life comes from non-life, how mind evolves from life, and of how spirit emerges from mind (Peacocke 2007). Rather than looking for signs of intelligent design in a perfect and completed universe, theologies of emergence celebrate the cosmos' potential for novelty, suffering, and redemption. At the moment of the Big Bang, or even a billion years after it, who might have predicted that thinking beings would now be attending conferences on evolution? Who can predict what novelties the universe will engender in the next 13.7 billion years, hinted at by John Haught's "theology of promise" that celebrates the freedom given by God to the universe? (Haught 2003, 39-40).

---

6   From Joel Primack and Nancy Abram's chapter, "The Epic of Cosmic Evolution," in this volume, p107.

5. Evolutionary transcendence: My most persistently recurring idea as
    I climbed Iztaccíhuatl was that the quarks of the primordial "flaring
    forth" could become maize farmers and mountaineers, scientists and
    theologians. We know of nothing in the universe more complex than
    the thought processes of the human brain, and the evolution of this
    capacity has enabled the cosmos to become conscious of itself (Coyne
    2002, 64-66). Czech philosopher Erazim Kohák has written that
    human beings live at the intersection of the dimensions of time and
    value: "It is in time that humans find their place in nature; it is as bear-
    ers of eternity that they find their justification" (Kohák 1987, 103). In
    the evolution of *Homo sapiens*, the universe has transcended itself.

6. The dynamic cosmos as mystery: Although for biologists evolution is
    quite properly a puzzle to be unraveled, for theologians it is more than
    that: it is also a mystery before which we remain silent. Ultimately, words
    proved inadequate for describing my impression, while on the mountain,
    of the great arc of evolution, or my awe at the fact that the cosmos exists
    at all. Beneath the structures and processes exposed by evolutionary bi-
    ology, there is something incommunicable about the epic of evolving life.
    Francisco Ayala contends that "as far as science is concerned the origin
    of the universe will remain forever a mystery" (Ayala 1998, 113). The
    apophatic, "unspeakable" nature of theology written from an evolution-
    ary perspective is perhaps most acute when we confront the problems of
    suffering and death, for which we have no adequate explanation. Writ-
    ing at the culmination of a life dedicated to exploring the contours of
    evolutionary faith, biologist and theologian Arthur Peacocke expressed
    his own serene acceptance of death as an essential component of an
    evolutionary cosmos, and the conviction of life everlasting, though it be
    opaque to biological science (Peacock 2007, 192).

What is at stake theologically in an ancient, dynamic, and evolving universe?
Theology is a living dialogue between scripture, tradition, and the cultures in
which it is embedded. The great religious traditions—Hinduism, Judaism, Buddhism, Christianity, Islam—were all born in a brief window of fairly hospitable
terrestrial conditions, a climatic stability that influenced their theologies accordingly. We know that the Earth will not in the future be nearly so welcoming
of large-scale life (Ward and Brownlee 2000, 101-128). In the near term, long
periods of widespread and life-scouring glaciation will recur, after which—as
the Sun's luminescence raises temperatures and the solar winds strip away the
atmosphere and oceans—macroorganisms will begin to die off. In the practical order of things here and now, of course, this eventual fate hardly matters to

us, but it does put our assumptions of cosmic stability into relative perspective. Large plant and animal life ultimately will have thrived for only one twelfth of the Earth's total existence, and human life will have occupied only a minute fraction of that twelfth. After humanity's disappearance, the Earth will continue on revolving for another three billion years as a reddish planet with only microbial life, and then possibly for another four billion years in a lifeless state (Ward and Brownlee 2002, 129-138). How can we rethink theology to reflect not only an ancient, dynamic, and evolving universe, but also an Earth that is only temporarily hospitable to complex and intelligent life? The theological issues at stake in such a fully evolutionary understanding of the world are many and varied.

The epic of evolution raises profound questions not only about the future of humans, but about the future and meaning of life in the cosmos. What should we assume about emergent rationality in some of our fellow species on this planet? If intelligence has survival value can we confidently assume that no other species will emerge into moral and spiritual awareness? If only a fraction of the 10^{22} stars in the universe support potentially life-bearing planets around them, what might we assume theologically about the future of rational extraterrestrial species? Is "salvation" unique to Earth or relevant to the cosmos as a whole? Can we adapt to an evolutionary paradigm the ancient Christian doctrine of *apokatastasis*, of the restoration of all beings to communion with God? If so, would it include all individual beings that have ever lived, or only representatives of all species? If the latter, at what stage of their evolutionary development?

Conclusion

We began by asking how theology might respond to the "evolutionary epic" as articulated by cosmology, geology, biology, and other related sciences. Ancient faith traditions have everything to gain from a bold and incisive engagement with the epic of evolution. Not only does the universe story resonate with our personal encounters with the natural world, but it also challenges us to articulate classic theological doctrines afresh. Peacocke and numerous other thinkers have developed a panentheist theological model—the roots of which run deep into Western tradition—in which the universe exists within God. In the fifteenth-century Cardinal Nicholas of Cusa applied to the universe as a whole the saying that God is "a sphere of which the centre is everywhere and the circumference nowhere." The panentheist model can serve theology by interpreting the Earth and its precious cargo of evolving life, and indeed, the entire universe, as all existing as but one miniscule point within the divine plenitude.

As my experience on Iztaccíhuatl attests, both the wonders of the ancient, dynamic, and evolving universe, and the promises of theological tradition bring me back to the apophatic state, a silence before the great and splendid mystery. In the final testament he penned shortly before his death, Arthur Peacocke reflected that:

> Over the years I have given much thought and spilt much ink on the nature of God and God's interaction with people. Not surprisingly the subtler nuances of my deliberations have fallen away before the absolute conviction that God is love and eternally so. This remains the foundation of my prayers and thoughts for "underneath are the everlasting arms" (Peacocke 2007, 192).

Evolutionary theism resonates with Christian theology at its deepest, most mystical level, for it is within the divine plenitude that, in Saint Paul's words, the whole creation groans and travails, awaiting consummation (Romans 8:22).

Author's Note

Peter M. J. Hess serves as Faith Project Director with the National Center for Science Education in Oakland, California, facilitating dialogue between communities of religious belief and proponents of evolutionary biology. He teaches at Saint Mary's College in Moraga, California, and is co-author with Paul Allen of /Catholicism and Science/ (Greenwood Press, 2008). With his wife Viviane, he has two sons, Michael and Robert. He is an avid rock climber and mountaineer.

References

Alvarez, W. 2008. The character of Big History: A geological perspective. Paper presented at the Evolutionary Epic Conference, Makaha, Hawaii.

Ayala, F. 1998. "Darwin's devolution: design without designer," in *Evolutionary and Molecular Biology: Scientific Perspectives on Divine Action*, ed. Robert J. Russell, *et al.*, 101-116. Vatican City: Vatican Observatory Publications.

Barbour, I. G. 1997. *Religion and Science: Historical and Contemporary Issues*. San Francisco: HarperCollins.

Berlinski, D. 2008. *The Devil's Delusion: Atheism and Its Scientific Pretensions*. New York: Crown Forum.

Collins, F. S. 2006. *The Language of God: A Scientist Presents Evidence for Belief*. New York: Free Press.

Coyne, G. V. and Omizzolo, A. 2002. *Wayfarers in the Cosmos: the Human Quest for Meaning*. New York: Crossroad.

Dawkins, R. 2006. *The God Delusion*. London: Bantam.

Delio, Ilia. 2008. *Christ in Evolution*. Maryknoll, NY: Orbis Books.

Dillard, A. 2007. *Pilgrim at Tinker Creek*. New York: Harper Classics. Original work published in 1974.

Hess, P. M. J. 2001. "Eschatology and the Reintegration of Worldview: John Donne to Teilhard de Chardin," *CTNS Bulletin* 21, 3-11.

Hess, P. M. J., and Allen, P. 2008. *Catholicism and the Sciences in the Modern World, 1400-2000*. Boulder, CO: Greenwood Press.

Kohák, E. 1987. *The Embers and the Stars: A Philosophical Inquiry into the Moral Sense of Nature*. Chicago, IL: University of Chicago Press.

Haught, J. F. 2003. *Deeper than Darwin: the Prospect for Religion in the Age of Evolution*. Boulder, CO: Westview Press.

Haught, J. F. 2007. *God and the New Atheism: A Critical Response to Dawkins, Harris, and Hitchens*. Louisville, KY: Westminster John Knox Press.

Miller, K. 2003. "An Evolving Creation: Oxymoron or Fruitful Insight?," in Keith B. Miller, ed. *Perspectives on an Evolving Creation*. Grand Rapids: Wm. B. Eerdmans Publishing.

Mooney, Chris. 2005. *The Republican War on Science*. New York: Basic Books.

Nichols, T. L. 2003. *The Sacred Cosmos: Christian Faith and the Challenge of Naturalism*. Grand Rapids, MI: Brazos Press.

Peacocke, A. 2007. *All That Is: A Naturalist Faith for the Twenty-First Century*. Minneapolis: Fortress Press.

Peters, Ted and Martinez Hewlett. 2003. *Evolution from Creation to New Creation: Conflict, Conversation, and Convergence*. Nashville, TN: Abingdon Press.

Pope Pius XII. 1951. *Humani Generis*. Rome: Vatican.

Primack, J. and Abrams, N. 2006. *The View from the Center of the Universe: Discovering Our Extraordinary Place in the Cosmos*. New York: Riverhead.

Southgate, C. 2008. *The Groaning of Creation: God, Evolution, and the Problem of Evil*. Louisville, KY: Westminster John Knox.

Ward, P. D. and Brownlee, D. 2002. *The Life and Death of Planet Earth: How New Science of Astrobiology Charts the Ultimate Fate of our World*. New York: Henry Holt.

Wildiers, N. Max. 1982. *The Theologian and His Universe: Theology and Cosmology from the Middle Ages to the Present*. New York: Seabury Press.

Życiński, J. 2006. *God and Evolution: Fundamental Questions of Christian Evolutionism*. Trans. K. W. Kemp and Zuzanna Maślanka. Washington: Catholic University of America Press.

Index

photosynthesis 61, 292
photosynthetic life 32
Planck length 113
Planetary Superorganism 32
planets 24, 33, 82, 109, 115,
        180, 331
    formation of 81
    Goldilocks 24
    life-bearing 343
    on crystal spheres 108
    rocky 111, 338, 340, 341
plate tectonics 14, 98
Plato 256, 260
pollution event 32
Pope Benedict XVI 291
post-modernist 147, 148
pottery and ceramics 65
practice (contemplation) 161
    forms of 162
    Tree of Contemplative Practices 163
prehending 324
Primack, Joel 186, 287
primordial conceptual order
        324, 325
primordial nature of God 324
progressive relaxation 268, 269
protein intake increase 62
psychotherapy 267, 268
puberty rites 266

Q

quanta of experience (events) 322
    actual occasions 322, 325
    modes of perception 323
    moments of experience 322,
        325, 326
    prehending 324
quantum mechanics 113, 116
quantum physics 128, 246
quantum theory 246, 247, 248

R

radioactivity 97
radiometric dating techniques 97
rationalist 149, 171
reconciliation 171
    Jacob and Esau 286
red giant 33, 34
reductionism
    methodological 180
    scientific 305
reductionist 127, 171
    anti-reductionist bias 180
    tendencies of scientists 230
regenerative process 308
relativity theory 138, 246
religious traditions 260, 342
    of Europe 92
Rembrandt 314, 315, 317
Rift Mountains 27
rites of passage 266
ritual engagement 308
Russell, Bertrand 322
Rutherford, Ernest 97

S

sacraments 295
sacred relation 189
salience 75, 76
    emotional 266
salvation 337
San Bushmen 254, 257
San People 277
Schanberg, Saul M. 238
Schooling Nemo 282
scientific
    cosmology 107
    discovery 109, 161
    paradigm 149, 338
    principles 150

Hopefully we will give ourselves sufficient time to learn to cope with the brave new world we have created. We are smart—but *are we smart enough?*

Kathy Schick and Nick Toth

The Humanity Conference and Book Series

captures the work of outstanding scientists, philosophers, theologians, historians, sustainability and environmental experts, futurists, artists, and poets as they illuminate and celebrate humanity's evolutionary path.

The Evolution of Religion
Studies, Theories, and Critiques
Book 2008

The Evolutionary Epic
Science's Story and Humanity's Response
Book 2009

Look for:
Science, Wisdom, and the Future
Humanity's Quest for a Flourishing Earth
Conference 2009, Book 2010

Humanity in the Cosmos
What does it mean to be human in a vast cosmos?
Conference and Book 2011

The conference and book series was inspired by Russell Genet's book
Humanity: The Chimpanzees Who Would Be Ants

All books in the series published by the Collins Foundation Press
www.CollinsFoundationPress.org

Website for the Conferences
www.EpicandFutures.org

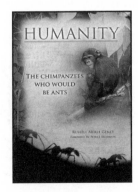
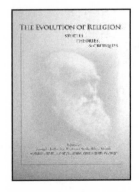

For the Evolutionary Epic Conference participants

Photo by Linda Palmer

Until we meet again - aloha!